Healing With The Horoscope

By Maritha Pottenger

Dedicated To
J. Marc Matz
With Love
And
Muffin
Because I Miss Her

International Standard Book Number 0-917086-45-7
Printed by Whitehall Company

Published by Astro Computing Services
PO Box 16430
San Diego, CA 92116

Cover design by Lynn Nelson

Also distributed by Para Research, Inc.
Whistlestop Mall
Rockport, MA 01966

Contents

SECTION THREE — Demonstration

Acknowledgments

In a very real way, everyone I have ever known (and many others) have helped to create this book, but there are a number of people I would like to single out for additional thanks.

My mother, more than anyone else, encouraged me to take power and responsibility for my own life, to choose to create my own realities. Her loving support has been and remains constant.

Two special friends, Laurel Siegel-Gord and Pamela Crozat, have always been available to talk, to ponder meanings, to consider relationships, to love and to share.

J. Marc Matz has taught me more about projection than anyone else I've known. Looking in the mirror through relationships is not always fun, but exceedingly useful for growth and change.

Jim Eshelman encouraged me to **do** a "counseling book" and provided needed motivation and impetus to get it finished.

A number of friends have been supportive and understanding, especially when writing took me away from other activities; offered ideas and encouragement; made useful suggestions and criticisms: Helen Ewald, Ann Anderson, J. Marc Matz, Dave Yamauchi, Helen Kessler, Jackie Siegel, Daniel Berenson, Brian Clark, Nancy Kelly-Hedges, Sarah Shaw and Deborah Wheeler.

Mary Dell and Harry Ginsberg gave me the benefit of their knowledge and supervision in furthering my counseling skills. Many ideas and inspirations I owe to them. Errors and interpretations are, of course, my own.

A number of clients have shared their lives, hopes, feelings, dreams and thoughts with me. They have given, and continue to give me opportunities to grow and develop as a person as well as a counselor. I am in their debt.

My family has assisted in all ways: editing (Mark and Bill), saving files when the computer and I had disagreements (Mark and Rique), cooking (Rique and Mom) and being there (all of them).

To anyone else I have inadvertently omitted: my thanks!

Preface

An Open Letter to the Reader

Humanity is on the edge of a revolution more fundamental than those wrought by Columbus or Copernicus. Current discoveries in physics, combined with psychological insight and research, open literally infinite vistas to human consciousness. We are just beginning to feel the first faint glimmering intimations of the powers wielded by our minds.

Counseling fields and human relationships are transforming as our understanding of reality undergoes radical shifts. As our conceptions of causality alter, so do our ideas about human interactions. Our healing potentials have dramatically increased.

This book is aimed to meet some of the needs of helper/healers in the counseling arena, with special focus on astrologers, but I hope you won't read it for the sake of your clients alone. Join me in a voyage of exploration of ideas that excite me more than I can describe! Some of the newest information about human consciousness is mind boggling. Experiences once dismissed as wild dreams are now becoming possible.

So don't get this book simply to be a better savior to your clients. Use it as an aid to living a truly powerful, productive, absorbing and satisfying life. Read it **for yourself!**

Foreword

Until I began writing books, I never read forewords. Becoming an author opened my eyes to their usefulness. Forewords are where we can explain ourselves and offer tips to guide the reader.

This book will be a mixture of theory and abstract concepts with concrete examples and illustrations, plus exercises for further development by the reader. Readers who prefer to have a broad outline in mind might read Chapter 29 (a summary checklist) first. For people less fond of philosophy and abstractions, I suggest you skip over the portions of Section One which seem too professorial. Later, if desired, you can return to the initial chapters which give the theoretical background and research support for ideas illustrated in later chapters.

Section Two of the book is designed to stimulate readers to carry the ideas presented further, with their own interpretations and adaptations. It is likely to be most valuable if you use the poems, exercises, illustrations and discussions as jumping-off points for your own pondering, examining and feeling. Some readers may wish to read the associated "applications" chapter after each theory chapter, thus: Chapter 1 followed by Chapter 17; Chapter 2 and 18; 3 and 19; 4 and 20; 5 and 21; 6 and 7 with 22; 8 and 23, etc.

Section Three presents a transcript from an actual consultation. This is not presented as a role model, but to help illustrate how many different directions the counselor can take. There are many roads to travel. In a number of places during the consultation, I could have chosen other interventions. I hope readers will follow the consultation with their thoughts and feelings searching for alternatives. What else could have been done or said? How might you have phrased that? What might you have done? What would you not have done? What do you feel was overlooked of significance?

A horoscope is a condensed blueprint of a human being. It can help us enter into the life of another human being, into all his or her numerous complexities, contradictions, ambivalences and wondrousness. The possibilities are immense; the choices before the counselor are immense. The more we stretch our minds and hearts for alternatives, the more we will be able, with each client, to consider a number of possibilities. When we allow ourselves a universe of choices, we can find the more fulfilling ones for the moment, and do not have to stay tied to a view that will not be viable for the client or for us.

It is my hope that this book will help to demonstrate to counselors the vast power we have over our lives, the infinite potentials stretching before all of us.

Introduction
Therapy in 2050 (What Kind of Counselor Are You?)

Read the following scenarios and choose the one that most appeals to you:
In the year 2050 counseling will be carried out...

...in spotless, germ-free clinics by scientifically trained technicians. Troubled people will undergo an extensive variety of tests. They will then receive the appropriate dosage of medication, hormone, drug or surgery to depress the appetite, elevate mood, banish hallucinations and delusions, eliminate traumas, raise self-esteem, etc. Biochemical breakthroughs will remove the scourge of mental illness as effectively as vaccines have eliminated smallpox.

... by women trained in mystic arts, hypnosis and modern magic. These women, clad in comfortable, flowing garments work out of their own homes. The client relaxes in the cozy environment and enters a near trance state. The wise woman establishes communication with the unconscious. Her major role is mediator, to facilitate finding solutions satisfactory to both the conscious and unconscious. The "Modern Mystic School of Therapy" reclaims the Eternal Feminine, uniting left and right brain functions. "Health means wholeness: intuition with wisdom."

. . . in small neighborhood centers throughout the country. Attractive, physically fit men and women will lead troubled souls through breathing exercises, stretching and massage. Samadhi tanks, jacuzzis and swimming pools will be on the premises for use. Exercise and nutrition will be promoted. "A healthy mind is a healthy body."

. . . by computer. A trained operator will punch in all relevant data, e.g., age, sex, cultural background, symptoms. The computer will search its data banks and quickly spill out a personalized behavior modification program with explicit goals and record keeping specifications. The program will involve the individual and significant others in his or her life who will be instructed on the use of a packet of counters, reinforcements, instructions, and so on. Daily or weekly checkups will allow the computer to assess progress and make modifications as needed in the regime. A "lie detector" scale in the program will screen for client falsehoods. Modern treatment will be straightforward and streamlined.

. . . in warm, friendly offices by supportive therapists. These healers always trust and believe in the client. Due to the total and unconditional acceptance of their therapists, clients learn acceptance of themselves. In a loving atmosphere, troubled souls learn to appreciate themselves, and become capable of risking and changing to be happier. "Love conquers all."

. . . by friendly, but detached, healers who explain carefully, until it is clear, to every client that his or her problems are his or her creation and personal responsibility. The healer tells each unfortunate individual, sincerely, "I **know** you can do what needs to be done." The healer is available to clients, but never offers sympathy for pain, nor solutions, nor suggestions. Generally, healers follow a Socratic method of asking questions. They also live appropriate role model lives. This modern approach is the "Truman School of Therapy" in honor of President Harry ("The Buck Stops Here") S. Truman. "Responsibility is Power."

. . . by wise seers who use their expert knowledge to determine the path of a client's life. These wise men tell their clients what to expect next, when to take action and when to avoid it. "Fore-warned is Forearmed."

. . . only in groups. Trained facilitators will take the client's complete history. Then the client, if indicated, will be matched to a homogeneous group: same sex, same ages (within three years), same occupation, socioeconomic status, religion, sexual orientation, etc. If indicated, the client will be sent to a heterogeneous group, with clients as different from one another as possible. Groups will include leaders and "leaderless." Through interactions with one another, troubled souls will learn to understand and change themselves, or just accept what they are unable to change. "If you did it alone, was it real?"

* * * * * * * * *

I imagine some readers will find one scenario a favorite. Others probably want to pick and choose from each, but not be limited to one. And some of you may feel all the choices are extreme and undesirable. Such *reductio ad absurdum* examples can help to lead into several points:

1. There are a variety of theories about the **causes** of "mental illness" and "emotional distress." Our beliefs determine our methodology in seeking to help people. Those who suspect physical causes look for physical effects and cures. People who believe the root is emotional look to interventions dealing on an emotional level. Others seek a blend of the two.

2. There is presently no agreement on which, if any beliefs about people are most accurate. There is no **one** correct way to deal effectively with all troubled people. Different people respond favorably to different approaches. Different definitions of mental health abound.

3. It may be that searching for the one, "correct" theory of human psychological functioning is a blind alley. Information from psychology, physics and other areas can be interpreted to suggest that human beings are just as much **inventors** or **creators** of reality as **discoverers** (or uncoverers). Individual "realities" may require individual solutions.

SECTION ONE

Theory

Chapter 1
What Is Reality?

Philosophical questions may seem an odd place to start a book on counseling, but the issues are vital. Since our beliefs about people and the "real" world affect all that we do, including how we counsel, it behooves us to examine those beliefs.

The human brain operates as a selective filter. Our world offers us large amounts of data; we screen out much of it. Workers in the psychology of perception have long observed that "from a myriad of impinging stimuli, we are aware of only certain objects and certain attributes of the objects" (Reference 37, p. 5). Probably the largest gap between Americans and more "primitive" cultures is our underutilization of our noses. Cultures that still hunt, and are less ensconced in concrete and steel than we are, gain a tremendous amount of information through smells and odors which most Americans just would not perceive.

We also censor, interpret and alter our experience. "The world is not merely revealed to us; rather we play an active role in the creation of our experience" (37, p. 5). For example, seeing an almost-circle , most observers tend to fill it in (complete the gestalt). Humans tend to create patterns, whether or not the pattern is "objectively" existent. Another common example is the image that can be seen as a vase, or as two faces in profile (49, p. 24). Or the ambiguous drawing that some see as an old, hunched-over woman with a scarf, while others see a young, lovely woman with a necklace (48). For illustrations, see Chapter 17.

It becomes almost impossible to talk of sensory reality **outside** of the interpretive framework we bring to it: what we see, hear and feel is influenced by our conditioning, training and heredity.

Out of the entire visual spectrum, we see only a small portion--and notice far less in America than in cultures that depend more on visual acuity. Similarly with our hearing, taste, touch, and so on. Eskimos can recognize more than seventy different kinds of snow, a perceptual skill vital in their environment (46). Most nonskiing southern Californians, like me, probably recognize only one kind of snow. It is possible that with sufficient time, training and motivation, I could learn to recognize seventy different snows. (I hope so.) It is also possible that I would be too set in my ways to change.

One of the most striking examples of people's seeming inability to change a **perceptual set** (an established framework, a stable way of experiencing the world) comes from an experiment by Postman and Bruner. They showed subjects, for very brief moments, a series of playing cards. Subjects were asked to identify the cards. Some of the cards were **anomalous,** such as a black three of hearts or a red eight of spades. In the beginning, subjects "fit" the cards into their existing framework (their previous experience of playing cards). The black three of hearts might be identified as the three of spades or as the three of hearts, with no sign of distress by subjects. Then the experimenters gave the subjects increasingly longer moments of time to examine the various cards. Subjects began to exhibit discomfort. Most began to hesitate. Their identifications were no longer quick and sure. They would say things to the effect of, "I think that is the three of hearts, but there is something wrong with it." Eventually, most subjects would produce the correct identification without hesitation, sometimes quite suddenly. After dealing with a few anomalous cards, they had no difficulties with the remainder.

For whatever reasons, some subjects could not seem to adjust their conceptual categories. Though viewing at forty times the amount of time needed to identify a normal playing card, these subjects still "missed" on more than ten per cent of the anomalous cards. They also often showed strong distress, saying things like, "I can't make the suit out, whatever it is. It didn't even look like a card that time. I don't know what color it is now or whether it's a spade or a heart. I'm not even sure now what a spade looks like. My God!" (10, p. 218). (I can imagine myself saying, "Snow is snow! How can you say this white fluff is different from that pile over there?")

Even scientists, usually considered the epitome of objectivity, filter and interpret their observations. Thomas Kuhn has written a seminal book on the subject: *The Structure of Scientific Revolutions*. In it, he points out that scientists make assumptions about the nature of the world, and then act on their assumptions. Kuhn suggests that scientists filter their perceptions selectively, based on their beliefs about truth, reality and the nature of the world. Radical shifts in scientific viewpoints, according to Kuhn, are fairly rare. Such shifts in how scientists see the world Kuhn refers to as **revolutions**. Copernicus contributed to one such revolution by declaring the Sun was the center of the solar system. Before that revolution, everybody "knew" the Sun went around the Earth. After all, they "saw" it every day.

With a scientific revolution, the basis of one school of thought in science is transformed. That is, a new world view supplants the old. The accepted explanations for how things work are altered. The people who make such a revolution, according to Kuhn, are, "Almost always... either very young or very new to the field whose paradigm [model] they change" (45, p.90). For, as Max Plank said, "...a new scientific truth does not triumph by convincing its opponents and making them see the light, but rather because its opponents eventually die, and a new generation grows up that is familiar with it" (45, p. 151). Or, as Ayn Rand put it, "The entire history of science is a progression of exploded fallacies, not of achievements" (61, p. 81).

There are a number of clear illustrations of the above in the history of science. For example, the smaller size of women's brains was once cited as "proof" of their "natural" mental inferiority (until someone finally noticed that women's brains are **larger** than men's in terms of percentage of brain weight to body weight).

A recent issue of *Scientific American* gives another good example. The January 1982 issue looks at what was being said one hundred years ago by scientists. Many of the accepted ideas were scientific "proofs" of what we now consider culture bound stereotypes. One (1882) article referred to differences between the sexes. The article noted that there were more females than males born and more old women than old men. The author concluded that this demonstrates that male dominance over females is the "superior phase of evolution," since it occurs in "superior species and races, adult age and the superior classes of society" (73, p. 8). By contrast, claimed the author, women are equal or greater in number than men only in "inferior races and species, young persons, the aged, and inferior classes of society." His final conclusion was that there is a predominance of women in the most primitive stage of evolution; equality is an intermediate stage, and the highest stage of evolution is male dominance.

Notice the article does not even question the use of such assumptions as "superior races,""superior classes" or "superior species." Today's scientists cite the larger number of women than men surviving to old age as evidence of the greater biological sturdiness of the female human. Usually the "X" chromosome is given some of the credit here. Presently, males are conceived in greater number than females, but are much more subject to spontaneous abortion and miscarriages. About 106 males are born to every 100 females, but males are more subject to disease, accidents and war. By age fifty, women outnumber men (22, p. 998). Most current scientists suspect estrogen plays a large, protective role in the greater longevity and resistance to disease of women over men. Sex roles may also be of major importance. In the past, women did not smoke as much as men, which helped to keep cancer rates down. Women do not usually fight in wars. And, women do not have the accident rate that men (especially when teenagers and in their twenties) have. Certain stress related illnesses, e.g., heart disease, are on the rise among women as they enter more fully into the tensions of the executive world and other formerly "male only" preserves.

The point is not what is actually "true" or "false" in this case. Rather, the point is that scientists, as well as the rest of us humans, **interpret** their "facts" within a framework of assumptions. Basic assumptions are rarely questioned. One hundred years ago, male superiority to females was a "given." Everyone (except a few "crazy" radicals) just "knew" it. So information was not interpreted in terms of: "What might this show about men and women?" but rather, in terms of: "How does this illustrate the superiority of men?"

Kuhn indicts scientists for seeing only what their world view includes. They are often "blind" to conflicting evidence. Perceptual psychology suggests this is not a blindness belonging to scientists alone. Being human seems to mean interpreting the world, fitting things into a framework of meaning. This applies to scientists, to astrologers, to religious leaders, etc. We need a framework in order to operate in the world. "...we as perceivers also seek to understand and predict the world in order that we may behave in it to our advantage" (37, p. 8).

If our world had no order, no way of deciding what was important and worth noticing, and what we could filter out and ignore, we would be overwhelmed by sensory data. The major function of the brain is to **filter out** certain perceptions from a huge mass of possible input. That filtering is assisted by our assumptions of what is significant and meaningful, based largely on past personal history. "...our past experiences and purposes play an absolutely necessary role in providing us with knowledge of the world that has structure, stability and meaning. Without them, events would not make sense.

With them, our perceptions define a predictable world, an orderly stage for us to act on" (37, p. 9).

Kuhn's description (of this process):

> ...that enterprise [science] seems an attempt to force nature into the preformed and relatively inflexible box that the paradigm [model] supplies. No part of the aim of normal science is to call forth new phenomena; indeed those that will not fit the box are often not seen at all. Nor do scientists normally aim to invent new theories, and they are often intolerant of those invented by others. Instead, normal scientific research is directed to the articulation of those phenomena and theories that the paradigm already supplies (45, p. 24).

In other words, scientists, and the rest of us humans, make certain basic assumptions about the nature of the world and the nature of reality. "Facts" are interpreted in terms of basic assumptions. (Indeed, what is defined as a **fact** is determined by basic assumptions.) These fundamental assumptions, or models of the world are rarely changed. They are so basic, the scientist almost never thinks of them, much less questions them. Data which contradicts one's basic world view is generally dismissed, or not even seen — by "scientists" and laypeople alike. A thousand years ago, people "knew" the Earth was flat. It was too "obvious" to ever be questioned. Two hundred years ago, many people "knew" that blacks and women were inferior people. History is replete with other examples.

For Kuhn, one of the functions of a paradigm or model is to "tell" the scientist what information should be gathered and paid attention to, and what is "meaningless" and of no concern. Without the paradigm, Kuhn points out, scientists end up collecting masses of data and observations, with no sense of what is useful or not. This sounds very similar to the dilemma of the observer who does **not** have an interpretive framework. "The notion of the existence of an 'objective observer' who sees the world accurately because he has had no past experience or is disinterested is patently false. If such a person did exist, we would have to predict that he would not see a structured, stable, and meaningful world" (37, p. 10). Indeed, we might suspect that such an individual would see the "blooming, buzzing, confusion" that early psychologists guessed was the experience of the newborn infant.

Kuhn likens a change in the scientific paradigm to a change in one's visual gestalt (configuration). One is looking at the data in a new way, making different interpretations. When we change our world view, we learn to see new gestalts. For Kuhn, it is not just interpretation, however. It is almost as though: ". . . after Copernicus, astronomers lived in a different world" (45, p. 117). Or, as he says on page 121: ". . . though the world does not change with a change of paradigm, the scientist afterward works in a different world." We act as if our view of reality **is** reality.

Children provide further evidence of a selective filter. What we know of child development implies that the development of a world view, and subsequent attempts to fit all data into that view of reality, is not a characteristic of adult scientists alone. Piaget's work with children certainly suggests that children go through a variety of changes in thinking about how the world works.

One Piagetian example focuses on recognizing what he called "conservation." A child may be shown two equal glasses (A & B) with equal amounts of liquid in them and asked if the glasses contain the same amount or not. If the child says that the amount is the same, the experiment continues. Step #2 is for the experimenter or the child to pour liquid from one glass into another, perhaps a low, wide glass (C) or a tall thin one (D).

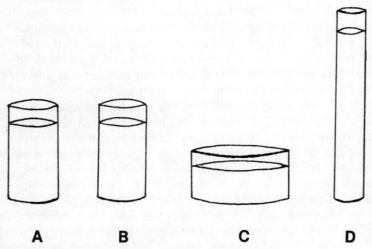

A   **B**   **C**   **D**

Again the child is asked if the liquid in the new glass is the same amount as in the original one or not. Piaget and others found that young children often say, "No, they are not the same amount." When asked why, the children explain because one glass is so tall or so wide.

Piaget theorized that the children had not yet incorporated the idea of constancy (**conservation** of continuous quantity). Instead, according to Piaget, young children focus on one dimension (such as length or width) and base their conclusions on that dimension alone. Older children recognize the conservation principle and will point out that the amounts must be the same because nothing has been added or subtracted from the liquid.

Children's eventual perceptions do tend to end up remarkably similar to those of the people around the children. As children grow, much of what they interpret in the world is influenced by family patterns and interactions. "The family's foremost function is to define reality and the child's relationship to it — essentially to teach a child what is and is not possible" (46, p. 96). Culture also plays a large role in molding a child's perceptions: "...very large number of human potentialities are in principle available to us. But we are born into a particular culture which selects and develops a small number of these potentialities, actively rejects others and is ignorant of most" (78, p. 170). For example, children are born with the capacity to make the sounds of all languages. The language(s) we learn when young channels our linguistic abilities. Unless exposed to a variety, we become limited to certain tones. For example, adult Japanese often have difficulty distinguishing between "l" and "r" sounds, especially in combinations, like "bled" versus "bread." English speakers have difficulty managing the tonal qualities in Japanese and Chinese.

When and where the filtering starts is an open issue. Some schools of human development argue more vehemently than others for the concept of the human child as a *tabula rasa* or blank slate (written on somewhat by heredity and largely by environment). The question of the existence, or nonexistence, of a consciousness or entity we might call a soul is an area of debate for some, unquestioned faith for others and immediate dismissal for others. I choose to avoid the issue for the moment.

People have successfully conditioned late term fetuses *in utero*, so some learning takes place before birth. Presumably, even in the womb, the fetus has a large variety of stimuli to which it can react. R.D. Laing has suggested that perhaps our intrauterine experiences are impressed psychologically on our awareness before we are born. He suggests that physical experiences (comfort, nourishment, pain, etc.) may help mold psychological attitudes (e.g. security, self-esteem, anxiety) (56). And, we may continue to repeat old patterns of discomfort. For such reasons, he suggests some schizophrenics need to be reborn, literally and metaphorically, in order to deal as an adult with cues from long ago which signalled not being wanted to the fetus. It seems likely that here, as in the outside world, we play an active role in creating our experience. (Even if Laing is correct in his speculations, not all children reacted to discomfort in the womb by becoming schizophrenic.)

Once the child is born, s/he receives an even vaster amount of information to filter and interpret. Children vary in their sensitivity to a variety of stimuli; they vary somewhat in temperament, even as newborns. These differences would obviously affect each individual's selection process. A more sensitive child, for example, might react more negatively to pain or more positively to pleasure than a less physically reactive child. Certain responses appear innate, such as the startle response to loud noises. But even with such "automatic" reflexes, the individual variations are considerable. When, where, how our filtering responses begin is an open question. That they exist seems extremely likely in terms of our present knowledge and interpretation.

The earliest filtering and selective processes channel later ones. It's like building a canal; we tend to keep using the same passage over and over again, rather than building new ones. This is one of the ways we create stability in our world. We constantly seek to repeat what is a familiar pattern in our perceptions. "We select certain facets of the situation and stick with them" (37, p. 6).

As the child grows, s/he continues to interpret reality, based on "Past experience, language and present motivational state or goals for the future" (37, p. 9). The present is "fit into" the model of the past. Many different schools of psychotherapy have noted this human tendency to repeat old, familiar patterns of long ago in new contexts, where they are uncomfortable rather than helpful. Example: the child who copes in a family by whining will not generally find whining useful as an adult, but may continue in that "stuck" behavior, not "knowing" (consciously) any other way to be.

It is important to remember that children are always filtering and interpreting. Psychological theories which talk as though the child were merely absorbing the output of the parents and family create a divisiveness, and tend to end up blaming the parents for the condition of the child.

Some of this adversary relationship appears to be rooted in the linear nature of our language. Take, for example, the sentence: "Juvenile delinquency is due to a lack of parental discipline." This establishes a simplistic cause and effect relationship, ignoring the effects of peers, the school system and a number of other factors. Also, the juvenile delinquent is seen as merely reacting to parental discipline or the lack thereof. There is no acknowledgment of what part the child plays in selecting delinquency out of a range of possible behaviors. This linear view also holds in other languages, as the Italian family therapists point out in *Paradox and Counter Paradox.*

They refer to the "tyranny of linguistic conditioning" (60, p. 51).

> Finally we were able to realize how much our belonging to a verbal world conditions us. In fact, since rational thought is formed through language, we conceptualize reality (whatever that may be) according to the linguistic model which thus becomes for us the same thing as reality.
>
> But language is not reality. In fact, the former is linear, while the latter is living and circular (60, p. 52).

They continue, "This traditional [linear] view easily leads to the temptation to use an arbitrary punctuation: correlating the symptom to the symptomatic behaviors of the 'others,' according to a causal connection. Thus it happened, not infrequently, that we found ourselves indignant and angry with the parents of the patient" (60, p. 55). They suggest, rather than seeing the behavior of parents as "causes" of the symptoms of children, to use a "circular model" where the behaviors can "be considered simply complementary functions of the same game" (60, p. 53). That is, children raise parents as well as parents raising children.

Alfred Korzybski and Benjamin Whorf suggest that the Indo-European languages tend to trap us into a linear model of life, disregarding relationships, encouraging us to think in terms of simple cause and effect. We easily confuse language and reality, falling into false assumptions. Language tends to isolate what exists in continuity. We can lose sight of change, process and movement. As Marilyn Ferguson puts it: "Life is not constructed like a sentence, subject acting on object. In reality many events affect each other simultaneously" (27, p. 149).

The manner in which adults filter experience and simplify a very complex world is often not very different from how children interpret the world. Freud, Adler, Jung, Berne and numerous other theorists have noted how often people repeat old, childhood patterns even when grown up. Most psychotherapeutic systems agree that people have a tendency to live their lives in patterns. They often repeat destructive patterns. T.A.(Transactional Analysis) refers to a **script,** a life plan people follow.

The general idea is, as astrologer Rob Hand so neatly put it: "People would rather be right than happy" (36). We often seem to live out our lives as if **proving** (to ourselves and others) that our basic assumptions about life and people are correct, even if these assumptions are highly uncomfortable ones with which to live. Haley notes that even distressing symptoms are often preferable to "living in an unpredictable world of social relationships" (35, p. 15). An example is the woman who has a basic belief: "You cannot trust men." She spends her life finding untrustworthy men and avoiding, or not seeing, trustworthy men. She gets an unhappy, frustrated life, but the presumably satisfying feeling of being "right" about men.

There is an old, flip definition of neurosis: "Neurosis is the pattern of defeating yourself by repeating yourself." What strikes many therapists about troubled people is that they are so often **stuck**. They don't see their options. They ignore other choices. They do the same, self-defeating, exasperating patterns over and over and over again.

I am suggesting, and have company in the psychological community, that a basic human drive is to make models. Scientists are not the only ones trapped by their assumptions about reality. Given that the world is full of **much** more input than any of us can absorb (in our present states), we learn to start filtering, probably in self-defense. The filters we adopt reflect our individual choices, and are considerably influenced by our language(s), culture and family background. We learned what to pay attention to, and what to ignore. I learned to pay attention to machines (TV, cars, refrigerators); the Eskimo child learned about snow. I'd be highly incompetent in the Far North, and she might have difficulty crossing a New York street.

We humans get ourselves into trouble when, as Korzybski says, we forget that "The map is not the territory." Or, as John Grinder, a proponent of NLP (Neuro-Linguistic Programming) puts it: "The menu is not the meal." We make assumptions. We interpret our "reality." We ignore some aspects of our environment. We fold, spindle, and mutilate our experience to fit our preconceptions of how people, the world, life is. We forget that our **view** of the world **is not** the world. Just because the earth **looks** flat, does not mean it **is** flat.

When we are sufficiently troubled, we may visit a psychologist, minister, astrologer or other healing/helping professional for assistance. Though specific techniques and methods vary tremendously, the underlying process of a therapeutic interaction appears fairly universal. The initial step is to enter the client's **world view** or "reality." This has been called rapport, or establishing the therapeutic relationship. Most descriptions of the process include some kind of recognition that it includes meeting the clients on their home ground and seeing things from their perspective. The goal is to help clients **change** their world views. As Frank Farrelly puts it: "The provocative therapist is constantly trying to do both: get inside a frame of reference and then change it" (26, p. 120).

As we might suspect from Kuhn's dissection of scientists, ordinary people are also singularly unwilling to change their world views. This is generally labelled "resistance" by the therapist. A variety of techniques are utilized to help effect changes. As with most specific tools, some work with some people, and not with others.

My major quarrel with most current systems of psychotherapy is that few of them address the issue of model building directly. Most operate by trading models. They offer a new model to clients, be it the Id, Ego, Superego model; the Parent, Adult, Child model; the Unconditional Love and Acceptance model; the Planet, House, Sign model, etc. For many clients, the new model does lead to more fulfilling lives than the ones they had previously, because the new model gives more choices than the old framework they were using. A change in models will often be experienced as an "opening up" in the life — horizons broaden, vistas increase. However, it is not a cure-all. It is **still** a model, and no model is as complete as reality. The very process of constructing a model or framework of interpretation implies generalization, condensation. We cannot include everything. The better the model, the more useful a description it is for us in dealing with "reality." The worse the model, the less useful, the sooner we run into holes ("unexplored territory" on our map), deletions and distortions.

There are a few people in the history of psychology who have been pioneers, emphasizing models and warning against becoming stuck in one way of viewing the world. Dr. Roberto Assagioli, founder of Psychosynthesis, recognized that we all strive for a conceptual framework to explain reality. With Psychosynthesis, he attempted to correlate similarities with other models, reduce exaggerations, and come up with a conception of human personality "nearer to reality than previous formulations" (1, p. 16). He emphasized that all models are tentative and hypothetical, and warned against getting too tied to one view of reality.

Alfred Adler studied people's **lifestyle**: a map of cognitive organization each of us develops to help us understand, predict and control our experience. Lifestyle is based on our perceptions, so inevitably contains some mistakes. People are prone to several "basic mistakes" in Adler's terms. These include (18, p. 57):

1. **Overgeneralizing.** This usually involves an implicit "all" or "always." The world is experienced in absolute terms. There may be strong dichotomies. Things are black or white. For example, "The world is hostile."

2. **Impossible or unrealistic goals** for "security" or "happiness." For example, "I'll be okay if everyone likes me."
3. **Misperceptions about life** and its demands. Severe forms include hallucinations and delusions. Milder forms include decisions like: "I'm a very unlucky person."
4. **Denying or minimizing one's own worth.** Adler described what Berne later popularized as the game of "Stupid."

George Kelly built an entire personality theory on the idea that each of us behaves as if we were a scientist. We create and test hypotheses about significant others. In other words, we make models. Kelly's central notions include that people strive to understand, interpret events of importance creatively, and are free to endlessly revise their theories about the world. (Only small or superficial changes are easy or common. Kuhn and others note how rarely people revise their theories about the world.)

Albert Ellis' Rational Emotive Therapy (RET) is based on the idea that people's beliefs, attitudes, philosophy and opinions are largely internalized as **self-talk**. Self-talk, or internal dialogue, helps create self-defeating emotions and behaviors. Ellis induces people to change their beliefs and attitudes, and emotions and behavior follow. Ellis recognizes the ideas of Korzybski and other semanticists, and sometimes calls his approach **semantic therapy**. For example, if a client says, "I always do badly at parties," Ellis would have the client say instead: "I usually do badly at parties," or "I've done badly at parties in the past, but that doesn't mean I cannot do better in the future."

Frank Farrelly and other Provocative therapists recognize the subjectivity of each individual's world. Farrelly notes that, as children, we tend to interpret, overgeneralize, and make decisions based on inadequate samples and distorted perceptions. As adults, we often continue to act on this inadequate or distorted information. For example, we may decide, "Everyone rejects me," after three people say "No," (inadequate samples and overgeneralization). We further decide, "I must not be lovable," (interpretation and distortion of data). The role of the therapist is to "provoke" clients into examining and changing their assumptions about the world.

Richard Bandler and John Grinder, along with other practitioners of Neuro-Linguistic Programming (NLP) emphasize that we all create "maps" of reality and then act as if they were true. They give three major ways in which we trip ourselves up with inadequate information.

1 . **Generalization.** For example, A man has a bad sexual experience and generalizes to: "I'm no good at sex," or "Women are too demanding," or "Sex will always be frustrating," . . . *ad nauseum.*
2 . **Deletion.** We leave out important aspects of our environment. Selective attention, or inattention, helps keep our perceptions stable. The die-hard male supremacist will just never "see" any successful women. He won't notice them.
3 . **Distortion.** This is valuable in art and science. We use it to dream, paint pictures, plan for the future. In it, we misrepresent reality. A not so healthy example would be the person who reacts to all criticism with: "You do not like me." Or the person who reacts to all praise with: "I'm perfect, so I don't have to do anything."

Even the above pioneers in recognizing how we construct reality do not always emphasize it in their counseling. And many schools preach as though their view of reality were the one and only "true" or "real" approach. I believe the most successful therapeutic intervention involves creating an environment where clients can realize that they are constructing models! Rather than saying, "Your map is deficient; mine is better; try it." I would have healers teach, "Once you realize that you are creating it all yourself, you can create a more useful map at any given moment. You can have millions to choose from!"

I think many Eastern philosophies have seen this more clearly than we have in the West. Many of the *koans* and parables about enlightenment stress the unwillingness of the teacher to provide answers. The students must find the answers for themselves. (This is one reason for Sections 2 and 3 of this book. I'm hoping to stimulate readers into finding their own answers.) Part of the illusion is that there is **one**, right answer. Sheldon Kopp's book addresses some of these issues with the provocative title of: *If You Meet the Buddha on the Road, Kill Him!*

Jay Haley has drawn a parallel between the experience of the student seeking enlightenment through a guru and the experience of a client in psychotherapy. Haley quotes Alan Watts on the enlightenment experience. Watts emphasizes that seekers must find truth for themselves; to simply be told is insufficient. Students are led to act on their assumptions, to go with their delusions until they realize their image of what is does not work. The Zen master traps students in paradoxical situations where they must confront their visions of reality. Then they can cast about for a new "reality." Haley, in his work, encourages the client to ". . . behave in his usual ways, while he undergoes an arduous ordeal which makes it difficult for him to continue in his usual ways. The response to this paradoxical situation is a type of response which the individual has never made before and he is thereby freed from the repetitive patterns he has followed in the past" (35, p. 85).

This also reminds me of Fritz Perls' use of what he called "skillful frustration." Perls saw his job as therapist to frustrate the clients' attempts to get Fritz or others to take care of them, until clients were forced to use their own resources, find their options, discover and tap their own potential. This is in line with the Perls definition of maturity: moving from environmental support to self-support.

Western education and the scientific model in the past have dealt with one, and only one, "correct" answer to each question. In the West, we have travelled the path of dichotomies, exclusive polarities. Something was real or not real; right or wrong. People were masculine or feminine. Something existed or did not exist. Eastern philosophies have had another perspective: the yin and yang, where each polarity has the other within it. A change is coming over our land, however. Today's physics is beginning to sound like philosophy from China or India. Books like *The Tao of Physics* note that we are moving away from a model of linear, materialistic causality towards a model of an interactive interrelated universe (where light can be both a wave **and** a particle). Consider the following:

> Vaccha asked the Buddha,
> 'Do you hold that the soul of the saint exists after death?'
> 'I do not hold that the soul of the saint exists after death.'
> 'Do you hold that the soul of the saint does not exist after death?'
> 'I do not hold that the soul of the saint does not exist after death.'
> 'Where is the saint reborn?'
> 'To say he is reborn would not fit the case.'
> 'Then he is not reborn.'
> 'To say he is not reborn would not fit the case' (49, p. 77).

From Robert Oppenheimer:

> If we ask, for instance, whether the position of the electron
> remains the same, we must say 'no';
> if we ask whether the electron's position changes with time,
> we must say 'no';
> if we ask whether the electron is at rest, we must say 'no';
> if we ask whether it is in motion, we must say 'no'(58, p. 40).

Concepts like the quarks have physicists sounding like philosophers and mystics. Quarks get from here to there before they have left here. People studying quarks use concepts like "reverse time" (67). Dr. John S. Bell published work showing quantum effects are not just here or there, but both! His work suggests our concepts of space and time are no longer adequate. Bell found that if paired particles (identical twins in polarity) fly apart, and the experimenter alters the polarity of one, the other changes instantaneously. They remain "connected" in some mysterious sense. Marilyn Ferguson quotes Dr. Nick Herbert regarding this oneness of apparently separate objects: ". . . a quantum loophole through which physics admits not merely the possibility, but the **necessity** of the mystic's unitary vision: 'We are all one' "(27, p. 172).

Dr. Herbert discards linear causality and talks of "cosmic glue," the idea that everything is the cause of everything else. Robert Anton Wilson, in an excellent article for the layperson on "The Science of the Impossible," gives the illustration of an old Sufi joke. Nasrudin is out riding and sees a group of horsemen. Thinking they may be robbers, he leaves hastily. Actually his friends, the group of men pursues him. Nasrudin gallops into a cemetery, jumps over the fence and hides behind a tombstone. His friends come up and ask why he is hiding there. Nasrudin's reply (illustrating cosmic glue): "It's more complicated than you think. I'm here because of you and you're here because of me" (79, p. 84).

Dr. Herbert does not speak of causality, but of "influence," which acts every which way in time. This strikes startling parallels in the work and words of family therapists. Bateson, Haley, Satir, Palazzoli and others have suggested that the causal, linear model is not effective for human relationships either. Haley suggests: "The ills of the individual are not really separable from the ills of the social context he creates and inhabits" (35, p. 2). Palazzoli et al., in discussing families, warn against the "trap" of searching for individual reasons and causes. Stay with the system, they emphasize. Palazzoli et al. note: "None of the members of the [family] circuit have unidirectional power over the whole, although the behavior of any one of the members of the family inevitably influences the behavior of the others" (60, p. 5). But it is not the cause. All the behaviors are interlinked and interweaving; each influencing and being influenced by the others. (There is not one "right" answer.) Compare this description to Marilyn Ferguson's description of modern physics: "In place of a real and solid world, theoretical physics offers us a flickering web of events, relationships, potentialities" (27, p. 171).

Mystics and psychics have long said that our linear, causal concepts of time do not fit their experience on other levels of reality. Linear causality, even in the physical world, has been challenged on a variety of fronts. ESP, fire walking and other "miraculous" activities do not fit into the standard framework of materialistic (physical causes) science. Yet many reputable people believe they exist, or may exist.

People who totally deny even the possibility of psychic phenomena are demonstrating the rigidity of their view of the world and unwillingness to change. As Otto Liebmann has pointed out: " Disbelief in miracles' is . . . to have **absolutely no doubt** as to the unconditional, objective, and universal principles of the causal principle" (16, 10). LeShan comments:

> When we are certain that a phenomenon such as fire walking **does not happen**, we are really saying, 'My basic knowledge of how the universe works is so complete and so accurate that the cosmos holds no more surprises for me. I know all the real truths and the details will all fit them.'
>
> How sad, and how reminiscent, to know that someone feels this way. We all did when we were immature. (When we were 'young' we knew better.) It feels familiar to hear this statement of certainty. I would wish this belief back for myself; it made a more comfortable world to live in. If only experience and life would not keep teaching most of us how little we know (49, p. 183).

LeShan calls this kind of certainty immaturity. Buddhists might call it unenlightened. Psychologists call it delusions of grandeur in a form only slightly different. But we can all fall prey to it. I suspect one of the attractions is the feeling of certainty, of being "right." Living in an uncertain world is rather frightening (as all of us in the nuclear generation are aware, even if we deny it often). As Yalom puts it: "Paradigms are self-created, wafer-thin barriers against the pain of uncertainty" (84, p. 26). Studies have shown many people have a low tolerance for ambiguity. We tend to "make" things fit (close the gestalt), "decide one way or the other." Perhaps good mental and emotional health will begin to include a healthy tolerance for ambiguity and a circular, interactive model of human relationships. Physics is abandoning linear causality; psychology is questioning it greatly. As we live in an increasingly complex world, the ability to visualize alternate possibilities, to imagine more than one "correct" answer may become a survival characteristic.

Marilyn Ferguson's *Aquarian Conspiracy* is all about the potential "paradigm shift" (change of models) we are currently facing. She notes the new model of reality means giving up certainty: "A sense of freedom requires uncertainty, because we must be free to change, modify, assimilate new information as we go along. Uncertainty is the necessary companion of all explorers" (27, p. 107). As I indicated in the introduction, incredible realms are opening up to all of us with this newest exploration, transcending most of the envisioned limits to the human psyche and experience. "Reality" may be grander and more immense than any of us dreamed.

The newest information suggests mystics were closer to "reality" all along. We can truly visualize William James famous quote:

> Our normal waking consciousness is but one special type of consciousness, while all about it, parted from it by the filmiest of screens, there lie potential forms of consciousness entirely different.
>
> We may go through life without suspecting their existence, but apply the requisite stimulus, and at a touch they are there in all their completeness. . . .
>
> No account of the universe in its totality can be final which leaves these other forms of consciousness quite disregarded (41).

Chapter 2
The Question of Meaning

What is the purpose of life? Is there any purpose to life? These and similar questions have haunted philosophy, religion, science and billions of people for thousands of years. I am not about to suggest answers or solutions. I wish to point out that the questions are important to those of us who work with people. What we believe to be (or not to be) meaningful in life will affect our perceptions of the world and other people. The kind of counseling we offer is based on our assumptions and our beliefs. Our feelings about life (joy, hope, optimism, anxiety, pessimism, anger. . .) will be felt by our clients and have an impact.

The basic materialist scientist's viewpoint is that life has no inherent meaning. People are assumed to be the current point in development of a long line of evolution begun by chance — the random coming together of the necessary atoms under the optimal conditions. The existentialist school of philosophy continues the materialist assumption that physical matter is the only reality, sees death of the physical body as final, but asserts that humans make their own meaning in life. This viewpoint is followed by a number of people in psychology, including therapists. Sheldon Kopp asserts: "There are no hidden meanings. It is a random universe to which we bring meaning" (44, p. 223).

The existentialist counselor generally stresses personal responsibility, but often displays underlying pessimism. Kopp again: "The world is not necessarily just. Being good often does not pay off and there is no compensation for misfortune. You don't really control anything. You have a responsibility to do your best, none the less [sic]'' (44, p. 223).

By contrast, various religious and mystical viewpoints assume an inherent meaning to life. The meaning may be ascribed to a Higher Power (e.g. ''God's will'). It may be given as various human values, such as love, good works, faith, hope, charity, progress and learning. Of course, all such values are subject to the interpretations and perceptions of their proponents.

There are psychological schools of thought which assume meaning to life. The strongest emphasis is probably given by Victor Frankl, who founded Logotherapy after surviving imprisonment in German concentration camps during World War II. He assumes humans have an instinctive ''will for meaning.'' Frankl insists counselors must treat the spiritual ills of mankind, not just physical, emotional and mental ills.

Assagioli, founder of Psychosynthesis, also emphasized the spiritual. He felt religious, mystical, inspirational experiences were real and factual in a pragmatic sense: effective, and producing change in the outer world. He rejected materialism. The Psychosynthesis model for the human personality includes a higher self of which our personal ''I'' feelings of self-awareness are but an imperfect reflection. Awareness of the higher self is assumed to be what has been described as cosmic consciousness: an ecstatic sense of being one with the universe.

Jung believed in ESP (psychic phenomena) and emphasized the human drive for transcendence, the ''pull from above.'' Ira Progoff, who originated the **Intensive Journal**, puts great importance on meaning. He feels people have rhythms and patterns to their lives, which are a part of a larger pattern and rhythm, in the infinite. ''A major quality of the psyche is its sensitivity to the large patterns of meaning in the universe. It **reflects** these in man[kind]. The psyche is a mirror of the patterns of meaning that give form to the infinite. Naturally, the reflection is not the reality, but it does indicate that the reality is actually there'' (69, p. 81).

Progoff cites the example of Herman Melville feeling drawn to go to sea on a whaling ship long before he envisioned *Moby Dick*. ''He did not decide it, and yet something within him forced it to be. He wrote of this in his letters to Nathaniel Hawthorne, and the tone of their correspondence implies that they both recognized such a factor in their lives'' (69, p. 77). This is the factor Progoff considers our ability to sense meaning and patterns, often unconsciously. Progoff's image of humans linked to the infinite has echoes in the modern physics view of an interactive, interlinked universe.

Not everyone assumes that a Higher Power provides the meaning. Maslow, Rogers, Perls and others have postulated a drive for self-actualization in the human being — to become all that we are capable of becoming. For such counselors, the purpose of life is to unfold more and more of our potentials. There are not necessarily any divine overtones to the self-actualizing urge.

A large number of people also mix the two basic polarities, seeing some meaning and some randomness (luck and misfortune) in life. The degree to which we perceive chance and randomness as operative in the world will influence our perceptions of responsibility, free will and people's power over their lives. The more randomness we perceive, the less likely we are to believe in the personal power and responsibility of ourselves and our clients. Since the empowerment of people is one issue in counseling, questions of meaning have ramifications for healers. (I will discuss responsibility and free will issues in greater detail later.)

Astrologers, like psychologists, fall across the spectrum in their beliefs about meaning. I am bringing up the issue here because it will affect how we counsel. The counselor who accepts only the physical world and cannot conceptualize other realms will have a very different world view than the client who feels s/he has had a mystical experience. One person's madness is another's reality. Assagioli points out the potential for conflict in such a client and counselor mismatch (where the client is undergoing a spiritual awakening in Assagioli's terms):

> The lot of the latter is doubly hard if they are being treated by a therapist who neither understands nor appreciates the super-conscious functions, who ignores or denies the reality of the Self and the possibility of Self Realization. He may either ridicule the patient's uncertain higher aspirations as mere fancies, or interpret them in a materialistic way, and the patient may be persuaded that he is doing the right thing in trying to harden the shell of his personality and close it against the insistent knocking of the Superconscious Self. This, of course, can aggravate the condition, intensify the struggle and retard the right solution (1, p. 55).

It would be equally hard for a materialistic client to cope with a mystical counselor who insisted on interpreting everything in terms of cosmic meanings, and would not stay with the physical focus the client trusted.

Confronting a competing world view can help us to examine and perhaps widen our own, but that outcome tends to be most likely when in the context of a warm, supportive relationship. Insisting at the outset that our views are **the truth** is likely to merely turn off clients who see another reality. If we can enter their reality first, we have the possibility of changing ours and/or theirs, perhaps to create a larger, more complex and inclusive view of the universe. Our definitions of meaning or absence of meaning will affect our judgments of good and bad. As counselors, our values affect the people with which we work. Counselors who value love and make it central in their lives, will emphasize it in their work with their clients and will live it. Counselors who feel discipline is vital will stress that. People who believe growth and progress is not possible without pain and suffering will encourage their clients to experience both.

The beliefs we hold, the assumptions we make, affect our perceptions, our clients and our own experience of the world. I am asking readers to question. The less locked in we are to one way of perceiving "truth, reality and meaning," the more potential for us to change our lives and the lives of our clients.

Chapter 3
Theoretical Model

If we accept the proposition that reality is at least partially subjective, we can take as one of life's tasks the ability to make as effective a map as possible for the moment. I would like to suggest one such map — a tentative model of human functioning. This model is not offered as any absolute truth, but as one of many potentially useful ways to interpret "reality." It will, hopefully, enable us as counselors to practice in a manner that assists people in living more fully and happily.

As with any model, I will make certain assumptions, and operate within them. I hope here to make my assumptions explicit so readers can know where they agree and disagree with me. My goal is to have the assumptions allow for the widest range of human functioning and contentment. Hopefully, the wider and more flexible the map, the more useful for dealing with the vast territory of human beings.

In this model, people get themselves into difficulties when they forget they are not perceiving an objective reality, but rather are reacting to their interpretations of their subjective perceptions. Or, as Bandler and Grinder put it in *Structure of Magic*, Vol II: "In coming to understand how people continue to cause themselves pain and dissatisfaction, it is important to realize that they are not bad, crazy or sick. They are, in fact, making the best choice that they are aware of; that is, the best choice available in their model of the world" (4, p. 17).

From this perspective, "unreasonable" behavior often becomes "reasonable," as Frank Farrelly explains: "It was a very frightening experience, but exhilarating too, to go into another person's world, into whatever limbo or 'corner of the universe' she inhabited. . . . Then her behavior made sense, it all hung together, it was eminently 'rational' " (26, p. 7).

Therapy thus becomes the process of helping clients to recognize that they create maps, and assisting them in designing more fulfilling, more inclusive models of the world. Once our map is altered, our behavior and experience are also altered.

Assumptions

Assumption One: Reality is at least largely subjectively determined. People experience their perception and interpretation of the world, much filtered by past experience, present needs, and future goals.

Assumption Two: Human beings have a drive towards wholeness, self-actualization, or to become all that they are capable of becoming. Self-actualizing urges encourage people to expand their perceptual frameworks, manifest their potentials and encompass more possibilities.

Assumption Three: People have a competing drive for stability. They create patterns in their perceptions as a method of gaining a sense of control and predictability in their experience of the world. Maintaining one pattern too long can lead to unfulfilling events and relationships. (What was fulfilling once is no longer fulfilling. The pattern becomes a prison.)

Assumption Four: Changing people's perceptions, including ideas, attitudes and beliefs, will change their experience in the world, including behavior. Much pain and unhappiness can be banished this way.

Assumption Five: The astrological model is one useful way to conceptualize human personality. Correlating the twelve sides of life symbolized by house, planet and sign, with twelve ways of being in the world, or twelve human motivational drives can be a helpful map for a number of people.

Within this framework, I make a few secondary assumptions, which I will call corollaries. One is that people have many more resources at their disposal than they are aware of in day-to-day life. The act of creating a model of our experience means condensation, generalization and filtering. Some data is ignored; some is changed. It seems logical that any "ultimate" reality is much larger, more complex and inclusive than our interpretations (models) of it. We do have a useful tool at our fingertips, however. The whole wealth of the unconscious can be tapped to serve us. I also see this clearly in the horoscope, where many talents and abilities are shown to exist, and the client is often unaware of some of them.

The concept of an "unconscious" is one which divides some psychologists from others. The world presents us with many more stimuli in any given moment than we are aware of and can immediately describe. Yet, in other circumstances (under hypnosis, or during surgery when portions of the brain are stimulated), people will often recall, in great detail, experiences that they were not fully aware of at that time. So, it appears that there is a part of us which pays attention to much more than we know in our conscious, daily dealing with "reality." I choose to call this portion "unconscious." Another word would do as well if the reader prefers. The working definition would be a part of our experience which we do not "notice" at the time, but which is available for later use. This definition recognizes the unconscious as one of our greatest tools. It is a resource of multiple possibilities, that can carry us beyond the limits of awareness in our everyday minds.

I like Adler's concept of using unconscious as an adjective rather than a noun. What is unconscious we do not (yet) understand. I believe that most successful interventions will include some unconscious material. As Milton Erickson pointed out, clients come to us **because** they cannot handle what is going on with their conscious resources. If they could, they wouldn't be there. It only makes sense to tap into unnoticed resources for additional information and assistance.

Corollary One: with a universe to choose from, there are always multiple possibilities.(some unconscious).

A second corrolary is that **all** desires are potentially positive. If we assume that people are doing the best they know how in a given situation, we can at least ascribe a positive **intent** to what they are doing, even if the behavioral and experiential outcome is pain. Our task then, as a counselor, is to help clients find proper contexts for their behaviors. For example, assertion may bring pain and suffering in one context, but joy and accomplishment in another. This is a **corollary** to my work with an astrological chart. I believe that **everything** in the horoscope (and in the individual's psyche) **can be** used in a positive, fulfilling fashion. We merely need to find the proper channel, the appropriate time, place and form of expression.

Corollary Two: With an entire universe to choose from, there are always positive options. (Or: evil is potential good — in need of transformation.)

A third corollary concerns subjectivity. I assume that my map of reality is very unique. It does not exactly match anyone else's. I can strive to enter the worlds of my clients as fully as possible, but to call myself "objective" is a lie. As Steve Lankton puts it: "...our maps of reality...are ultimately highly personal and idiosyncratic. No one else completely shares your way of making meaning, the associations and anchors that have developed over the course of your personal history" (p.46, p. 84).

Corollary Three: With a universe to choose from, no other person will make the same exact choices as I, nor see the world exactly as I do. (Similarly, no one will have the same exact horoscope as I do.)

Since we are both sending out information constantly and receiving data continually (mostly on the unconscious level), to say that I can be unconditional and merely reflect back to the client is also untrue. "It is as though the unconscious minds. . . (of counselor and counselee) were carrying on a conversation of which their conscious minds did not know. . . . [it is] what the counselor really is which exerts the influence not the relatively superficial matter of the words he utters" (53, 97).

Or, as Steve Lankton puts it in *Practical Magic*: "As a therapist you can't **not** influence your client despite any intention to avoid being 'manipulative' or 'interfering with the process.' Your client will always be responding, in some way, to your words, voice tone and tempo, gestures, posture, breathing, facial expressions, etc." (46, p. 74). And:

> According to this writing, it is not possible **not** to influence someone's experience and produce a response. A response is considered to be anything from verbal output to skin color changes, eye movements, gestures or breathing. I take any of these to be an indicator that a person's internal state has altered, that his experience has been influenced.... since consciousness is limited, we are really only cognizant of a fraction of the stimuli that we are continually responding to anyway (46, p.20).

Lankton continues, "The issue of responsibility in therapy and communication thus becomes very clear cut: each person will influence the other to varying degrees for a variety of outcomes" (46, p. 35).

Corollary Four: With a universe to choose from, the responses I make have meaning and intention. They are not random, nor are they neutral.

It also follows that the influencing process works both ways. I influence my clients, and they influence me. Or, as Rollo May quotes Jung: "The meeting of two personalities is like the contact of two chemical substances; if there is any reaction, both are transformed. We should expect the doctor to have an influence on the patient in every effective psychic treatment; but this influence can only take place when he, too, is affected by the patient" (53, p. 79).

Corollary Five: In an interconnected universe, any meeting has meaning and affects the individuals involved.(Remember Bell's experiment with two light particles which, once in contact, continue to react as if still in contact, no matter how far apart they are in space.)

Thus, I assume I will affect, and be affected by, my clients. My job is to be as effective in my influence as possible. I can measure my creativity in interactions by the impact on my clients. If I bore some, turn others off, excite and inspire some, it is likely I am operating in too stereotyped a fashion, probably trying similar techniques with different people. This is a form of insisting that the clients come into my map of the world. If instead, I can enter their map (as fully as possible), I have the option of suiting my influence to each individual client, and generating a useful response. Here, I would define useful as one which involves the clients changing their representations of reality so as to include more possibilities, encompass more territory.

I can also measure my effectiveness by its impact on me. If I do not change, if my clients do not shake me up, surprise me at times, I am probably closing myself off from a great deal of learning and growth. If I know all the answers and understand all my clients, I am probably deep into my biased perceptions and old habit patterns. The "expert" role leaves little room for learning and personal transformation.

In short, I shall judge myself most effective when both clients and I are able to expand our world views, encompass a bit more of "reality" than we did before.

Chapter 4
Information From Other Models of Counseling

If we judge models in terms of their utility (more or less effective), a reasonable question becomes: which models of psychotherapy and counseling have been most useful in helping people lead happier, more fulfilled lives? There is a fair amount of research on outcomes of psychotherapy. Some of it suggests that psychotherapy may have little effect on people's lives. Eysenck's trail-blazing study found that two thirds of people in therapy got better, and two thirds of people on the waiting list got better. People have criticized his work, but it certainly raised questions of efficacy. Bergin suggested that differences between treated and control groups in psychotherapy studies were confused because the treated groups contained both positive **and** negative changes.

Carkhuff and Berenson looked at Eysenck's data and that of other people, building upon Bergin's ideas. They found, in general, people on a waiting list gradually improving. Often, it appeared, they requested therapy while in crisis, and eventually (with or without therapy) the crisis subsided. People in therapy, although averaging a two thirds improvement rate overall, got both better **and** worse on an individual basis. Some people were considerably improved by therapy; some appeared worsened by therapy! (Having met people traumatized by astrological consultations, I believe astrologers can harm as well as heal.)

A recent book on the subject, *Psychotherapy For Better or*

Worse, addresses the issue of negative effects in psychotherapy with a survey of the literature and responses from a number of clinicians regarding what might be considered negative effects, and what might produce them. The authors (Strupp, et al.) comment: "It is clear that negative effects of psychotherapy are overwhelmingly regarded by experts in the field as a significant problem requiring the attention and concern of practitioners and researchers alike." (77, p. 83) This is a concern I hope astrologers share. Many of the points in the book can be applied to astro-counselors as well.

Negative effects are defined as including such things as increase in the number or severity of problems faced by the client; clients attempting to overreach themselves through counseling; clients becoming disillusioned with their therapist and therapy (for many a "last hope"); clients' abuse or misuse of counseling (e.g., overintellectualization, using psychological jargon as a label or excuse and not changing, etc.). Many of these possibilities have parallels for astrologers. Astro-counselors lacking in empathy and other skills may aggravate the problems of their clients. Counselors enamored of their healing role may, knowingly or unknowingly, encourage dependency in clients, who then manufacture more problems in order to return to their dedicated counselor. Just as some people see a therapist as a "last hope," so do some individuals go to astrologers as a last resort. Disenchantment may be devastating. Astro-counseling is prone to intellectualization because it is mostly "talk therapy." It is easy for counselor and client to understand things "in their heads," but never take action. They may label a situation, and feel that is enough. (Does the label indicate a direction to take, options to try?)

The authors list a number of factors associated with negative effects in psychotherapy: deficiencies in therapist training and skills; inadequate or inaccurate assessment; personality traits of the therapist and technique problems. Training for astrologers is even less systematized and less subject to peer review than for other counselors. This does not automatically make astrologers unqualified. As will be pointed out below, caring for people, and skill in working with them, is more important than educational background *per se*. Astrologers committed to a high standard of excellence in their field will strive to update their training and knowledge, and provide supervision for others to learn as well.

The question of what training is appropriate for the astro-counselor is a difficult one. Astrologers' views on the qualities and training of a successful counselor will reflect their assumptions about reality and basic values. Several organizations have attempted to come up with tests of competence and suggestions for licensing. Research demonstrates that empathy and other personality characteristics in the counselor are much more important than credentials in the form of degrees or whatever. Nonetheless it is true that some clients are reassured by credentials. Complex issues such as this require a great deal of discussion among many people. I think peer review can be a potent tool. If we pay attention to what we do, and what other astro-counselors do, and have ongoing communication, the likelihood of everyone honing their skills becomes greater.

Inaccurate assessment is a large danger in astrology as in psychology. Where people, in all their complexities, are involved, it is easy to misjudge. Remaining flexible, checking out one's interpretations, keeping an open world view help the astro-counselor avoid becoming dogmatic, or insisting that a certain interpretation of the chart **must** be so.

On the question of personality, Strupp et al. note: "It has long been known, of course, that the therapist's personality makes an important contribution to the quality of the therapeutic relationship he creates as well as to their outcomes" (77, p. 125-126). Clearly the personality traits negative for a therapist would also be negative in an astrologer. Among personality characteristics to be avoided, the authors include voyeurism, sadomasochism, coldness, obsessiveness, seductiveness, fascination with fads, readiness to exploit, pessimism, limited self-examination, narcissism, lacking genuineness, unconscious hostility, needing clients to change a lot and greediness.

Among technique problems, Strupp et al. include false assumptions regarding the range and potency of therapy, especially a therapist feeling omnipotent and omniscient. The issue of omnipotence is particularly crucial to the astro-counselor. A horoscope can give us more information than most psychologists have in the first few months. It is tempting to overvalue its power. Astrologers' needs for status, control or power may encourage them to believe they know and understand more than is the case. (These issues will be discussed more fully in the sections on power and on projection.) Too many clients are prone to see the power of the infinite universe as lying behind their astrologer's every pronouncement. The dangers of playing the omniscient savior are addressed in Jerome Frank's *Persuasion and Healing* and Guggenbuhl-Craig's *Power in the Helping Professions* as well as other sources. The most common outcome of omniscient fantasies on the part of a counselor (astrological or otherwise) is that the client feels disillusioned and angry when the counselor turns out to be human and fallible.

Counselors can also do grave harm with their need to be "right," insisting on certain interpretations. Or, counselors out of touch with their own conflicts may work out anger, hostility, or control issues with clients rather than the people the astrologer is close to. Zip Dobyns and I are regularly told horror stories about what this or that astrologer said to a client. An amazing amount of negativity is put out by some astrologers who may enjoy the sense of power over a client's life (as clients cringe in anxiety). Or, the astrologer may be unconsciously expressing hostility, and the client is a handy target.

Mistakes around goals are cited as possible problems in counseling, including not discussing the reality of certain goals; not reaching **mutual** agreement on goals; having too demanding goals, or expecting clients to reach the goals too quickly and goals which are not in the client's best interests. All of these points are useful to astrocounselors as well.

Another error mentioned was misplaced focus: too much internal or too much external. Also criticized were technical rigidity (unwilling to change procedures, treatment; not seeing the client's individual needs; lack of thoughtfulness and understanding); overly intense therapy and misuse of interpretations. Misuse of interpretations has already been mentioned in terms of assessment. The other possible problems fall generally under a lack of empathy and flexibility. The personality traits of the counselor begin to look more and more important! (This is borne out by the research concerning what leads to positive outcomes in therapy.)

A warning was issued against the mismatch of therapist and client, e.g., using attack therapy with a fragile client, or aversion therapy with a masochistic client. Problems in therapist to client relationships were mentioned, including too much or too little rapport; **countertransference** (therapist reactions, problems, unresolved conflicts coloring his or her interactions with clients) and failure to maintain professional distance, especially in sexual involvement with clients. Any of these could be issues with astrological clients as well. (One male astrologer told attractive female clients that they had sexual problems, but he would be happy to help them work out their blocks.) Countertransference will be discussed in more detail subsequently.

Communication problems were another arena the clinicians mentioned. These included failure by the therapist to communicate clearly **and** determine if the patient understood, plus patient distortions, omissions, falsifications. It is important to be sure one is understood. Too often, counselors put out excellent insights, or ideas, but fail to check if the client has really grasped or understood what the counselor was communicating. Thus, vital, important material may be lost because the counselor never realizes the client didn't "get it." Clients, like all humans, will distort, falsify and omit some of their perceptions. Being aware of this can help us work with it, watching and listening for omissions. The horoscope can also provide us an additional viewpoint on the client, and may suggest clues about where to look for more details, or questions, or ways and directions in which to explore further.

Another potential danger mentioned was breach of confidentiality. Confidentiality is a client right which some astrologers are very lax in protecting. I have seen and heard astrologers mention clients by name, or with so much biographical information that the client is identifiable. Often, horoscopes with full birth data and names printed clearly on them are left lying about. (I've been guilty of this myself.) Astrologers do not always get client permission for the cases and examples they use. (Because one never knows when you might need an example, I tend to ask a lot of clients if they mind if I use them as an example some time, assuming their identity is kept confidential. Most are thrilled to agree. It is generally experienced as an ego boost; they are important.)

Other issues brought up by Strupp et al. included refusing to refer a client out when called for, and labelling — especially when used as an excuse for repeated failure. Few people are able to be helpful to everyone who comes to them for healing. Sometimes, personalities do not mesh, or our world views may be too divergent, or the client may need specialized areas of expertise in which we are not trained. For this reason, it is useful to have a referral list. My list includes trained and qualified psychotherapists, a polarity therapist, a nutritional therapist, an astrologer specializing in business clients and two astrologers who are willing to do specific predictions. Having a list is one step. Using it is another. If we define ourselves as an omniscient, omnipotent savior, we are unlikely to refer people out. We will try to help everyone. Therefore, it is useful to know one's own limits. For me, a major limit is a client with whom I have a strong negative reaction (strong enough to make my effectiveness unlikely) and any client for whom I do not see hope. If I cannot see any potential for my clients improving their life situations, I believe I should send them to someone who can offer them hope. (The next section will discuss the prime importance of hope in helping people improve their lives.)

Strupp et al. conclude with an appeal for more careful training and preparation of therapists. They note that academic achievement has no relationship to one's skill, or lack of skill, as a clinician. This point is also emphasized by Carkhuff and Berenson and NLP (Neuro-Linguistic Programming) practitioners. Astrologers can take note and great pleasure from this observation. It reaffirms that an astrologer need not go to school for years and years, or take dull courses to be a helpful counselor. People skills — not book learning — are most important.

Strupp et al. suggest tailoring training programs more carefully to necessary people skills, and include the possibility of requiring that all therapists undergo some personal therapy themselves. Zip Dobyns' exam after her *16 Day Astrology Intensives* includes a delineation (by the student) of his or her own chart. The focus is on the student's strengths and weaknesses, particularly as might influence working with clients. For example, the counselor who tends to hold back anger had best realize that and work with it. Otherwise, clients are likely to become targets for hostility, unknowingly. Once a counselor recognizes such a tendency, s/he can find more fulfilling ways to channel the aggressive energy, such as working out physically, being active in sports or fighting for a worthy cause.

Clinicians in Strupp's book emphasize the importance of flexibility on the part of the counselor and caring for people. And, not to forget world views, we read: "A competent therapist, it goes without saying, must be capable of understanding the client's perspective" (77, p. 128).

Other people have attacked the problem from the opposite point of view. That is, rather than attempting to determine the origin of negative effects, they attempt to determine the origin of positive effects. The authors of *Psychotherapy For Better or Worse* warn that this leads us into very muddy waters. They note that in the past, positive outcome has tended to be judged on an individual basis, e.g., the patient felt better; the therapist attained the goals s/he set initially. The authors suggest a model having three parts for judging therapy outcomes. They point out that mental health professionals have one set of standards, usually involving a personality theory regarding what "mental health" is, which may be at odds with the attitudes of society and the individual being treated. The client has another set of standards regarding successful outcomes, usually including feelings and success in certain outside activities (relationships, work, recreation). Society also has standards of good health which tend to involve stability, fulfilling one's roles, social predictability, etc. These three "parties" to the positive and negative outcome of psychotherapy will not necessarily be in agreement!

As an example, suppose a woman has been fulfilling her role as wife and mother at the expense of repressing her anger at an emotionally cold, intellectually inferior husband. Through therapy, this woman realizes her needs for love and mental stimulation. She has an affair and divorces her husband. Is this a negative or positive effect? For her? For the husband? For the children involved? The example is given by Ann Appelbaum, who suggests our judgment might depend on the kind of life the wife is able to build for herself afterwards, the state of the children, etc.

Current political policies aimed at pushing women back to traditional roles (regardless of their personal preferences) clearly demonstrate that societal interests are **not** always one with individual fulfillment. Thus, the question of negative and positive outcomes does become a complicated issue, like most of life. As the authors of *Psychotherapy for Better or Worse* indicate, with increasing insurance and so forth, other "third party interests" are likely to enter into the therapeutic relationship more and more. The issue of how the rights of the individual and the rights of society are going to be combined becomes an important one for clinicians to examine.

One of the best examples of such a "conflict of interest" question is found in the Broverman, et al. study of what clinicians judged to be mental health. The descriptions given for a mentally healthy "adult" were identical to those for a mentally healthy "male." The "mentally healthy female" was quite different: weaker, more likely to cry, less interested in math and science, more dependent, less assertive. In short, all the traditional sex role stereotypes were found widespread among definitions by "helping, healing" practitioners.

Such practitioners would encourage a man to cope and be responsible in instances where they would expect and encourage a woman to be dependent and seek someone else to cope for her. A recent *L.A. Times* article called "For Women Hooked on Legal Drugs" noted the prevalence of drug addiction among women, particularly to such drugs as tranquilizers. Some doctors are more prone to give a woman a pill, but expect a man to "**do** something" to take care of the situation. This further encourages women to stay gentle, quiet (tranquilizers!) and dependent. Broverman et al. noted that such stereotypes were widespread among psychiatrists, psychologists and social workers. It is my experience that they are widespread among astrologers as well. The individual woman who does not fit into the stereotype would be out of luck. Such a woman might experience a personal, highly negative outcome in therapy that society and the sexist practitioner judged as positive, or vice versa.

This is **not** to suggest that the individual is always right and society is always wrong. Such generalizations are usually deadly. I merely wish to stress the issue and suggest any counselors look closely at their values, the ways in which they wish to serve, or not serve society, and why. Unspoken, unexamined assumptions are the most dangerous. I'm asking everyone to question, question, question!

Chapter 5

Research on
Positive Outcomes

Quite a few researchers have attempted to discover which theories of human functioning "work" the best, which succeed most often in helping troubled people feel easier, more fulfilled. A number of studies have focused on **therapist variables,** qualities manifested by the counselor which seem to correlate with increased healthy functioning in the client. Researchers include Berenson, Cannon, Carkhuff, Collingwood, Foulds, Rogers, Truax and Wolf among others.

When queried on reasons for improvement, clients generally emphasize the quality of the therapeutic relationship, the humanity of the counselor, not specific techniques or insights. Heine looked at clients and found they ascribed improvement to relationship factors, regardless of the school of the therapists. Feifel and Eells found clients attributed successful therapy to relationship factors, while therapists put it down to technical skills and techniques. Blaine and McArthur found patients emphasizing the personal relationship between counselor and client. For some, encountering an accepting authority figure was an important experience. Other clients mentioned changing their self-images and their perceptions of others. Therapists emphasized making the unconscious conscious and correlating childhood experiences with present symptoms.

Fiedler studied expert clinicians from a variety of schools (Freudian, Adlerian, Rogerian, etc.) and found much similarity in their view of the ideal therapeutic relationship and also the kind of relationship they did establish with clients. (This differed from clinicians who were not experts, even if from the same therapeutic school as experts.) Carkhuff and Truax have emphasized that effective therapists establish a warm, accepting, understanding relationship with their clients. Seeman and Parloff found clients who were liked, or felt themselves liked, by their therapists were more likely to improve in therapy.

Terms vary slightly from one investigator to another, but one common theme was a focus on what might be called the **empathy** of the counselor. Carkhuff and Berenson defined "empathic understanding" on a continuum, where the therapist varied from not really understanding clients, detracting from their experience, forcing the therapist's point of view upon clients; to a level where client outputs and therapist responses were "interchangeable," expressing the same meaning; and on up to where the therapist was able to successfully deepen clients' experiences, enable clients to articulate feelings and perceptions only dimly felt or groped at. Rogers found a similar variable to be important.

Rogers, Berenson, Carkhuff and Truax also all emphasize **respect**: positive regard for clients' feelings, experiences and potentials. (The degree to which this positive regard should be "unconditional" or not is a matter of disagreement for researchers.) Respect begins with self-respect and includes communicating human warmth and understanding. A therapist's attempts to understand are a vital portion of respect (and the ability to enter another person's "reality"). Respect can include spontaneity and sharing honest feelings (thus tied to self-disclosure, immediacy, confrontation and congruence).

We must face at times the conflict of: Do I respect where clients seem to be **now** in their lives, or do I respect where I believe the clients **could be** in their lives? This issue splits psychotherapy--into schools that call themselves **directive** versus **nondirective**. Directive therapists will push clients, provoke them, give orders, give advice, and are willing to "take charge" to some extent in order to get clients moving in a direction the therapist judges as positive. Naturally, this is fraught with the perils of biased value judgments. Guggenbuhl-Craig warns us that an immense amount of evil is done in the name of good (e.g., the Crusades and "Holy Wars"). Counselors may judge as "good" what clients feel is very "bad."

Conversely, some clients flourish under directive therapy, appreciating the sense of stability and security, and happy to avoid some of the responsibility. Yalom points out that highly directive therapists tend to be counterproductive. Clients are less likely to develop their own confidence, willingness to take risks and responsibility. But a middle ground is effective with some clients. Some people seem to need a "push" from outside to start developing their potentials.

Nondirective therapists try to always "follow" the client and never "lead." They encourage clients to bring up issues and concentrate on what clients define as important. As indicated earlier, one cannot be totally nondirective. We influence clients (often out of awareness) with inflections, gestures, grunts and other subtle cues. This kind of subtle influence does not seem to be as destructive to client confidence and willingness to take personal responsibility as the highly directive counselor. But the less aware counselors are of their unconscious cues, the more potential for unknowing influence and possible harm.

A danger in so-called nondirectiveness is that both counselor and client may get very passive and collaborate to avoid dealing with important issues. Both parties need to keep alert and examine their relationship for subtle forms of influence and manipulation.

I am not suggesting one path or the other, merely asking readers to consider the issue. Most astrologers are fairly directive in that they are often bringing up issues which they see in the chart, whether or not the client indicates a willingness to get into those issues. The question then comes, what if a client seems unwilling to get into certain areas? What do you do? What if you judge those areas as fundamental and essential? My personal inclination is to consider each individual situation on its own merits. But there are often no easy answers.

Another counselor dimension emphasized is **genuineness** or **congruence**. This is the ability to be in agreement in one's various levels of communication. All of us communicate in gestures, body language, tone of voice, etc., as well as the words we use. Congruence means the counselor is in agreement within himself or herself. The different levels of his or her communication support one another. There are no internal contradictions. Incongruency means one part of the message is in conflict with another part. Receivers of incongruent messages tend to feel confused. Therapists who are able to be congruent most of the time are seen as more effective in aiding clients. Congruence includes expressing our ambivalence — when present — verbally, rather than saying one thing with our words and another with our bodies. People **do** have internal conflicts and contradictions. Congruence means clarity — not total agreement.

When we are pulled in different directions, we say so: clearly and directly.

Another useful skill is the ability to focus on specifics. Carkhuff and Berenson called this **concreteness**. It includes getting down to the basics, not wandering off in generalities or abstractions. Virginia Satir and others have emphasized the need to define who, what, when, where and how. In fact, one of Virginia Satir's definitions of successful family therapy is when each member of the family is able to make clear statements beginning with a definite subject (who), followed by an active verb and a clear object (what). (Examples of concreteness, congruence, empathy and respect in astrological consultations appear in the Practice Section of this book along with a few suggested exercises to enhance their development in one's self.)

Some researchers and practitioners value **confrontation**, where the therapist brings a client face-to-face with discrepancies (e.g., between the client's verbal speech and what his or her actions imply, between what the client is saying and what the counselor experiences as happening). Frank Farrelly has based a whole therapeutic school, Provocative Therapy, on (often humorous) confrontations of clients. Carkhuff and Berenson quote Douds on the importance of confrontation and honest expression of feelings: "...how pathetic it is to hear a therapist remark that he almost laughed, cried, got angry. What would happen to a child who was raised by a parent who almost expressed his real being? The child might turn out to be **almost** human!" (15, p. 12).

Carkhuff and Berenson see alienated individuals as searching for the "one insight which will provide a solution to life." (Shades of our linear model with **one "right"** answer!) But, "There is no one solution, only a series of confrontations" (15, p. 177). They note that high level counselors confront clients more often with their assets and resources rather than their limitations. Low level therapists are more apt to focus on client "shortcomings" (as defined by the therapist, of course).

Self-disclosure (sharing one's honest feelings and reactions) by the therapist has also been suggested, in the proper time and place, as aiding the healing relationship. Existentialists, especially, stress honesty and self-disclosure in their counseling interactions. Sidney Jourard was a major spokesman for the importance of relating personally to the client. Timing is vital, of course. Yalom notes:

> There is no way around the conclusion that the therapist who is to relate to the patient must disclose himself or herself as a person. The effective therapist cannot remain detached, passive and hidden. Therapist self-disclosure is integral to the

therapeutic process. But how much of self does the therapist disclose? Personal life problems? **All** feelings toward the patient? Boredom? Fatigue? Flatulence? (84, p. 411)

When appropriate, it is often very reassuring for clients to hear their astrologer has coped with similar dilemmas, e.g., "I have a lot of Taurus in my chart, and really do struggle against the temptation to overindulge." Examples of how I or other people have handled similar dilemmas can help the client see the astrologer as human, and offer the sense of company: "I'm not alone in my conflicts and occasional 'craziness.' " The important issue with self-disclosure is honesty and spontaneity. If we share ourselves openly and directly, clients will generally sense our sincerity and involvement and appreciate it. "Self-disclosure" designed to show how we always handle life the "right" way and make the "correct" choices is rarely helpful.

Collingwood and Renz studied the importance of **immediacy**: dealing with the feelings between client and counselor in the here and now. That has also been a focus given major importance by Fritz Perls in his Gestalt work, Frank Farrelly and a variety of humanistically oriented counselors.

Yalom's Curative Factors

Irvin Yalom is another researcher who has focused particularly on groups. He discusses twelve curative factors which lead to success in group therapy (85). Yalom bases these factors on therapist and client reports, research and his own clinical experience. Some of them appear to work in individual consultations as well. They are:

1. Imparting of information (suggestion, advice).
2. Self-understanding.
3. Identification with others (including the counselor).
4. Instillation of hope.
5. Universality.
6. Corrective recapitulation of the primary family group (or family reenactment).
7. Altruism.
8. Interpersonal learning: input (how others perceive us).
9. Interpersonal learning: output (improving skills in interpersonal relationships).
10. Group cohesiveness (not a factor in individual consultations).
11. Catharsis.
12. Existential factors.

Information

Therapists vary in the amount of direct information, suggestions and advice they offer. Transactional Analysis and other modalities come close to straight teaching (including the blackboard!) during therapy. The giving of information is usually of major importance in the astrological consultation. Many astrologers judge themselves as separate from counselors because, as astrologers, they provide information or "teach," but do not "counsel."

Knowledge about something previously unknown can greatly reduce anxiety. People tend to be uncomfortable with uncertainty (as emphasized in the work of Frieda Fromm-Reichmann and Yalom). Anxiety about the meaning or severity of one's symptoms may be more disabling than the symptoms *per se*. Anxiety is diminished by the lessening of ambiguity, and the reverse holds. Anxiety disturbs perception, aids ambiguity. Anxious people are less capable of organizing and perceiving visual cues. Perceptual distortions can lead to more ambiguity and more anxiety: a vicious cycle.

Yalom comments on the importance of a belief system to both client and therapist:

> . . . patients are enormously reassured by the belief that their chaotic inner world, their suffering, their tortuous interpersonal relationships are all explicable and therefore governable. Therapists too, are made less anxious if, when confronted with great suffering and voluminous, chaotic material, they can believe in a set of principles which will permit ordered explanation (85, p. 75).

Frankl places tremendous emphasis on people's need for meaning, and George Kelly built his theories on the assumption that all of us continually seek to generate hypotheses and build models about our world, and the people in it, for better understanding.

Yalom also notes (85, p. 75): "Frequently therapists will cling tenaciously to their system in the face of considerable contradictory evidence" — even evidence a result of their own investigations and research. (Shades of Kuhn!) Astrologers are also prone to ignoring evidence which contradicts their basic assumptions. A good example is provided by the research of Michel and Francoise Gauquelin. Their findings have been replicated and seem very solid, yet many astrologers refuse to accept, or even consider, the information because it is contrary to their beliefs about planetary meanings. They cannot fit the findings into their current astrological system, so they prefer to ignore the findings, rather than consider changing or altering some of their astrological system. Astrologers may also ignore client feedback or responses which suggest a particular interpretation of the chart is inaccurate.

Yalom suggests that information giving and intellectual insight are useful, but perhaps not as valuable as many therapists believe. The fact that most clients remember the quality of the relationship and the **person** of the therapist, not specific techniques or ideas, suggests this factor may not be of major importance. This supports other studies which indicate that the quality of the relationship is much more significant than information given in both teaching and counseling.

Hope

In contrast, the instillation of hope appears to be vital. Yalom points to research correlating high pretherapy expectation of help with positive therapy outcomes. Faith healings and placebo treatments operate (often successfully) on hope alone. Jerome Frank has written a book (*Persuasion and Healing*) on the parallels between psychiatrists and witch doctors in using the placebo effect and other psychological mechanisms to effect cures. Several informal healing groups (e.g., Alcoholics Anonymous) use hope in testimonials, focusing on how others have succeeded, so "you can too!"

Jourard emphasizes that there is always hope: "Man's potential for survival, for adaptation, for rehabilitation, for recovery from illness and for growth seem barely to be scratched. Our concepts of man's limits have proven, century after century, to be too rigid. Man continually exceeds limits that science says are built into his tissue" (43, p. 58). Jourard suggests that one of the functions of a healer is to believe in a client's ability to transcend, until the client begins to believe on his or her own.

Hope keeps the client in therapy and can play a curative role on its own. However, hope can be overdone. Guggenbuhl-Craig points to the dangers of a therapist adopting an omniscient role in *Power in the Helping Professions*. Unrealistic hope is counterproductive. Astrologers must work carefully with this variable. Many clients ascribe the powers of the cosmos to astrologers, and hope for some highly unrealistic situations and events.

Universality

Feelings of universality come as a relief to many clients: the recognition that they are neither unique nor alone in their suffering. Yalom cites his experience in groups that common themes of inadequacy exist. (When revealing anonymously their top secrets, the most common response of group members was a feeling of inadequacy, a fear of not being liked if ever seen by others "as I really am." Many people expressed such a secret fear. Second in frequency was a feeling of alienation, fearing one could not really love or care for another person. Third most common was some kind of sexual secret.)

Universality is perhaps one of the strongest points of astrology. Through it, we see that everyone shares the same twelve sides of life, in varying degrees and emphases. Clients can learn that other people have similar conflicts, ambivalences as do they. One reason Zip Dobyns chose the word "dilemmas" to refer to the challenges of the various grand crosses in astrology, was to emphasize that these are a natural part of life, faced by all of us. Everyone is learning to balance their various sides, avoiding overdoing and underdoing the different parts of life symbolized in the horoscope. Humans share the same drives and desires, just in different combinations and amounts for each individual.

Learning others have similar problems is a healing experience for many. Astrology gives us many useful examples to share with clients, being careful to protect confidentiality, of other individuals who have mastered similar challenges to the one the client is now facing. We may share with clients, torn between their need for security and their need to take risks, gamble, do something big in the world (a common form of the fixed dilemma), how some of our other clients have handled that dilemma. For example, one chose to pursue a secure, but boring profession for ten years until he saved up enough to do what he found exciting. Another chose to work in a fairly lucrative, but unsatisfying, job for two days a week, and do what she really enjoyed the rest of the week. Another chose to keep her secure job and only do her exciting onstage activities (as a performing artist) for a hobby. There are many possibilities. Each client can choose the option that most suits him or her for the moment.

Altruism

Altruism is another curative factor. Discovering one can help others can be very healing, affirming, and lessen morbid self-preoccupation. It takes the individual out of the victim role. Group members often point out one another's assets and provide support. Jerome Frank notes that frequently, in other cultures, the patient is given a task, often a service to the community, to perform. Alcoholics Anonymous also operates in this mode.

Astrologically, this can be viewed as two sides of Neptune: the savior and the victim. Through helping others, the patient can leave behind a negative, powerless role (victim), and move into a positive, affirming, contributing (helper) role.

Family Reenactment

Yalom notes that group members often play out old family business. They **face paint** therapist and other group members into mother, dad, sister, brother, etc. New relationships are treated along old rules, old roles, old family ways of interacting. Clients rarely see this as an important factor. Yalom and other therapists tend to value it. Yalom suggests it is mostly worked through on the unconscious level anyway. In *Existential Psychotherapy*, he notes: "The past is explored in order to facilitate and deepen the present relationship. This is precisely the reverse of Freud's formula, where the present relationship serves as a means to deepen understanding of the past" (84, p. 350).

We can see the potential for face painting often in the horoscope. That is, the horoscope may indicate the potential of facing certain lessons with one group of people (earlier in our life), and if not resolved, the people (later in life) with whom we will face those same lessons. An example is the woman who had (among other configurations) a Moon in Pisces in the fourth house and Ceres (the Earth Mother asteroid) in the fifth house. All her astrologer had to say was that it looked as though her experience of her own mother was likely to be very tied to her ability to nurture her own children comfortably, and she might possibly repeat patterns she had with her mother with a child of her own. The woman began to cry.

She explained that she had been raised in a very traditional household where women did all the housework. She had two brothers, a father, and a mother who was ill. So, from a very young age, this woman was expected to do all the housework and pick up after her brother and father. She came to resent, not the dictatorial father who expected this, but the ill mother who was not doing "her" job. (We might suspect, of course, that being ill was a socially acceptable way for the mother to escape from some of the demands of the authoritarian father.) This woman now had a Piscean son whom she picked on constantly. She would feel very guilty, try to stop and end up criticizing and resenting him again. With the input from her astrologer, she put two and two together and realized she was reacting to this child the same way she had reacted to her ill mother. (The child was obliging by adopting the victim role, and already had health problems.) The client could see that much of her resentment and anger with this child was "leftover" from her relationship with her mother. (In psychological jargon, this is called "unfinished business.") The recognition meant a lot to her and gave hope for changing her attitude and behavior.

Interpersonal Learning

Interpersonal learning takes place individually and in groups. For some people, a therapy group is their first opportunity to learn about social habits which are interfering with their relationships. Awareness can then lead to change. Role plays are one technique used to deal with specific situations as well as facilitating the development of empathy and social skills. Clients might be encouraged, for example, to role play a job interview several times, until they felt comfortable.

Feedback, role plays and learning social skills can be encouraged in individual work as well. Self-observation and feedback from others help clients become more aware of their interpersonal behavior: strengths and weaknesses. Distortions can be recognized and dealt with. Clients can risk new types of behavior and expression. The microcosm of any consultation provides clients with opportunities to get feedback, recognize and come to terms with distortions. Although the astrologer is only one person and not a group, s/he is still a valuable resource for clients in practicing interpersonal relationships.

Identification With Others

Imitative behavior (identification with others) can be adopting attitudes or behavior from the therapist or the astrologer. Specific pieces of imitative behavior may be dropped later, but are useful in helping clients determine what they are **not**, as well as what they are. Whether s/he wishes it or not, the astrologer is often a role model for clients. People are most prone to imitate others in authority or who appear to have skills worth learning or power in life.

Self-Understanding

All of the above contribute to a client's self-understanding. The more fully and deeply we know ourselves, the more choices and options we recognize, the wider and more fulfilling our lives are. Learning about our many different sides and inner contradictions assists us in choosing the most appropriate avenues of expression in a complex world.

Catharsis

Clients often experience intense emotions. For many, intellectual insight alone is not enough. They need the impact of an emotionally laden experience. Oftentimes, they simply need to express some feelings, to get things out. This is the factor Yalom calls catharsis. Astrologers, too, get their fair share of clients who just need to talk, or cry, or get angry. At times, clients need to almost relive situations that they did not handle well previously. They may need to express a strong, negative or positive, emotion interpersonally. This represents a risk by the client. The group (or individual counselor) needs to be supportive enough to allow the risking and provide reality testing. (That is, the clients may wonder if their feelings were appropriate. The client may need reassurance that you still like him or her.)

Personal Responsibility

The existential factors Yalom considers include the following ideas (which are existential assumptions): the idea that life is unfair and unjust at times; the idea that there is no escape from death and some pain in life; the idea that we are ultimately alone, no matter how close we get to some people; the idea that we should face basic issues of life and death, thus becoming less caught up in "trivialities"; the idea that we are ultimately responsible for our own lives (84, p. 265).

Clients tend to rank these observations as important learnings in therapy. They especially rank one idea highly (fifth out of 60 factors in rank order). This is the factor clients cite as being so important in their improvement: "Learning that I must take ultimate responsibility for the way I live my life no matter how much guidance and support I get from others" (84, p. 265).

Yalom summarizes the research which demostrates that successful therapy includes clients accepting more personal responsibility for their lives. Clients learn to take power into their own hands for what they can do (and also learn of limits in relationships — what they cannot get from other people).

Synopsis

In summary, client reports on positive outcomes emphasize the importance of the therapeutic relationship and the human qualities of the therapist. Positive therapists' traits include: empathy, warmth, respect, congruence, concreteness, spontaneity, flexibility and the ability to share the self appropriately. Helpful counselors draw clients' attention to assets and strengths much more than liabilities and limitations. Successful clinicians work to create a positive relationship with their clients. Despite technical and theoretical differences in therapeutic modalities, clinicians in all schools who are most effective build a similar therapeutic relationship. Successful clinicians of different schools resemble one another much more than do the less skilled clinicians of any school resemble their more skilled colleagues.

Successful therapy creates an environment where clients are hopeful and feel liked by their therapists. Clients are able to experience universality, altruism, catharsis, self-understanding, identification with others, family reenactment, interpersonal learning, acceptance (of and by others) and increased personal responsibility.

A number of these variables interact and intertwine, as noted. A theme that comes through the research is the importance of flexibility and individual analysis. Carkhuff and Berenson comment: "There are no rules for functioning in unknown areas, and crises are crises because they are unknown areas for the therapist as well as the client" (15, p. 169). They continue: "Whole counselors, as well as their clients, often do not know where to go next; the whole counselor has the resources to enter the process without knowing the outcome" (15, p. 181). Successful astro-counselors make that same leap into the unknown, trusting their empathy, flexibility, warmth and understanding will enable them to cope in as healing a manner as possible.

Strupp et al. emphasize, "Orthodoxy, if it ever had a place in training programs, must give way to greater flexibility and breadth . . . tailor therapeutic techniques to the requirements of the patient" (77, p. 127). Carkhuff and Berenson suggest that counseling and therapy both are living and learning to be all that we can be. That process is continuous, lifelong, and never ends! They note: "The whole person trusts the unknown, perhaps more than the known; it may always be greater than the known and [s]he is bound to act upon it" (15, p. 144).

Chapter 6
The Reality of
Interpersonal Relationships

The Heisenberg Uncertainty Principle in physics tells us that the act of observation tends to affect what is observed. Perceptual psychology tells us that there is no "objective" observer. All of us interpret and create our own version of "reality." This holds true not just for physical objects, but also for people. Harry Stack Sullivan coined the term, **parataxic distortions** to refer to the human tendency to distort one's perceptions of others by relating wholly or largely on the basis of imagined or fantasized attributes in the other person. Our interpersonal needs affect and alter our interpersonal perceptions. We do not see other people clearly when we are anxious, when our self-esteem is threatened, or even when we are excited or introspective. Many people have experienced walking down a dark street at night, alone, where any other person seemed a potential mugger.

Transference

Transference, a concern of many therapists, can be seen as a subclass of parataxic distortions. In transference, the client perceives the counselor in a limited and/or distorted manner. Clients may react to therapists as if they were God, or parents or other significant people in the clients' lives. Clients may interpret criticism as praise and vice versa. Transference aids a client's sense of stability and security. Clients tend to react to current relationships as they reacted to early ones. They, thus, do not have to alter their world view, perceptions or behavior.

For example, the problem child who grew up abused and misused may believe the world is hostile. Acts, even of kindness are distorted or misinterpreted in the child's mind to be hostile or unkind. Or, the kind helper is continually provoked in an attempt to elicit harsh responses because the child is "used to" hostility and already knows what to do in that context. It is familiar and secure, albeit painful.

Our distortions tend to be self-perpetuating since we act on them, and our behavior encourages that continued distortion. The idea of a self-fulfilling prophecy fits here. If I expect criticism, I may adopt a defensive, unfriendly attitude to "protect" myself, and thereby invite the very criticism I fear.

Interpersonal feedback can help us to change parataxic distortions. If we discover that our personal interpretations of reality are quite different from consensual reality (the majority of people around us), we may change our interpretations. Initially, most of us tend to assume that other people feel as we do. To us, it seems "natural," the "only way to feel." Feedback from others can alter that. One client with strong Juno and seventh house placements mentioned that it came as a big surprise to her the day she realized other people did not feel the need to accommodate people which she felt. That recognition also gave her permission to be different, to not always appease people.

That, basically, is what much of counseling is all about: helping clients to realize that their maps of reality are insufficient, and in need of updating. Recognizing the reality of relativity helps the counselor to function. As Leslie Cameron-Bandler put it: ". . . what people tell us is **not** what happened, but instead what they consciously experienced as happening. . . . So, if two individuals come in telling two different stories about the same phenomenon, I know they are both right" (12, p. 34). Physicists used to argue about whether light was a wave or a particle. It acts as both. There is often more than **one** "right" answer, more than one useful model.

Ms. Cameron-Bandler continues: "They can't understand each other; they disagree about what reality is. Your job as a professional communicator is not to concern yourself with 'reality': your job is to concern yourself with process" (12, p. 35).

The challenge here is for counselors and clients to deal with transference as nondefensively as possible. Any perception, even a distorted one, is information and can be used to improve one's map of reality. Besides, if all we have to work with is subjective information, why waste time criticizing it for its subjectivity!?

Singer gives the example (in *Key Concepts of Psychotherapy*) of a young psychiatrist working on a ward with very disturbed patients. At first nervous and afraid, she gradually relaxed, and felt she was making progress. One day she heard her father was ill again. (He had had several previous illnesses, but had recovered.) She didn't feel very worried. But one morning when she came in to work, one by one each of her patients asked to see her and informed her that s/he was well and ready to be discharged from the hospital. Stunned by the unanimity, the psychiatrist concluded she had been more worried than she recognized, and her patients had responded to it. Their behavior implied: "We don't need you as much now; it is okay to leave." She took a leave of absence, and went home. Her father died a few days later.

Clearly, focusing on the "distorted reality" of patients, who were still disturbed, saying they were ready to be discharged, would have been counterproductive to all concerned. The psychiatrist learned her patients were very sensitive to her feelings (and protective). The patients learned some of their perceptions about others were highly accurate.

Many therapists emphasize the need to be open minded and nondefensive. Clients are often quite sensitive and skilled at reading parts of their therapists' personalities. Often clients will focus on aspects of a therapist's nature which the therapist would rather hide. Denying unpleasant truths about one's self limits one's own growth and can be a great blow to clients. The implicit message is: "You are mistaken **again**." It can be a vitalizing experience for clients to receive validation for their accurate perceptions!

Countertransference

The major trap for a counselor is to trust utterly his or her map of reality — forgetting it's just a map. Counselors who become convinced of the validity of their interpretations fall prey to countertransference (another form of parataxic distortions). Here, the counselors' anxieties, ego needs and defenses prevent them from perceiving clients, and the information they provide, clearly. Counselors react to incomplete and often distorted information.

Steve Lankton notes: "The unconscious nature of many anchors can occasionally cause complications in therapy...some aspect of a client's behavior or verbal narrative will set off associations from the therapist's own life and personal history. This is the classical countertransference phenomenon" (46, p. 58).

An example would be a client whose voice reminds the counselor of a detested sister. If unaware of this, the counselor may begin reacting to the client with the irritation and anger which was, and is, felt for the sister. An astro-counselor can also easily find a rationalization for her anger in the client's horoscope. Since astrologers are making interpretations of charts on a regular basis, countertransference is a particularly significant issue for us to guard against. Several astrologers joke: Find the sign an astrologer cannot stand and you will know the sun-sign of his or her ex-spouse!

Countertransference is generally seen as an outgrowth of a counselor's reluctance to know and/or learn something about himself or herself, striving to keep unresolved conflicts buried. These desires can motivate the counselor to (overt or covert) hostility against the client.

Singer emphasizes:

> Just as the patient's transference reactions are genuine aids in the patient's and therapist's quest for understanding, and just as transference is harmful to the therapeutic enterprise **only** when it remains unexamined and is permitted to lie fallow, so are countertransference reactions powerful tools in exploration and potent instruments for uncovering inner states which are damaging **only** if they are brushed aside, ignored, or not taken seriously (75, p. 298).

The major point is that any and all perceptions and distortions by both client and counselor provide information. We can react blindly, or we can choose to delve more deeply into our reactions, and extend our information, enlarge our maps of "reality."

Chapter 7
Who Me? Projection

One of the greatest tools counselors have for understanding both themselves and clients is a firm grasp of the defense mechanism projection. Projection is a subcategory under parataxic distortions — where our needs and fantasies influence our perceptions of other people.

The theory of projection is thus: people are prone to fail to recognize certain parts of themselves. We are often ambivalent, feeling both love and hate, attraction and repulsion, etc. Especially in Western society, we tend to be uncomfortable with such opposites. As Guggenbuhl- Craig puts it: "It is not easy for the human psyche to bear the tension of polarities. The ego loves clarity and tries to eradicate inner ambivalence" (34, p. 91). So, we tend to deny one side or another of ourselves. Especially, qualities we feel are negative are likely to be pushed into the unconscious, kept out of awareness as much as possible, partially for reasons of self-esteem.

Less obvious and therefore more likely to be missed by the counselor, is the tendency of some people to focus on their weaknesses and ignore their actualized or potential strengths because they do not support the clients' "Poor Me" images.

Freud felt that such denied feelings or qualities constantly seek to return to the light of awareness through dreams, symptoms and projection. The human self-actualizing drive postulated by Maslow and others would constantly seek to dig up any material we try to bury and keep unconscious. Self-actualization assumes an urge to become all that we are capable of, encompass all our potentials.

In projection, we see our own disowned qualities in someone else. In the original Freudian formulation, we **imagined** those qualities in the other person. For example, a very stingy individual feels his wife, family and children are all misers, but sees himself as practical or even generous. Outside observers feel the reverse is true. We say he has **projected** his stinginess (like a movie projector) and sees it "out there" in other people, rather than recognizing it within himself. For most of us, this is more comfortable, because we are able to condemn or criticize these projected qualities in others. It would be hard on our self-image to criticize the qualities in ourselves.

Most clinicians today feel there is at least a kernel of truth in almost any given projection, and often more. I, and others, find that people do not have to imagine qualities in others. Clients are bright enough and intuitive enough to find significant others who will exhibit those qualities the client needs to face! That is, if stinginess is an issue of concern to us, we will attract or becomes attracted to, a highly stingy or highly generous person in order to work out our own conflict in this area.

This includes the client to counselor relationship. Thus, as counselors, we work on issues relevant not just to our clients, but to ourselves. Guggenbuhl-Craig says: "Such an analyst recognizes time and again how the patients' difficulties constellate his own problems and vice versa and therefore openly works not only on the patient but on himself" (34, p. 130). And he suggests, "Part of the training of social workers, nurses, teachers, doctors, etc. should emphasize that the problems of the 'case' or the patient are one's own as well" (34, p. 153).

Along these lines, Jung said that no analyst can bring clients further than s/he has gone personally. Carkhuff and Berenson point out that therapists with lower levels of empathy, respect and other essential qualities than their clients will not be helpful and may do harm.

Fritz Perls put a lot of emphasis on facing projection and reowning parts of one's self. He once suggested that people start with the assumption that **everything** they experienced was a projection, and go from there. (Given that we all filter and interpret reality, this is not as absurd an assumption as it might first appear.) The authors of *Paradox and Counter Paradox* make a related assumption in their work with families. They act as if every feedback in the family system is an output of the therapists' behaviors.

Note that these positions, although extreme, give the counselor tremendous power. If we are involved in and a part of all that goes on, we have the power to affect and change it.

Recognizing projection gives the counselor an opportunity to learn and grow from each and every client. As in much of counseling, one's feelings and reactions are one's most valuable tools. Example: a client comes to me and shortly I find him to be amazingly self-centered. I am appalled by his lack of consideration for others. True, this may very well be an area in which he needs to work in order to improve his interpersonal relationships. However, I do us both a disfavor if I stop after labelling him selfish and inconsiderate. I must now look at myself. Why am I irritated by this man? I have discomfort with his self-centeredness. Therefore, it is a good bet I am uncomfortable with my own self-centeredness. So I criticize him for what I deny in myself.

Having gone that far, perhaps I can meditate on the values of selfishness. Under what circumstances is it useful? When is it "good" and not "bad?" And how do those judgments work in his life, not just in mine?

Unless I can come to understand how "selfishness" fits for him, our therapeutic relationship is doomed. When a counselor feels contemptuous of or looks down on clients, the clients sense it and, unless they are highly masochistic, will usually break off the relationship. (Why pay someone to sit in harsh judgment of you?)

Often, more information will broaden one's perspective. Perhaps I discover this man comes from a large, immigrant, poor family and has had to work and fight and push from the beginning, just for food. His "self-centeredness" makes more sense now.

A major point is that even though an issue may be very much a problem with a client, it can also be an issue with the counselor. And vice versa. One does **not** preclude the other. If a counselor realizes s/he has been fantasizing a lot, misperceiving and exaggerating an issue with a client due to his or her own personal conflicts in that area, it does not automatically mean it is **only** his or her agenda. The issue may still be significant (although perhaps only mildly so) for the client. Else, why did it happen with that particular client?

The key issue here is meaning. Our interactions with people have meaning. We do not pick fights out of thin air, have random likes and dislikes. People relate as they do for reasons, albeit somewhat subterranean ones at times. Much of the exchanges between people are not explicit. Or, as Guggenbuhl-Craig says, he is "struck by how much [more] transpires and is exchanged between two people than is ever expressed in word or deed" (34, p. 48).

It behooves us as counselors to scrutinize our behavior most intensely when we notice a common pattern in our clients. For example, If I get three "selfish, self-centered" clients in a row, my first question to myself would be: "What am I wanting and denying myself because it is 'too selfish'?" Perhaps I have been working too hard and want a vacation, but don't want to "desert" my clients for a week or two. Perhaps I am immolating myself on the altar of the family: working to keep an immaculate house, bake bread, etc. Perhaps I'm giving in or compromising in friendships or love relationships and feeling resentful and taken advantage of. . . .

My next question would be: "How am I creating selfishness by my attempt to avoid being selfish?" Ironically, our attempts to cut out a part of our own nature usually lead in circular fashion to doing exactly what we most want to avoid. So, if I sacrifice myself in a relationship, I will feel more and more resentful. I will get increasingly self-centered as I focus on all my unmet needs, and count the various ways in which my lovers/friends are not doing what they "ought" to for me.

Having a strong emotional reaction to a client is a fairly reliable sign that the counselor has conflicts to work out in that area. Generally, the counselor would like to do in some mild form what the client is overdoing and carrying to excess. Or, the counselor is also expressing the qualities the client demonstrates, but manages to deny that fact until forced to face it by the extreme example of the client. It's as if clients are fun house mirrors, who throw back in exaggerated, overblown fashion, our own conflicts and ambivalences for us to face and learn and grow.

I want to stress that it is not only "negative" qualities that are projected. People often give away very positive parts of themselves. (And "good" and "bad" are often in the eye of the beholder, as well. Independence can be positive in some arenas and negative in others.) I have seen clients deny their own beauty, intelligence, artistic talent and organizational skills. Instead, they attracted people into their lives who would manifest beauty, intelligence, artistic talent, organizational skills for them. Like often does attract like in the world: successful people hang out with successful people (if they define "success" similarly). Beautiful people often associate with other beautiful people. Often, however, clients are unaware of their likenesses. They may be denying their own intelligence, and recognizing it only in those around them. Sometimes I respond to such people: "If they are so brilliant, and you are so stupid, how is it you understand so fully their brilliance?"

It is this mirroring effect in relationships that makes them **so** valuable. The people around us present us with endless opportunities to know ourselves more thoroughly. They give us wonderful examples of sides of ourselves which we have not come to terms with. They show us what to do and what not to do in dealing with a side of our nature. We have only to pay attention.

Projection can be encouraged by culture, family, etc. For example, sex roles encourage the woman with Mars conjunct Uranus to find a man to live out her freedom urges, rather than being an independent, assertive, rebellious type herself. Unfortunately, the more she denies her **own** need for freedom, space and independence, the unhappier she will be. The analogy Zip Dobyns uses is feeding someone else when you are hungry. You keep on feeding them, and you get more and more hungry! So it is with projection. Instead of expressing a side of your nature, you are attracted to someone who "does it for you." But, the more we deny it inside, the more extreme examples we attract from the outside (the hungrier we get). So, a woman who denies her needs for independence attracts increasingly unstable, free soul type partners who do not hang around. Thus, she gets the space and independence she yearns for — but through the actions of another. If she is not conscious of those needs for freedom, she will be terribly unhappy at the instability and infidelity of her relationships! Once she recognizes her own need for freedom, she can choose more fulfilling ways to satisfy that need.

Here, the usefulness of the horoscope is almost unparalleled. I have found, over and over again, that the chart mirrors the likely projections of the individual. The horoscope pinpoints which qualities might be projected, and into which people.

Projection is most likely when a horoscope indicates a character heavily weighted in one direction, with a portion fighting to go another direction. For example, the man with a heavy mud (earth and water) chart who has Jupiter in Aries in the seventh is likely to find it difficult to integrate the freedom needs of that Jupiter (the restlessness it suggests and the need for excitement it implies) with his strong needs for security, fidelity, predictability and commitment. It is quite likely he will project that Jupiter onto a partner, and pick someone who is very freedom-loving, extraverted, exciting, dynamic and hard to pin down! The more he denies his own needs to sometimes cut loose, do his own thing, have fun, the more his partner is likely to overdo: be too spontaneous, too into excitement, overdramatize life, leave on an instant's notice. (Of course such a person would be attracted to the earth and water man because he is manifesting the responsibility, security and stability that the fire and air type needs to learn.)

The most common area of projection is in the seventh and eighth houses. Long associated with "other people," it is quite easy for the individual to deny that side of his or her character, and live it out through others. This can be encouraged by culture, family, sex roles and unwary astrologers. I feel very sad when I hear astrologers talk of placements in the seventh and eighth houses as if they had only to do with partners and other people. Everything in our charts is **us**. Those houses show parts of our own nature which we tend to meet through our close peer relationships. To talk of the planets there as only applying to partners is to encourage people to give away much of their talent and abilities.

It is most difficult to project planets in the first and second houses. In the first house, people may see configurations as a part of their physical bodies, but deny the connection to their "real selves," e.g., the "thin soul" in a "fat body" denies responsibility for one's physical being. In the second, people may project qualities into money, possessions, physical objects. Projection is much more likely in subsequent houses. In the third, we can project into neighbors, siblings, and other collateral relatives, e.g., a woman with Neptune in the third denied her own creative imagination, because she believed, "My sister is the artistic one." In the fourth and tenth houses, we can project into parents and other authority figures. This seems to be a particular issue when power is involved. For example, a very full fourth or tenth house with a strong stellium — Leo, Capricorn, Scorpio — may indicate a dominating, very powerful parent, overwhelming to the child, who never gets in touch with his or her own power. The parent may be seen as negative, and thus power is defined as negative. "I'll never be dominating like Dad!" So, instead the child stays passive and is a pushover even as an adult. Or, the parent may be seen very positively, but the child feels, "I'll never be as strong, competent, successful, capable as Mom/Dad," and so never tries. (I must confess however, that power is a strong issue in my chart, so perhaps I just attract these clients as mirrors for my own issues.)

In the fifth house, we are prone to giving away parts of ourselves to lovers and children. In our culture, especially, women are often encouraged to live some of their unfulfilled sides out through their children — a scenario uncomfortable and unhealthy for everyone involved! A good example of this was supplied by a woman with a chart full of Capricorn, Cancer and Virgo (and their houses). She also had Uranus in Aries in the fifth house which was square her Capricorn placements, square her Cancer placements, and in conflicting aspects to other planets in the chart. She was strongly identified with the "proper" side of her chart: duty, responsibility, doing the right thing. She had two daughters who were total rebels. They were free souls, thumbing their noses at the world, refusing to obey the rules, and pretty much running wild.

These daughters were doing all the independent, individualistic, freedom-loving, irresponsible things the mother's Uranian side would have **liked** to do. The mother, identifying only with her Capricorn, Cancer and Virgo, saw this behavior as disgraceful. The more she denied her free and rebellious side, the more she overdid her stable, responsible, following the rules side. Her daughters were wonderful, exaggerated mirrors of what she needed to face and find a positive channel for in her life. It was not that she should do what they were doing; they were overdoing the Uranus in Aries energy. She needed to learn to express that side of her nature **in moderation**.

Of course, there was a lesson for the daughters as well. The mother was mirroring to them the need for some stability, concern for society and its rules and regulations, etc. She was overdoing that; they were underdoing it. In family systems, it is misleading to say one behavior caused another. They are interlinked. Her excessive responsibility encouraged their excessive rebellion. But their extreme rebellion encouraged her extreme responsibility. It was a typical vicious circle.

But note, any of them could have broken the cycle by changing her behavior. If one individual changes, the system is altered, and others will adapt or find a new system (unless they can coerce the person who is changing into going back the way she was, which is usually the first strategy tried in family systems). The mirror was there for all of them to learn from; they only had to pay attention.

In the sixth house, we may project into colleagues and coworkers. The seventh and eighth, as mentioned, are easy. We project here especially into partners (business, marriage, living together) and close friends. Seventh house relationships also include client and counselor (in therapy, in the law, in astrology). In the ninth house, we may give away abilities or qualities to God or our version of the truth and meaning in life. The tenth includes at least one parent and other authority figures (boss, President, police officers, and so on). In the eleventh, we can project into friends, or groups, or causes.

And in the twelfth, we see it all as "secret enemies" or our own un-conscious. Blaming the unconscious is still projection if we separate ourselves from it, avoid personal responsibility. Yalom gives an amusing example of the therapist who responded to such a denial by a client with, "Whose unconscious is it!?"

One of the other fascinating phenomena revealed in the chart is the cyclic nature of our projections. That is, as long as we are not dealing with an important part of our nature, we will continue to attract people in our lives who will manifest it for us (often in overblown, exaggerated, uncomfortable fashion).

An example would be the woman with a Saturn, Pluto conjunc-tion in Leo in the seventh house. She first faced the power issue with father. (Saturn conjunct Pluto, Scorpio Midheaven). He was dominating and controlling, and she was unhappy in the relation-ship. She avoided marriage for fear (which Saturn can also be a key to) of being dominated and controlled by another man. Her percep-tual set was such to notice when men were dominating, controlling or punitive. She tended to not notice or not be attracted to men who were gentle. She continued to seek out, presumably unconsciously, men that were strong and controlling. And, as long as she denied her own strength, she felt threatened in such relationships. The goal, of course, was for her to recognize her own strength, and needs for power and control. Once she could integrate her own capacities to take over and take charge positively in her life (e.g., competitive sports, the business world, fighting for causes), she could be com-fortable in her interpersonal relationships. She could find other kinds of men to relate to, rather than drawing in men who expressed, in an extreme fashion, the controlling side of her own nature which she denied.

The Saturn-Pluto conjunction in the seventh showed the poten-tial danger of picking powerful (perhaps dominating) partners. (Remember, none of this is inevitable. We are talking about **poten-tials** in a chart.) Some people with similar combinations, more in touch with their power, just fight all the time with their partners about who is going to be in control. Integration means being able to take turns: each partner taking charge and responsibility in his or her areas of strength, each partner able to gracefully comply as well as take over. The Saturn also indicated that **unfinished business** in the relationship to father might be faced again in rela-tionships with partners (and faced, and faced, until we finally learn!). Psychology calls this **face painting**, and I mentioned an earlier example of a woman who was meeting her mother (in a sense) through her son.

Thus, we can use the horoscope as an extremely valuable map of possible projections, both for clients and for ourselves. We can strive to be aware of qualities we are most likely to project, and be on the lookout. Astrologers mention to me that they often will get clients in waves or cycles. The patterns are important. If I get a succession of "Poor Little Me" Piscean victims, I need to look at my yearnings to play omniscient savior and find where I'm feeling victimized in my life. If I get a succession of Piscean artists, perhaps I'm feeling a lack of beauty in my life.

If I assume that everything I notice about clients has some meaning (even if very small) for me as well, I will be a more effective counselor and a growing, changing person.

Chapter 8
Displacement & Repression

Displacement

There are two other defense mechanisms from psychology which I find useful in my understanding of the chart and people. These are repression and displacement. The latter refers to expressing what is a natural part of life in an inappropriate time or place. The typical textbook example is the individual who is angry at an authority figure and afraid to express it. So, s/he **displaces** the anger onto a safer target — perhaps a partner, perhaps a child, perhaps a pet. Displacement can be helpful, e.g., pounding the pillow instead of yelling at the boss, but it can also create difficulties in life, such as screaming at a partner when our desire is to scream at the boss.

Any mixtures in the chart are the potential for displacement. We may express an important part of life (one of the twelve basic ways of being) in an inappropriate arena. One example would be the person who has a blend of work and pleasure in the chart. This could include such things as strong Saturn-Venus aspects; Venus in Capricorn or in the tenth house; Saturn in Taurus or in the second (and to some extent, in the seventh or in Libra); Saturn conjunct rulers of the second; Venus conjunct rulers of the tenth, and other variations. The danger is that the work and pleasure needs may not be blended comfortably. One integration is to find a career which the person enjoys, providing beauty, comfort, pleasure to others as well as the worker. Artistic careers are likely. Or, the person may just get a lot of pleasure from work.

Examples of displacement include expecting the work to always be easy, pleasant, comfortable, and feeling critical when it is not. (This displaces the play attitude into the work arena.) Or, some people will displace the work attitude (judgmental, critical, searching for flaws, evaluating performance) onto the play arena, and inhibit themselves from enjoying the world. Instead of just getting pleasure (from food, drink, sensuality, beauty), such people criticize themselves, feel they don't "deserve it," or are constantly watching and judging their own performance. One can go on and on.

The basic idea is that all parts of life (and the horoscope) **can be** fulfilling, in the appropriate amount, place and time. If we are putting a part of our nature into an area (or at a moment) where it is not fulfilling, we merely have to find another time and place to express that need. That does not make the need "bad" — just outside its proper context.

I would like to draw a clear distinction here between desires or motivations and actions. For example, I consider rape a destructive action. I do not believe there is an appropriate context for that act. However, for most people, part of the motivation behind rape is a need for power, and a feeling of rage against one's powerlessness. (So, a victim who appears weaker is selected.) I do believe there are appropriate times and places in life to express a power drive (fighting for a worthy cause; competitive sports, games, ethical business competition). Feelings, urges, emotions are a part of being human. What we do with them, where and how we express them, is up to each of us.

Repression

Repression is the concept of pushing certain desires into the unconscious because we do not want to face them, or deal with them. We may feel they are "bad." These submerged issues continue to seek to return to awareness. The most common outcome of long-term repression (ignoring one of our basic needs) is physical illnesses. The unmet emotional needs can eventually create hormonal and other imbalances which lead to physical (health) problems. Astrologically speaking, repression is easiest where water (unconscious) is involved: planets, houses **or** signs. Every chart will have a great mixture, so there is some water in a large number of combinations. I do not find it helpful to try to guess the physical difficulty from the chart. However, the reverse can be tremendously useful.

If we look to the part(s) of the body involved, we can use astrological correlates to see what emotional needs are not being faced. For example, cuts, burns, accidents, surgery, headaches, and sinus colds are all associated with Mars. Usually, in some way, people suffering from the above problems are not dealing with their needs for free self-expression. They may be blocking themselves from doing something they do want to do, or forcing themselves to do something they do not want to do. The person who does not want to cook dinner often burns himself or herself on the stove. Blocked anger is often an issue. The physical problem or accident points a finger to us, saying: "Look at this part of life, and find some way to do it comfortably. Otherwise, you'll end up doing it with discomfort."

For a fuller discussion of these issues, see *The Mutable Dilemma*, especially the Pisces 1980 issue. To just summarize briefly, if there are throat problems, or difficulties with the body's handling of sugar, look to the person's need for pleasure and beauty in life (Venus). If the arms, hands and/or lungs are involved, issues could be around thinking, communicating, relationships with siblings and other relatives (Mercury). Lung difficulties also may involve Neptune. (It is usual to have several factors in combination.) Stomach problems suggest examining our needs for dependency and nurturance: warm, emotional commitments in our lives (Moon). Heart problems relate to our sense of pride, ability to be center stage, our ambitions, our ego needs (Sun). A focus on the intestinal tract suggests issues around our sense of craftsmanship, being able to be productive, to do a good job for its own sake (Virgo). Kidney problems (Libra) suggest the partnership arena is a key. Bowels, bladder, sexual organs point to our handling of joint resources, including money and sex (Pluto). How well are we sharing or not sharing that area of life with an intimate other? Liver difficulties suggest a focus on faith and values (Jupiter). What or whom do we trust, if anything or anyone? Back problems and all forms of premature rigidity and crystallization (arthritis, gout, arteriosclerosis) suggest a Saturnian issue. Perhaps we are taking on too much responsibility. (No wonder the back gets tired!) Perhaps we are overdoing rules, regulations, following the structure. Accidents, ankle problems and sudden upsets imply we need to consider our drive to be unique, unconventional and do our own thing. Are we feeling confined (Uranus)? Feet and all sorts of dissolving illnesses can be connected to Neptune. Are we pursuing our dream in life? Are we playing victim, rather than doing a healthy artist or realistic savior number?

And there are lots of mixtures, of course. Allergies are often connected to the mutables, so we have the mutable dilemma concerns. Are we overextended, trying to do and know and learn everything? Do we lack a focus? Are we torn between our many goals and values? Are we unsure what we believe? Do we lack a direction? Are we perfectionistic, wanting more than is possible from some areas of life (e.g., partner, work, parents, self)?

Sometimes illness is the only way a body can get a workaholic to slow down and take a vacation. Sometimes major health problems are a means for the person to get the nurturing s/he would otherwise never allow others to proffer. (Strong Atlas types tend to always take care of others, but may have difficulty leaning on and being dependent on someone else.) Or, illness may be the only way the person knows to get attention or affection. There are usually **lots** of reasons.

The point is to go from the problem to the chart and then to what the person can **do** about it! As an illustration, here are two examples from my own life. When I travelled to Europe in 1980, for the first time I was totally alone, on my own. I was also scheduled to lecture a number of places. I am good at repressing my anxiety, so I managed to produce all the symptoms of an incipient ulcer. It was quite painful. I started living on milk and eggs, and said: "Stomach. Okay. Cancer needs. I'm away from home, probably homesick. I don't have anyone to lean on to help me out. I'm probably feeling very scared and insecure." My solution was to write home even more, and write lots of my friends unusual postcards. My typical card is bright, cheery, how well everything is going. Instead, I wrote to several people about my "ulcer," my concerns and worries. I also allowed myself to ask for more support in my European environment. All the astrologers and students and friends I met were very supportive. I just had to ask. The "ulcer" left. A few weeks later, I had so completely forgotten, I ordered curry in a Belgian restaurant. It was great, and I had no problems, and have had none since!

The second illustration was very recent. The final work on this book was being done in a great rush to try to get it out for the A.F.A. So, I was editing and revising day and night. I told friends not to call, and did nothing but work for weeks. My lover was not happy at my refusing to go out to movies, or relate much at all, but he did his best to be supportive. I developed a sore throat — not serious, but annoying. So, I thought: "Throat. Venus. Taurus. Pleasure principle. I'm feeling deprived and perhaps unloved, so my throat acts up. " I took just two hours off to go out to lunch with my lover and another friend whose birthday was that week. Within a few hours, my sore throat (of two days) had disappeared.

The idea of repression emphasizes how much information we can get from our bodies, if we only pay attention. Most problems start small. If we listen to the signals, we can fix situations, resolve issues, before the problems get too large. We have a number of warning signals. The longer we wait, the stronger the signals become. (I had a few twinges of pain in my stomach before leaving for Europe — anticipatory anxiety I am sure. But I ignored them, declaring, "I don't get ulcers!")

This concept of repression needs to be handled with care with clients, because many are prone to feeling guilty rather than powerful when it is suggested they have helped to create their own illnesses. The point is not to get into what started it all. The point is to determine what the clients **need**, what drive(s) are being frustrated, leading to this. Then, clients — alone or with counseling — can determine more fulfilling ways to meet those needs, to satisfy those drives.

I am not suggesting that people forsake medicine. (There is not just one answer!) When illnesses have manifested in the body, physical interventions are often necessary. However, dealing with the emotional roots of illness can help us avoid repeating our unpleasant physical problems. The idea is to treat causes and not just symptoms. The most effective treatment will address the **whole** person: physical, mental, emotional and spiritual. Restricting ourselves to one channel is limiting. A good diet and exercise program promotes health. A positive attitude assists well-being. Meditation and spiritual studies support the balance of our organism. If we take care of ourselves and watch the early warning signals, we can deal with our conflicts and good health (on all levels) can be the norm it ought to be rather than the exception it often is.

Chapter 9
Responsibility & Free Will

There are other intertwining issues that affect how much we as counselors learn from our clients and vice versa. Many counselors and astrologers are ambivalent or conflicted in regard to their beliefs about human free will versus determinism. This issue divides psychology (humanists versus behaviorists) and astrology as well as other fields.

Most counselors find that acting as if people have free will works. Taking responsibility for one's life seems to be an essential part of the therapeutic experience. Rollo May lists the acceptance of responsibility as one of people's four tasks of personality. Judging by client self-report and some clinical labels (e.g., depressed), clients who assume more personal responsibility tend to get better. Clients who see the power as external tend to continue feeling helpless, depressed, and are less likely to improve. Yalom (84, pp. 261-268) discusses some of the research in this area.

A man named Rotter designed a scale to measure internal versus external locus of control, basically whether people feel they are in charge of what is going on, or outside forces are doing it. He notes:

> . . . the individual who has a strong belief that he can control his own destiny is likely to (a) be more alert to those aspects of the environment which provide useful information for his future behavior (b) take steps to improve his environmental conditions, (c) place greater value on skill or achievement reinforcements, and be generally more concerned with his ability, particularly his failures, and (d) be resistive to subtle attempts to influence him (71, p. 25).

However, at least in the past, our scientific training has tended to support the idea of environmental determinism. The old, mechanistic view of the universe was reflected in psychology's mechanistic view of mankind, be it Skinner, who considers only physical, measurable events "real," or other scientists, who reduce human beings to computers. Example: Dean E. Woolridge thinks it is possible to build cybernetic machines "completely indistinguishable from human beings produced in the usual manner" (82, p. 172).

Many psychologists see people as products of their culture and upbringing. Behaviorism and environmental determinism still dominate most university psychology departments. This often leads to conflicts and ambivalences. It can result in a counselor sending out double messages: on the verbal, explicitly conscious level, "You are in charge of your life," but implicitly, "You poor dear, you're an innocent victim."

Even in the past, some theorists have rejected the materialistic assumption that only the physical is real. For Jung, the pull from above, a transcendent urge in human beings, was undeniable and just as real as physical bodies. For Assagioli, founder of Psychosynthesis, mystical experiences were as real and true as physical ones. Frankl, founder of Logotherapy, emphasizes that people have a spiritual, as well as mental, emotional and physical part to be dealt with.

However, most psychologists and other theorists about human nature fell into the trap of trying to be "scientific," which meant dealing only with physically observable data. As modern science changes with radical shifts in physics and our view of reality, our definition of "scientific" will also change. Meanwhile, Yalom offers some helpful thoughts on the subject of free will for people caught in the middle.

One example is of an experiment where schizophrenic and normal children were placed in a potentially rewarding environment, full of pinball machines, TV's, electric organs and trains, and similar toys. Coins were available to activate the machines, but only when a light on the machine was on. If the light was off, a coin would just keep the machine shut off even longer. Normal kids figured this out quickly and had a great time. The schizophrenic children did not master the setup and experienced the same environment as frustrating and unpleasant. Can we say the environment determined that experience?!

Yalom quotes Bandura, a behaviorist discussing freedom and determinism who emphasizes that the behavior of a bunch of people in water up to their necks would be very similar despite their different personalities. Yalom points out that overt behavior may look similar, but each person has control over how s/he feels. He quotes Epictetus (84, p. 272):

> I must die. I must be imprisoned. I must suffer exile. But must I die groaning? Must I whine as well? Can anyone hinder me from going into exile with a smile? The master threatens to chain me: what say you? Chain me? My leg you will chain — yes, but not my will — no, not even Zeus can conquer that.

Each of us has strengths and weaknesses, but we are responsible for our attitudes towards our handicaps. Alfred Adler noted that two children might have the same disability and react entirely differently. One might build his life around the "victim of fate" excuse with his handicap: "Oh, if only I'd been born without this...(asthma, club foot, cleft palate, fill in the blank)...what I could have done." Another might find in her "disability" a motivation for "striving for superiority" working even harder to overcome any handicaps. Alfred Adler himself (a weak and sickly child) is a good example of this, as is Milton Erickson. Admirers of Erickson feel he treated every setback (including a crippling bout with polio) as an opportunity and challenge to develop in new ways. Helen Keller could have remained deaf, dumb and blind, defining herself as a helpless victim. Instead, with much help from Annie Sullivan, Helen Keller chose to take action, transcend her "limits" and became an example and inspiration to millions of Americans and to the handicapped all over the world. Frankl emphasizes the importance of responsibility, saying, "The conditions do not determine me, but I determine whether I yield to them or brave them" (24, p. 55).

Yalom and others carry responsibility even further, pointing to how one's psychological state influences one's physical condition. Psychosomatic medicine recognizes this with ulcers, asthma, colitis, arthritis and other ailments. The treatment O. Carl Simonton is doing with "terminal" cancer patients demonstrates the impact which taking personal responsibility and control can have even with that much dreaded disease. The very act of taking charge is life-affirming, it seems. Biofeedback research is showing the vast extent to which we can control our own bodies with our minds and emotions.

Total determinism or freedom seem equally untenable. The Skinnerian view would say we are products of our environment. But what if we operate on and alter that environment? Did the environment determine our alteration of the environment? But then it is the environment that is being determined, not us. Where does it begin or end?

We run into a similar chicken and egg problem with free will. If we have total free will, why are we born with different sets of talents and handicaps? Some would argue we set up our present circumstances through past lives. If so, how do we begin?

It seems reasonable to me to accept some environmental determinism and some free will. I suspect the limits to free will are far beyond what most of us assume. Yogis who stop and start their own hearts, fire walkers, people like Jack Schwartz who stick skewers into their arms and do not bleed demonstrate that many of the physical limits we assume do not have to operate unilaterally.

As our physics turns more mystical, it begins to look very much like reality is (at least largely) a state of mind. If so, we may be becoming more freer in a historical sense, because we are less bound by assumptions and outmoded mind sets.

What does seem to work, therapeutically, and in "real life" is responsibility. If we **believe** in our power to affect ourselves and/or situations, we are likely to be effective. If we do not believe we have that power, we rarely try. History, psychology, astrology are full of examples of people who transcended the limits other people said were impossible. Roger Bannister, the first man to break the four minute mile, refused to accept the prevalent opinion that running a mile in less than four minutes was "impossible." Now sports people are wondering if we will one day break the "barrier" to a three and a half minute mile!

Yalom lists several commonly used defenses against awareness of personal responsibility. One is compulsivity. People may set up their lives to feel they have no choice; they "must" do such and such (even when painful). Many people displace personal responsibility, e.g., onto therapists, parents, society, the planets. Some people play "innocent victim," setting up games (see Berne in *Games People Play*) or situations where they will be dumped on, and feel innocent: "I didn't do anything!" Some clients "lose control" or become temporarily irrational. Their behavior will show secondary gains (payoffs), e.g., revenge on someone. They will also often get nurturance from others by "falling apart."

Some people seem to know what to do, but never do it, never take their well-being into their own hands. Such dependent types are often still fantasizing that an omniscient parent/lover/therapist will ride into their lives and make it all perfect.

How does a counselor help a client take responsibility? First, by believing it him or herself.

> The therapist must continually operate within the frame of reference that a patient has created his or her own distress. It is **not** chance, or bad luck or bad genes, that has caused a patient to be lonely, isolated, chronically abused, or insomniac. The therapist must determine what role a particular patient plays in his or her own dilemma, and find ways to communicate this insight to the patient. Until one realizes that one has created one's own dysphoria, there can be no motivation to change (84, p. 231).

Many clinicians warn against trying to demonstrate responsibility through clients' verbal descriptions of their lives. Clients distort the data to fit their world views. It is much more effective to use here and now behavior which they exhibit in therapy. The behavior of people in a counseling situation mirrors their behavior in the outside world. Clients will run the same numbers, try to play the same games with their therapists as they do at home, at the office, etc. The therapist can point out and underline such incidents, showing the parallels between the client's conflicts in therapy and conflicts in the outside world.

For example, a client who is highly judgmental and critical has rationalizations for his criticism of the people in his life. Trying to defend the other people is likely to go nowhere. More potential lies in pointing out how he criticizes in the consultation as well. If he sees the pattern, he has the option of changing (although critical people often prefer continuing to blame others rather than changing themselves). Yalom and many other clinicians emphasize that a therapist must be in touch with her own feelings. They are "a therapist's most important instrument for identifying a patient's contribution to his or her life predicament" (84, p. 235).

The issue of free will and determinism is particularly important to astrologers. The division among astrologers regarding causality seems to be:

1. "The planets are doing it. The interaction of gravity, electromagnetic force fields and other, as yet unknown, physical forces **causes** events on Earth."
2. "I do not know who/what is doing it." Jung's concept of synchronicity applies here. "A" correlates with "B" but it is **not** a causal or linear relationship. The planetary positions correspond with human professions, character traits, but neither one causes the other.

3. "We are doing it." The planets are symbolic of psychological states. We create our own experience through our beliefs and attitudes; the planets merely mirror it. We do not make the planets orbit, and the planets do not cause things to happen in our lives. The relationship is symbolic only. In some variations, God (or some Higher Purpose) is assumed to have created the planetary correspondences for our use.
4. Some mixture of the above.

I would like to note that viewpoint #1 is quite compatible with electional astrology, mundane and business work, but not as helpful for counseling. If we are controlled by external forces, then we are powerless and have no motivation to change or to do anything. "What will be, will be." Some try to soften the materialistic approach by saying the stars "impel" but do not "compel." This can still be hard on feelings of personal power and responsibility.

There are, nonetheless, quite a few clients who will be comforted by this approach. A number of clients come to astrologers eager to abdicate personal responsibility. They want to hear that the planets are doing it. They want to be told when it will stop, and when something better will begin. They do not want to hear that they have any responsibility for what is going on in their lives.

Reassurance about when a situation is likely to end is all that some clients really want (and they will usually make that clear). Yalom and others point out that anxiety about a problem is sometimes more crippling than the problem itself. Allay the anxiety, and the client may begin to cope very well.

Similarly, clients who want to be told that the planets do it may be buoyed up by the astrologer's support of that world view. This can ease guilt feelings ("It's **not** really my fault.") and help self-esteem ("I'm not such a failure after all.").

The deterministic approach tends to be most effective when emphasizing concreteness. Astrologers using this world view require clear information about the life situation of the client. They then can deduce which astrological patterns are probably symbolic of that life situation and calculate when the patterns will end. For example, a client may describe feeling anxious, depressed and insecure. I find transiting Saturn conjunct the Moon in the chart, and may decide that symbolizes the current anxiety. I can calculate that Saturn will be out of orb in two months.

This information may help to reassure the client, but if s/he feels s/he has already been burdened too long, it is going to be small consolation to hear that some of the patterns continue for another two months. So, I will emphasize what s/he can do with those aspects that is positive. I will explain that Saturn is the reality principle, and the Moon is connected to our emotional security needs. People generally feel most secure when working, accomplishing and contributing during such periods. When Saturn has strong aspects, it symbolizes our need to be very realistic, especially in regard to what is our responsibility and what belongs to someone else. I would encourage the client to examine his or her life to be sure s/he is carrying out all proper responsibilities, but not taking on more than his or her share. Trying to avoid necessary duties or taking on too much of the load can contribute to guilt, anxiety, insecurity and depression. The point is to leave the client with some options, something she can do, above and beyond waiting for a pattern to end.

A perfect example of personal power and responsibility is illustrated by three clients, coming close together, all coping with Moon conjunct Saturn aspects. One woman worked very hard writing songs, and was so successful, she was flown to England to write more. One man wanted life to be easy, was into positive thinking in terms of something for nothing, and suffered frustrations and setbacks the entire period. Another woman took on a job she was afraid she would not be able to handle at the beginning of the aspect, and did marvelously. She felt she deserved a vacation, so then did nothing. The aspect was still in orb, symbolizing her inner need to accomplish. She was suffering anxiety attacks (partially due to guilt). Each client will handle a situation in his or her unique way!

The danger in operating out of a deterministic world view is it can help undermine a client's belief in responsibility and free will. Clients often come to astrologers wanting a convenient excuse for their various problems. Eric Berne warned against the avoidance of responsibility in therapy through the game of "Wooden Leg." ("I'd like to do this or that, but I can't because of this wooden leg...") Astrologers do this constantly to themselves and clients. Example:, "Your problems with men are because you have Venus square Mars." (Implication: "Therefore you are stuck. Too bad.") Or, "No wonder you had an unhappy childhood. You have Saturn in the fourth house." (Implication: "You poor dear, the planets and your parents had it in for you.") Or, "I cannot sign the contract until next week. Mercury is retrograde." (Implication: "Even if I did my best, Mercury would mess it up.") Whose life is it, anyway?

The synchronistic and symbolic approaches leave more room for free will and responsibility and have more potential for useful therapeutic growth. I mention this not to convert anyone to one philosophy or another,but so one knows what world views (which maps of reality) are most functional for various purposes. It behooves astrologers to consider what world view they would most profit from under various circumstances.

For reasons of self-esteem, most people tend to take more responsibility for the "good" things in their lives, and ascribe setbacks and failures to "bad luck" or other external circumstances. As long as we do this, we have little or no hope of changing those circumstances. The assumptions we hold about personal power and responsibility in life will have an influence on our clients. The question becomes what "mind set" we deem most useful in various circumstances. Responsibility means power. If we helped to create a situation, we can help to alter it.

This is not an issue I intend to "solve" for anyone. My personal belief is that we confront the dilemma with every client, and I believe such thorny issues are best decided on an individual basis. The mixture of free will and responsibility versus determinism and ordained events we practice with each client is up to us. Note that these are **not** mutually exclusive. We can have some of each!

Some of the questions I might ask myself when pondering this issue include:

1. How anxious is this client? What kind of reassurance is likely to be most helpful?
2. How strong are any guilt feelings? Is the client likely to equate responsibility with guilt and wrongdoing rather than with power? If so, what can I do about that?
3. How much self-confidence does the client have? Is s/he able to act on her own desires? Is s/he prone to giving away the power? Is s/he a dependent type?
4. What is the level of self-esteem this client has? And how might my input affect that self-esteem?
5. Am I helping to establish a pattern with my approach? (e.g., a pattern of confidence, dependency, anxiety, etc . . .).
6. What can the client do to improve the situation? What options does s/he have? Are my statements closing off or opening up possibilities?

Chapter 10
The Issue of Power

Current understanding of the many subtle interactions that take place between people above and beyond their words suggests that, as counselors, we **are** influencing people. It is unavoidable. One question becomes how much of the influence is in awareness, and how much is happening on a subliminal level (where they influence us as well). This brings in the issue of power in the helping professions. When we set ourselves up as counselors or astrologers who offer expert knowledge to people about their lives, we take a position of power. The expert is willing to affect the lives of clients because s/he assumes that s/he will offer helpful information. And most of us do go into healing professions because we want to help people.

At the same time, power is a component of status in our society. Powerful people tend to be admired, often affect large numbers of other people and often have high status. Healers need to be aware that their desire for status and admiration can influence their yearnings for power. There is an extra issue for women, who are socialized towards avoiding direct power, but encouraged to "take care of" people. It can be tempting to slip into the role of controlling (too much) with the assistance one is offering.

Adolf Guggenbuhl-Craig has written a book on the subject: *Power in the Helping Professions*. He is highly aware of polarities and emphasizes that none of us operates out of exclusively pure motives. Even the most idealistic, yearning-to-save-humankind individual usually has some drive for power. In order to help, we must take some power. We must also believe that we know what is right (at least to some degree). There is the potential of tremendous abuse here, if we try to force our vision of "right" and "good" on others. Guggenbuhl-Craig uses Jung's term of the **Shadow** to refer to those parts of our nature which we deny, term as negative, and relegate to the subterranean parts of our being. Most of us try not to see our own Shadow side.

The more we deny it (as in projection), the stronger it becomes. Thus, warns Guggenbuhl-Craig, it is the most idealistic healers who are in strongest danger of falling into their Shadow lust for power. He suggests being constantly on the lookout for such polarities, trying to train ourselves to be aware of our internal ambivalences. Noting that friends are often as oblivious to our Shadow side as we ourselves, Guggenbuhl-Craig suggests: "In such cases enemies can be very useful; we should study their statements with care" (34, p. 29).

He also suggests concentrating on Shadow issues in therapy, much as others suggest dealing with one's own projections as a counselor. "By constantly trying to spot the workings of our psychotherapeutic shadow, to catch it red-handed, we help our patients in their own confrontations with the dark brother. If we fail to do this, all the patient learns from us is how to fool himself and the world" (34, p. 30).

A counselor's needs for power can contribute to tendencies to project. An example was the female astrologer who lived a miserable, unhappy life, feeling helpless and hopeless. When clients who were successful came to her, she was full of terrible doom and gloom — just awful predictions. One can suspect she was (unconsciously) wanting her clients to experience the same misery she felt in her life. How much happier she could have been if she had just used those successful clients as mirrors, realizing they reflected her inner yearning for success and achievement.

Guggenbuhl-Craig warns against falling into the trap of appearing omniscient. Many clients come, begging and hoping we will give them all the answers, the ultimate meaning and truth of the universe. "Any analyst, on the basis of this particular theory, can pretend to himself and his patient that he is capable of penetrating every event...This procedure gives the patient a momentary sense of security and the analyst a pleasant sense of himself as an omniscient magician" (34, p. 78). This is an especially likely occurrence with astrologers whose clients see the entire weight of the cosmos in the astrologer's lightest words.

Since we are all human beings, sooner or later we fall off the pedestal. The damage to our self-esteem may be small, however, compared to the wrath of a disillusioned client. By playing the omniscient savior role, we step into the fantasies of many a client who has been yearning for just such a perfect, omnipotent figure to make his or her life all wonderful. Trying even for a moment to fit that bill is to set one's self up for much unpleasantness later.

Even more destructive is the counselor who insists on being "right," even when given client feedback suggesting s/he may be misinterpreting. One example is a woman who was told by an astrologer that during an upcoming (Martian) period she would have an auto accident and be raped! She responded with disbelief, saying she was on a spiritual path and did not believe those events would take place. What happened during the period was a power struggle in an organization with which she was involved. Her side won the battle for control of the organization.

Too many astrologers fall into the omniscient trap, believing they have the power of the universe and can predict anything. The end result is that some clients are given destructive, anxiety producing predictions which usually turn out, after much concern, to be false. Clients have had their own deaths, husbands' deaths, deaths of children and equally horrific events predicted. Some astrologers use (hopefully unconsciously) their "insights" to breed more dependency in their clients. I mentioned the male astrologer who sees sexual problems in the charts of all his attractive female clients, and offers to help them out.

Adolf Guggenbuhl-Craig warns that some therapists begin to live vicariously through their clients. They become so absorbed in the conflicts and struggles of their clients, they neglect their own lives. They may neglect their relationships, sex lives, other areas of vitality and joy. They become like psychic vampires, living off the emotions and reactions of their clients. This breeds even more dependency in the clients, because the therapist dare not let them get well and depart. It also is highly destructive of the therapist's potential growth and development.

When we wield our authority in someone else's life, we send out the implicit message: "You are incapable of taking care of yourself, so I will do it for you." This can be a very damaging message to a client, so I try to resort to it as little as possible. Yalom's work emphasizes the importance of personal responsibility in getting better and leading happier lives. To attack those feelings in a client is a course to be taken rarely and with great caution.

One possible use is in crisis situations, e.g., a client (or friend) calls who has just been raped. As a counselor (as a friend), I want to know where she is and what her physical condition is. It is imperative she get to a safe place, if she is not already in a secure location. And she needs to be treated for any physical injuries, along with the emotional ones. The woman may be in shock and not thinking clearly. I may be very directive if she appears distraught.

Similarly, some therapists become very authoritative with suicidal patients: **"Don't do it!"** One technique is to have clients pay a session in advance and stress at the end of each session, "Now, I am expecting to see you at . . . ." The client contemplating suicide has to cope with breaking his or her promise (to be there) to the therapist. Oddly enough, that guilt can give clients pause. Other therapists are available for crises, and depend on the client calling or coming by and the therapist's ability to talk the client out of suicide. Some therapists have a contract with client, where the client literally promises not to kill himself or herself for a specified period of time (again, enlisting the aid of guilt and the power of the personal responsibility of the patient).

If clients are being physically abused, I do advise (flat out) them to leave. If a client is dead or hospitalized, therapy becomes much more difficult. I think the harm to someone's self-esteem and feelings of personal power can be lessened if we are as clear as possible and put our actions in a time-limited framework. Example: "Right now, I believe it is very difficult for you to take care of yourself. I want you to get to a more secure situation so you can take over your life again."

A client may also tell me, directly or by inference, she does not need my suggestions. It is important that I know when to back off. Refusing to allow a client her own responsibility and power is like a parent wrapping a child in cotton and trying to protect the child from any unpleasant experiences. You end up with a parent (counselor) who has to do everything, and a child (client) who never grows up. Besides the harm to their clients, overly directive counselors can be harmful to themselves. Such counselors may stunt their own potential development by becoming overly involved with clients' lives, by missing out on potential learning when they do not examine their own projections, by not seeing an exchange in the counseling encounter. As long as the counselor feels s/he is doing all the giving and providing, it is easy to become drained, resentful, and so on.

The concept of the Rescue Triangle from T.A. fits nicely here.

The Rescue Triangle

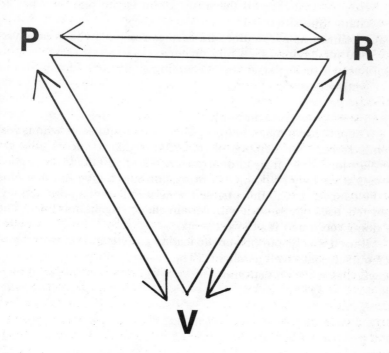

The idea of the **Karpmann (or Rescue) Triangle** is that often life offers us three roles to choose from: persecutor, rescuer and victim. There are legitimate victims, e.g., someone who cannot swim and is drowning needs assistance. Illegitimate victims fall in the rescue triangle. These are people who feel helpless and hopeless but actually can take action to improve their lives. Such victims define other people (or life circumstances) as persecutors: wicked and nasty, making life difficult for the poor victims who cannot (in their minds) do anything. So, they look for a rescuer, a noble soul to take care of things and make them all better.

This is a lovely "hook" for many counselors. Most of us like feeling helpful. So we often rush in with assistance "automatically." If we rescue illegitimate victims, the rescue triangle assures us that we will soon have the opportunity to become a victim ourselves. Once you get into the triangle, it is like musical chairs. You get to try on all the roles. The usual sequence goes:

1. Victim arrives, and offers "hook" ("Help me!") to counselor.
2. Counselor tries to help.
3. Help is unsuccessful (because victim is the one who has to change the situation).
4(a). Victim turns persecutor and berates rescuer (who is now victim) for having failed him or her.
4(b). Rescuer turns persecutor, becoming angry with victim for not getting better.

The merry-go-round continues.

There are two major warning signals to a counselor who is rescuing, rather than helping, clients. One signal is clients who get weaker (or worse) instead of stronger. Negative effects are a good clue that we may be doing **too much** for our clients. Another clue is the counselor who finds herself consistently feeling drained, exhausted, used or resentful with certain clients. Again, it is likely s/he is doing too much for those clients.

If used wisely, our power can lead to growth and transcendence for ourselves as well as clients. The responsibility for our use of power lies in our own hands.

Chapter 11
Universal Processes Of Counseling

Step One — Establishing Rapport

In my reading of a variety of psychotherapies, I am struck by the similarity of process among different schools. It seems many healers take similar steps, even though they come from different theoretical positions. I see most counselors as utilizing their empathy, respect, congruence and immediacy in an almost universal first step of establishing rapport with the client. Across a number of different approaches, I find an agreement that the first vital step in a counseling relationship is the establishing of rapport. In terms of the model of this book, rapport can be defined as the ability to enter the other person's version of reality.

Leslie Cameron-Bandler says: "Of first order is to acquire the client's trust and confidence" (12, p. 164). Steve Lankton emphasizes, "meeting the client at his model of the world and establishing a conscious and more importantly, unconscious affinity with him" (46, p. 59).

When human beings interact with one another, a number of factors can influence feelings, thoughts and perceptions. Some of these factors are provided by the physical and psychological setting of the meeting. As healers, we have a fair degree of control over the physical setting we create, although time, money and the structural constraints of our property will set some limits.

First impressions are often highly important; someone's initial ideas about you will color subsequent interactions. So consider carefully the kind of information and image you wish to convey. For example, if you want a very serious tone, choose the colors of your cards, stationery, advertising, working area accordingly. If you want a mystical aura, that will affect the environment you create. You choose your image.

I advise creating surroundings that are, as much as possible, reflective of your persona as a counselor. Do you tend to be warm, involved, emotionally expressive? Do you tend to watch and wait and observe? Are you extremely rational? If you strive to create an image that isn't a part of your own nature, you are likely to feel constrained by an uncomfortable and unfamiliar role, and clients are likely to feel disappointed and let down.

Clients who project their grandiose expectations onto a counselor are terribly disappointed, disillusioned and often angry when the counselor (eventually) shows through as a human being. If we allow ourselves to be put up on a pedestal as being wonderful, knowing all the answers, we set ourselves and the client up for trouble. For that reason, I strive to be particularly clear about what I **cannot** and **will not** do as a helper.

Consider the following questions in terms of who you are, and what you want your clients to know about you. There are no "right" answers to these questions. What is correct for one person is not suitable for another. I'm suggesting you analyze and appreciate your own personal style.

How do clients find you? Do you advertise? If so, where? In astrological publications? In the yellow pages — under astrology, magic? . . . Do you depend on word of mouth — satisfied clients referring others? Do you have a network of people (therapists, doctors, healers) to whom you refer, and who refer clients to you? Do you have a business card, stationery, etc.? What image does your card present to people? What information do you wish to convey to would be clients — whether through cards, referrals, advertising and layout? People will read into the information you do provide, so strive to be as clear and unambiguous as possible with the information you want them to know correctly. One decision to be made is how much information to include in any brochures or promotional literature which you distribute. Some biographic information is essential. You can choose to make that formal (such as degrees, training) or informal (feelings, character, likes, dislikes) or both. An outline of the sorts of work you do is necessary, e.g., lectures, workshops, private consultations. If you have particular specialties, it is usually good to mention them: relationships, for example. Specific details such as price or time needed are subject to change and generally not useful in your literature.

What is your first contact with clients? Do they call on the phone? If so, who answers: you; a secretary/receptionist; a member of your family; an answering machine...? Again, there is not **one** right answer to any of these questions. The important point is to ask yourself what you want to convey, and set up the situation accordingly. Clients will often feel a sense of importance and seriousness if a secretary or someone else handles your calls. Some may see it as excessively formal. What are you most comfortable doing?

Do you choose to see clients in an office? In what part of town is the office? What other professions (if any) have offices nearby? Do you have a receptionist? Do you make your own appointments and usher in your own clients? Do you have a waiting room as well as a consulting room?

What sort of furniture do you have? Does it look expensive, in perfect taste, comfortable, Salvation Army material? How is your consulting room arranged? Do you have a desk? If so, do you keep it totally neat and clean; full of papers and books, but relatively neat; totally chaotic? Do you sit behind a desk when working with a client? Do you sit in a chair? Where do they sit? Is there one place where you put clients, or do you offer them a choice of seats? How do any carpets, pictures, decorations affect the image and feeling of your consulting room?

If you work out of your home, in what part of town do you live? Do you set aside one room as an office, and use it only for seeing clients? Do you see clients in the living room, or other areas of your home? Who greets clients when they arrive: you, members of the family, friends near the door?

When clients arrive, are they ushered immediately to the consulting area? Do you offer them refreshments?

Does the consulting area offer assurance of privacy to the client? Is noise from the outside world (or rest of the house) a problem? Do you answer the phone while consulting? (Or the doorbell, if it is your home?)

Again, I do not intend to suggest that there are "correct" answers to these questions. Your choices will depend on the sort of atmosphere you wish to facilitate with clients. What is "right" for one person may be "wrong" for another.

Speaking in generalizations, an office seems very businesslike and serious to people. Clients are more likely to take you seriously, and expect to pay more for your services. They may also feel intimidated by the more formal atmosphere. Office furnishing may augment the cool, detached, business world theme, or may be used to create a more informal atmosphere within that world. A receptionist and other trappings will support your aura of authority, control and importance. Practicing in the "good" part of town will impress some clients. Similarly, living or practicing in a "bad" part of town will discourage some, if only from coming out at night.

Astrologers have a special problem with advertising. My experience is that the average person on the street goes to the yellow pages for astrologers when s/he wants "good day/bad day" astrology for gambling in Las Vegas, or whatever. For counseling, most people do not seek out the yellow pages. They depend on suggestions of friends and associates, referrals, or local clinics.

However, some kinds of literature can be useful. If, for example, you teach and lecture as well as counsel, it is helpful to have some brochures available on request which list the sorts of counseling services you offer. I know of psychotherapists who have several typewritten sheets they give to clients upon entering therapy. Those sheets include basic information such as fees, scheduling, what the therapist expects of the client, what the client can expect of the therapist, and so on. I recommend this highly. When expectations are explicit, they can be discussed and people can negotiate. When both parties have unspoken expectations, they can easily get into feeling hurt or taken advantage of. (See Section 2 for example literature.) Of course, issues can be discussed verbally. One does not have to overwhelm one time clients with literature.

Your style of dress sends subtle cues to your clients. Do you want to be perceived as soft, gentle, flowing, flexible and perhaps confused and illogical? Do you enjoy a formal, immaculate, precise and possibly rigid appearance? Do you consistently choose solid, dependable (but possibly boring and unexciting) colors? Or electric reds and blues that keep the client awake, but possibly uncomfortable? Is your style of dress seductive?

Many people will enjoy being offered coffee, tea or juice. Others will find it too informal, and prefer to get "down to business."

People will often be more relaxed and at ease in a home atmosphere. They may also overstay their time when it seems like "visiting" rather than "consulting."

Many clients feel interrupted by telephones. One can arrange to turn the phone "off" (so the ringing is not audible), or have a receptionist or family member available to answer quickly and take messages. Ignoring a ringing phone is often just as uncomfortable for clients as you actually taking the call. Many people "itch" to answer a ringing phone; they have difficulties letting it ring and ring.

Sitting behind a desk tends to increase one's aura of power and authority. The question is whether you wish to do that or not. The tidiness or messiness of your working area will affect some clients. There are people to whom either extreme is anathema. A happy medium is least likely to arouse negative responses. (Excess tidiness or neatness can be seen as rigid, obsessive-compulsive, exacting or critical. Excessive messiness can be seen as lack of order, uncaring, or the sloppiness may be generalized to other areas in the client's mind.) Having several chairs available to clients gives them choices, and some feelings of power and control. It also allows them to choose a level of closeness with which they feel comfortable, in terms of how close their chair is to yours.

Analyze your voice. Does it tend to be too soft, too loud, too harsh? Listen to your tone of voice. Does your irritation show in your voice? Does fear reveal itself through your voice? Can you use your voice for dramatic and persuasive emphasis? Working with a tape recorder can be extremely valuable, once you get past any initial self-consciousness. Turn on the recorder sometimes when you are going to be having ordinary conversation. It will help you become familiar with your normal patterns of communication. Remember, we all sound differently to other people than we do to ourselves. A recorder gives a closer approximation of what other people hear.

Similarly, a video tape can be a tremendously educational experience if you ever have the opportunity. Films can reveal annoying little habits we never notice, e.g., playing with one's hair, fiddling with pens or pencils, nervous tics and twitches.

Barring such technological riches, we all have people resources. Ask for feedback. Discuss with others how you come across. How is your eye contact? When are you most persuasive? What do they think of your voice? How do your postures, gestures and other body language affect them?

From the moment you greet the client onward, you are creating a psychological setting (or adding to and changing the one you began with the initial contact with this client). Is your manner basically detached and aloof? Do you avoid eye contact to a large degree? Do you wrap yourself up in your papers and notes, so as to ignore cues from the client? Do you feel uncomfortable when clients ask questions? Do you frown when clients ask questions, get impatient, dismiss the questions, or answer them perfunctorily?

Do you encourage and solicit participation by the client, asking open-ended questions? (For example, "How do you feel about that? How does this strike you? What do you think of that? What is your reaction?") Do you watch the client for nonverbal cues of understanding (or lack of comprehension), agreement (or disagreement), discomfort (or ease), anger or irritation, embarrassment or grief?

Do you power play the client? This can include not listening; insisting on being "right" even when the client indicates you are misinterpreting; maintaining a tone of voice, air of authority, position in the room and impatience that suggest you know it all; criticizing and putting the client down; being disrespectful of the client.

Rollo May, along with many others, emphasized the importance of using the other person's language in establishing rapport. This includes such minimal steps as avoiding jargon and overly technical terms. Taken further, it means attempting to learn how clients use their words, not assuming that we "know" the meaning of what they are saying. If someone says, "My lover hurt me," I can have an idea of what that hurt is. Depending on my model of the world, I may imagine the lover criticizing, rejecting, ridiculing, physically abusing, ignoring, or a multitude of other possibilities. If I assume I know what that client means by "hurt," I may luck out and be accurate. More likely, I will operate from my reality and be far removed from the reality of the client. Frank Farrelly (26, p. 119-120) tells us that a therapist's task is to translate her concepts into "terminology that is relevant and has significance for that client within his sociopsychological and semantic frame of reference." Then, we use the client's language to give new meanings and influence his thinking and perceiving.

And there are much deeper forms of empathy (a term for entering a client's world) than the words. Moreno, originator of Psychodrama, emphasized the bodily reactions of clients. He taught the technique of mirroring: adopting, as closely as possible, the posture, gestures, body language, breathing, expressions, movements of another human being. This was a highly successful method for "getting into" the other person, being able to feel what that person was feeling. Many therapists use the technique regularly. Steve Lankton quotes Fritz Perls as admiring another therapist who got into clients so thoroughly that he breathed in rhythm with them. Farrelly on this subject: ". . . nonverbal cues of caring are at least as crucial if not more crucial as the verbal cues" (26, p. 63).

Neuro-Linguistic Programming is one of the newer psychotherapies, and puts a tremendous emphasis on establishing this nonverbal rapport. NLP practitioners have taken the ideas of Moreno, Perls and others and extended them. NLP theorizes that Western people gather much of their interpretation of the world through three major sensory channels: visual (eyes), auditory (ears), and kinesthetic (tactile sensations, balance, motoric reactions). People are assumed to reveal the sensory channel they are using through eye movements and use of predicates, e.g., a visual person will talk of things becoming clear. An auditory individual might say, "I can really hear you now." A kinesthetic would need to "get a handle" on a situation. The NLP therapist will mirror a client's representational system(s), along with many other nonverbal behaviors. If a client uses a lot of visual predicates (such as clear, image, see, paint a picture) the counselor would deliberately search for and use visual predicates and images.

Such counselors observe the eye scan patterns of their clients. Most of us, especially when asked a question or when thinking something over, unfocus our eyes slightly and often look away. Many people have a pattern in where they look. For example, one client may look, most of the time, up and to the right. Another may look down and to the left. In establishing nonverbal rapport, one NLP technique is to mirror the eye scan patterns of the client.

Of course, eye contact in general is also important. Clients who hardly ever meet the counselor's eyes may be very shy, nervous, uninterested or perhaps threatened by what is being discussed. Generally, the more involved a client is with what is going on, the more eye contact s/he will make. It is important to get an individual measure, as people vary tremendously in the amount of eye contact they make. What is a lot for one client may be very little for another. The shy, inhibited person may make only a few fleeting connections with his or her eyes, even though very interested and involved in the session. A sudden break in what has been fairly good eye contact will often indicate the client is feeling vulnerable. A touchy issue may have just been broached.

Other nonverbal cues can help the counselor assess how

comfortable or uncomfortable her client is. Does the client appear basically relaxed? Is his body tight or rigid? Is his face open or is it tense and constricted? The eyes and mouths of most people give a number of clues. Watch for softness or hardness in the eyes trembling in the mouth, and other tics and twitches. Does the client sit quietly and calmly or make lots of agitating movements? Is the client's posture towards the counselor, in the middle, or backed away? Generally, leaning forwards tends to indicate receptivity, while leaning back tends to show relaxation or inattention. (See diagrams on p. 93.)

What is the client's voice like? Does s/he sound bored, cheerful, anxious, angry, . . .? Notice any pauses, emphases through timing or tone, breaks in the client's speech. They may be underlines to issues of importance. For example, a client with a normally pleasant voice was having conflicts with her partner. Whenever she mentioned him, her voice would deepen slightly and acquire an edge of irritation.

Be alert to small (and large) sighs, grunts and other noises. Small sighs may be inaudible but visible as an extra deep breath by the client. The counselor must still figure out whether it is a sigh of relaxation and loss of tension, of boredom, of frustration, or of something else.

Yawns carry information also — often disengagement or boredom, although they can indicate relaxation and comfort (and not getting enough sleep or oxygen). When does the client smile, frown or grimace? Is s/he preoccupied with taking notes, writing or doodling? Does s/he ever nod his or her head (implying agreement) or shake it (implying disagreement)? Such moves may be very small.

All of the above observations apply to the counselor as well. Are you relaxed and open in body posture, facing clients squarely and keeping good eye contact? What nonverbal messages are you sending out?

Skilled counselors emphasize that our first and most fundamental tool for understanding clients is ourselves: paying attention to how we feel. We need to listen to and observe our own reactions as well as those of our clients. It is a truism in the field that people will be in our consultations as they are in life. They do not change the pattern. Clients make the same assumptions, play the same games, operate out of their usual world views.

Thus, a counselor who finds herself becoming angry with a client can guess that perhaps a number of people in this client's life become

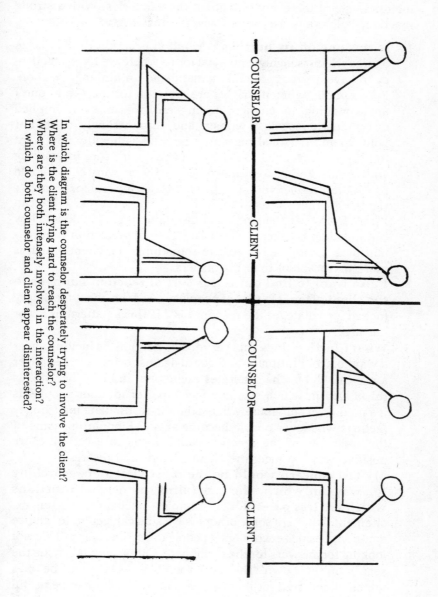

COUNSELOR CLIENT

COUNSELOR CLIENT

In which diagram is the counselor desperately trying to involve the client?
Where is the client trying hard to reach the counselor?
Where are they both intensely involved in the interaction?
In which do both counselor and client appear disinterested?

angry with him or her. The counselor's reaction is important information — about the client and about the counselor. With a strong reaction, I generally ask myself several questions:

1. **Is this one of my buttons?** (A button is jargon for any issue or area which is highly emotional for us where we have a tendency to have a strong, often automatic and unthinking, reaction. For example, women's rights are a button for me — and one I am unwilling to change. I am sensitive to even implied discrimination against women and react strongly to it. For political and personal reasons, I feel this is healthy and want to keep my reactions. But I watch them with care in working with clients. For me to push women's right on every client would be counterproductive — for the clients, for me and for women's rights.) In other words, what is the issue here for me? What can I learn from the situation? What assumptions am I making? How can I enlarge my world view? The issue of projection is important here. I may be reacting to something in a client which is more my problem than his or hers.

2. **I also want to find out if this sort of reaction happens to the client often.** Do a lot of people around the client feel angry (or sad, or whatever the response is)? Is this a pattern in his or her life?

3. **What function does this serve?** For example, is inciting anger a way to avoid intimacy and guard against being hurt? Is anger a way in which s/he generates excitement in his or her life? Is this a way in which s/he can feel superior to other people? Is it a method of self-abuse where s/he can restimulate inadequacy feelings whenever people become angry? Pinpointing some of the functions of the reaction can help us to ascertain more positive ways to meet the client's needs and desires.

4. **My last concern would be the most vital step, searching for ways in which s/he can fulfill the needed functions which are less painful.** For example, if a client is wanting excitement, what are some others ways s/he can generate intense emotions besides encouraging people to become angry? I am not looking for answers for the client here. Often, clients pursue the search on their own. The most valuable answers will be ones which clients find for themselves. The counselor can be useful in helping to pinpoint what needs and desires are behind (helping to create) an uncomfortable situation or problem behavior.

Rapport entails listening to and paying attention to clients, and to one's own feelings. Listening to words is not enough. One needs to listen for the message behind the words. The alert counselor watches for patterns. As an example, the client who apologizes constantly:

1. may be projecting the power ("I have to please other people").
2. may feel resentment and anger underneath at being "forced" to appease everyone.
3. may have low self-esteem.
4. may be very identified with the traditional, "feminine" sex roles.
5. may be manipulating others (in or out of awareness) feeling, "People are likely to feel sorry for me and do what I want if I constantly apologize for my existence."

As always, any such guesses or hypotheses are just that. We need to check them out. And, hypotheses do **not** have to be mutually contradictory. We will often find more than one desire operating. Once we know the motivation(s), the path is clear for clients to find more fulfilling ways to satisfy that motivation(s), or drive(s).

Rapport also includes honesty. Lying is counterproductive. Sooner or later, our lies are exposed, whether they are literal spoken lies or implied promises such as falling into the mystical, total savior role. ("I can help anyone. You don't have to do a thing. I'll make it all beautiful.") Being direct and candid with ourselves is just as important as being forthright with clients. As Guggenbuhl-Craig points out, if we avoid facing unpleasant truths about ourselves, we only role model deception to our clients. Honesty can incorporate congruence: sending out clear, unambiguous messages. Incongruence includes saying one thing with words, and something different with body language. If we constantly examine and confront ourselves, we will be more aware of our inner ambivalences and polarities and will be able to express them, rather than sending confused, mixed messages to clients.

If we are honest, respectful (of ourselves and clients); if we genuinely care about people and are able to demonstrate warmth; if we can put ourselves in the place of the client and imagine how s/he might feel; and if we are flexible we will easily establish a comfortable rapport with our clients.

Chapter 12
Step Two —
Gathering The Evidence

In many respects, a successful counselor is similar to a good detective. Both search for clues collect data, and make inferences and logical deductions on the basis of the information available. Both need a good grasp of human nature. Personally, I find the sense of being with and understanding another person far more exciting than tracking criminals.

From the moment of first contact on, we collect information from a client. If the first contact is by phone, we have the tone of voice, the timbre to listen to. We can be alert for indications of nervousness, stress, grief, confusion, casualness, joking, concern or terror. We have the information of the sex of the individual with whom we are dealing. Astrologers have, with the birth data, the age of the person. They may supply, or we may request, other background data, e.g., married or not, children, birth order, and so on.

The authors of *Paradox and Counter Paradox* emphasize that they begin therapy with the first phone call and are especially sensitive to power plays by clients. They watch for "peculiarities of communication, tone of voice, peremptory demands for all kinds of information, immediate attempts to manipulate by trying to make the appointment for a particular day or hour, attempts to reverse roles so that it appears as if it were the therapist searching for patients and not the family asking for help" (60, p. 11-12). Jay Haley (36, p. 16) gives an extreme example of a client trying to control the therapeutic relationship in the first phone call. He believes the first, immediate issue between therapist and client is who is to control what kinds of behavior in the relationship. Haley feels all relationships involve power plays and control issues, but judges people as symptomatic when they seek control while simultaneously denying they are seeking control. That is, such an individual is incongruent: sending out contradictory messages.

I feel a note of caution here is vital. When collecting information, we need to use concepts and labels with great care. As Steve Lankton warns: "...you can induce all kinds of behaviors in your clients and yourself by not questioning your therapeutic presuppositions" (46, p. 191). He uses the example of Fritz Perls who often made therapy sound like an "act of war between client and therapist" (46, p. 191).

Thinking requires language and labels, but we must not get too trapped by them. Palazzoli, Cecchin, Prata and Boscolo warn that "appearance is not necessarily reality" (60, p. 26). They trained themselves to think in terms of "to seem" rather than "to be" (60, p. 27). Example: "He seems sad," as opposed to "He is sad." Gestaltists might recall Fritz's differentiation between thinking (intellectual), feeling (in the body only) and imagining (theories, opinions about self or others). Thus, I **think** it's raining. I **feel** a lump in my throat. I **imagine** you are angry with me. Too often, we treat our labels and imaginings as reality.

I see counseling as a refining process. We generate hypotheses (like any good scientist) and check them against the data. As long as they hold, we continue to work with them tentatively. If a hypothesis (imagining) is contradicted by the data, we throw it out. (This is where any counselor must beware the human desire to be "right." Being "right" at the expense of one's client is seldom helpful.)

Generalizations and even stereotypes are one place to start generating hypotheses, but they must be used with extreme care. Too often, people apply stereotypes, forgetting that they **are** stereotypes. Then they continue trying to force their clients into stereotypical constraints. Stereotypes may help us see some of the assumptions clients are living their lives by. Using the stereotype means being able to see other possibilities, and helping the client realize there are alternatives, not locking the client into a mold.

Nonetheless, it is important to know about societal prescriptions on behavior such as sex roles. Men and women are socialized differently (in general) in our society. We need to be aware that a woman, in general, is less likely to be strongly assertive, physical, angry than a man; and that the majority of men tend to be less tender, gentle, nurturing than women.

The stereotype gives us a place to start, but not a place to end! And we have to be wary of relying too heavily upon it. Suppose a man calls and sounds very guarded, aloof and cool upon the phone. Upon erecting the chart, I find a very large stellium in Cancer. **One** hypothesis I would entertain would be that he has had trouble integrating his tender "feminine" side, due to sex role conditioning in our society. He may be afraid of his gentler, dependent side. Another hypothesis might be that he has never seen an astrologer before, and is uncertain about how one should act. (Note these two hypotheses are **not** mutually exclusive.) Another might be that he expected someone different when he called, perhaps an older woman than I. The important point is remembering that these, and any others, are all **guesses**.

Once the client arrives, I have further information. The style of dress will often give clues as to the kind of person I am seeing. Ethnic background is a source of more data. Additional biographical information may be offered. And: lots of nonverbal cues are now available for my enlightenment! My job is to check out my hypotheses. This can include checking some information against latter indicators. It can include directly asking the client. It can include exploring together for answers. However, if I make up my mind that one particular answer or aspect of a person is "right," I have closed myself off from noticing anything different in that area. My belief in the correctness of my judgment is going to create strong blinders in my observation of the client in that area.

Therefore, a major important step for me as a counselor is to — as much as possible — know myself. This means knowing my own blind spots, getting in touch with my own buttons.

I am not suggesting a counselor "should be" totally objective and value free. As indicated earlier, I think that is impossible. Human beings are evaluating animals. We make judgments. I don't feel total objectivity is possible. We are living inside our skins and that will affect our interactions with others. I am not suggesting we try to change ourselves, just that we understand and know ourselves.

This returns us to the earlier concept of world views. We all have a world view — an (often unconscious or subliminal, unexamined) image of what truth, reality, people and the world are. We operate under these assumptions. The closer "match" our assumptions have to **consensual reality** (other people's interpretations), the more effectively we tend to function. The more discrepancy, generally, the more pain and difficulties in our lives.

A successful counselor must not be tied to one world view. A necessary skill is the ability to see alternatives. This includes the necessary empathy and imagination to enter another person's "reality," at least to some degree. The most destructive counselors are the ones "laying a trip" on their clients. That is, they are insisting the client adopt the counselor's world view. (Of course, such counselors have no recognition that they are dealing with a map. They are convinced that their version **is** reality, and the client is mistaken, abhorrent, depraved or wicked.)

Stereotypes are a common area for limited world views. Many people take stereotypes as reality and treat whole groups of people accordingly. People are most prone to using stereotypes when they do not know the other person well, or are getting ambiguous clues. (This is more a danger in the initial steps of counseling, but if adopted, the stereotype may be defended by self-fulfilling prophecy tactics.) The counselor who cannot see past a client's age (or sex, or skin color, or sexual preference) to the individual — can do much harm. Such counselors will put out their moral judgments about right and wrong, good and bad, with the righteousness of a "true believer." (See Eric Hoffer on that subject.) They will be blind to large chunks of reality — whatever does not fit into their stereotypic image.

Nonetheless, if used with care, stereotypes can be a useful tool, a way to generate hypotheses. Alfred Adler gave us lots of information about the importance of birth order. Knowing that eldest children tend to feel responsible and are often more conservative than their peers may give us an effective clue with some clients. Being aware that youngest children may be pampered and spoiled, but are often very lovable and loving is potentially helpful information. Being aware that only children make up a higher proportion of high achievers (and also of people with severe problems) can aid us on occasion.

Similarly, we may make guesses about an individual based on his or her dress and general appearance. An overly meticulous, exacting appearance may suggest obsessive-compulsive tendencies, psychological rigidity. An extremely scruffy appearance may indicate rebelliousness, a lack of involvement with other people, a lack of caring for the self. Certain styles of dress invite reactions from others. A woman wearing an extremely seductive outfit is sending out a message to the world. (The message may be an interest in sex; it may be insecurity about her "femininity" and using sexy apparel to bolster her self-image; it may be a desire to tease other people but not follow through.) Similarly, with men whose clothes accent their sexuality. The behavior may be a power play, a reaction to insecurity, a threat, a tease, and so on. (Again, hypotheses need not be mutually exclusive either.)

With age, we have the awareness of cycles in people's lives. (See particularly Daniel Levinson, et al. in *The Seasons Of A Man's Life* and the work of Gail Sheehy.) For example, many people experience a "life crisis" around age 30: they feel terribly old all of a sudden; they begin questioning their lives; they feel time is rushing by and they haven't accomplished much. People often make major changes in jobs, relationships, self-images and/or other areas of their lives. Again, individual reactions will vary tremendously. Leslie Cameron-Bandler suggests that, "people who respond creatively to and cope effectively with this stress are people who have a rich representation or model of their situation, one in which they perceive a wide range of options in choosing their actions" (12, p. 79). People who experience such times as heavy crises tend to have more limited maps of "reality," and get into "stuck" places where they don't see (hear, feel) any other possibilities.

In gathering information from body language, we have a wide range of clues. These include the basic posture and positioning of the body; tone and timbre of the voice; loudness or softness of speech; gestures; movements; tics and twitches, plus a multitude of data from the face. To quote Steve Lankton, ". . . abundant information you can glean from the client's face color changes, pupil dilation, movement of the orbiscularis oculi, the oris, zygomatic and risorius muscles of the face, changes in respiration, posture, muscle tone in the face and neck and eye scan patterns" (46, p. 132).

A number of books exist on body language and they all deal in stereotypes and generalities. For example, a "closed" or "crossed" posture indicates a closed attitude; an open posture, an open attitude, etc. Sometimes, crossed arms may be only closing off the feelings of cold someone is experiencing! As with most generalities, it is okay to begin with a stereotype (remembering it is very limited) if we are careful to check it against each individual case. People have their own idiosyncratic body language as well as world view. We need to be alert, as counselors, to these unique clues.

Bearing in mind that these are overgeneralizations, we can be aware that closeness tends to go with liking and distance with dislike or not caring. People tend to sit closer to individuals they are fond of. Similarly, we stand a bit closer to people we care about. Different cultures have very different standards for the optimum distance at which to converse. Closeness for a northern European may be quite different than closeness for an Arab. People tend to draw inward a bit (bodily, gestures, facial expressions) when feeling attacked, or experiencing something they judge as unpleasant. They tend to "open up" or out (and pupils dilate) with more pleasurable experiences.

What is most helpful is training ourselves to observe. We have countless opportunities to watch people and make guesses (at bus stops, in lines, in lobbies, on street corners, at parties, and so on) about what they are communicating with their body language. With clients, we can check our perceptions against other information they give us. Many clients will have unique, personal responses, e.g., a muscle in the right cheek which twitches when they are nervous; tugging at an ear when anxious; a deepening in color of the lower lip when enjoying life, etc. As we train ourselves to be more and more observant, we will notice and learn more and more.

When in doubt as to what a nonverbal message may mean, one good check is to mirror it. Often we will enter another person's feeling reality when we enter it bodily. We can also ask, or look for additional clues elsewhere. And we can file it away in our minds, to be alert for in the future. Flexibility includes not having to have all the answers right now (or even ever).

As astrologers we tend to gather most of our information from the horoscope. The horoscope is also just another map, a way of conceptualizing reality. (I, personally, find it more valuable than any psychological tests.) But it is subject to our perceptions and interpretations. The careful astro-counselor will keep her astrological assumptions just as hypothetical as other guesses about the client. Any knowledge we think the chart gives us about that person needs to be checked against their life and experience. The map can become a trap.

Not testing such assumptions reveals a counselor's lack of empathy and respect. For example, One astrologer insisted that a client **must** be "cheating" on her husband, despite her denial, because she had Venus square Uranus. This astrologer clearly has a very limited world view since Venus square Uranus **always** means affairs to him.

Chapter 13

Step Three —
Changing Paradigms

Naturally, this three part division is artificial, useful mainly as a teaching tool. In actual counseling interactions, we simultaneously establish rapport, gather evidence and change paradigms. The three steps are totally intertwined and interdependent. Like most of life, the process of counseling is a circular, interweaving one, not a linear progression.

As was discussed earlier, people seek stability in their perceptions and experience of the world. Thus, many people are resistant to change. Yalom offers several insights which help clients mobilize their energy to change. These include the recognition by clients that: "Only I can change the world I have created" (84, p. 340). Once clients appreciate that they are creating much of their experience, they also realize they can change that creation.

Another insight is for the client to trust that: "There is no danger in change" (84, p. 340). Many people have catastrophic fantasies about what might happen if they change. Sometimes just facing the fantasies is enough. Other times, clients need to make changes slowly and gradually, lest an abrupt shift create major difficulties in their lives; (e.g., someone who is beginning to face buried resentments and tremendous rage may need to release it in small pieces over a period of time.)

Another factor which can work against change (especially if rapid) is the social system of the clients. Systems tend to perpetuate themselves. Generally, people in a partnership or family or other system have set up an implicit set of rules and ways to interact with one another. Everyone has learned them. If one person in the system changes, it upsets the balance. Often, the other people do not wish to change, to learn whole new ways of relating. The most common first reaction is that the other people will encourage, in subtle and direct ways, the changing individual to return to his or her former behavior. (That was more predictable.)

It is during this period that the emotional support of a counselor (or group of people dealing with the same issue, as in A.A.) is vital. The counselor provides a framework, a world view that says it is okay to change, to grow, and I will still respect and care for you as you alter. To oversimplify, it often is as though the family (or relational) system encourages the stability drive of the individual desirous of change, while the counselor encourages the individual's self-actualizing drive to grow, transcend, encompass more potentials. Of course, this is not universal. Families and other networks of attachment can be very helpful in change as well. They are most likely to be helpful when change is more gradual, giving everyone a chance to adapt more slowly, and when the other people in the system believe that they will get greater rewards and still satisfy the needs that were satisfied under the "old rules."

For the above reasons, it is often helpful to involve the significant others of clients in the change process. It is no joke that therapy can lead to divorce. When one partner changes radically, the other may decide s/he would rather leave the relationship than have to learn new rules and roles of relating. This can be used as a threat to the individual who would change as well, and needs to be faced and threshed out in the counseling.

A third realization by clients is: "To get what I really want, I must change"(84, p. 341). This includes the realization that reality is largely subjective (and we are in charge). It also often involves confronting internal ambivalences. Clients get unconscious needs met, often in ways that are very uncomfortable. Once the clients become aware of their underground needs, they can find more satisfying ways to meet those needs. This may involve a shift in the frame of reference. That is, clients may change their minds about what they "really" need.

For example, a client comes in, proclaiming all she "really" wants is some peace and quiet. She cannot understand why she is always arguing and fighting with the people she loves. Through the chart, discussion and examples, it becomes clear that fighting is her way of creating space in her relationships. She feels she "should" be loving and always "there" for her family, so she incites disagreements in order to withdraw emotionally. Once she realizes she needs to be independent, to do some things alone, she has choices. She can fight merely for the sake of habit, or for excitement. She can stop fighting. She can take space directly, adopt a hobby, go out more often, create other choices. She may take a look at her "should's" around the proper role of a good wife and mother. Peace and quiet may also become less important to her. An interesting parallel is the woman who consistently developed headaches when she was not expressing her anger. She came to appreciate her headaches as a dependable signal to her that she had some anger to face. This shift of turning liabilities into assets is a cornerstone of effective counseling. Clients have tremendous resources at their disposal. Sometimes all it takes is a slight shift in their viewpoint to turn a problem into a potential. The role of the counselor is to assist in the shift in perspective.

Clients often come to realize that they have mutually contradictory "needs." That is, they may want closeness, but they also want freedom. If they identify with one consciously, they declare: "This is what I **really** need." Meanwhile the unconscious is arranging life to include the other desire. When we allow both desires, we can find different areas and times in life to satisfy them.

The counselor also may have to deal with client fantasies that the "right man" or "right woman" or "right job" or some outside, omniscient, totally loving figure will eventually come along and make life perfect.

A fourth important conclusion is: "I have the power to change." Yalom emphasizes that this must be within the frame of reference of the client. In some cultures, the explanation of the problem will include magic. Unless the healer can offer a frame of reference that is relevant to the client, explanations are unlikely to lead to a sense of power or mastery. Within a given framework, however, the most helpful explanations are those which allow room for the client to feel a sense of potency, the ability to make a difference. The most useful world view is one which incorporates client power and responsibility.

Our ability as counselors to help clients alter world views is inextricably bound up with our skill and sensitivity in entering their world (rapport) and collecting information. The counselor who is able to feel with clients, see their points of view, understand their reality, finds that change is not as difficult as the above might suggest. The degree of ease or difficulty in change is closely related to a counselor's empathy, respect, congruence, and so on. The more sensitive the counselor is to the client's point of view; the more the counselor can present an explanatory framework that makes sense to that client, fitting all his or her problems into a logical world view which gives that client a sense of power to improve the situation; the easier and more rapid change will be.

Once rapport is established, many clients are amenable to (direct or indirect) suggestions from the counselor. As noted earlier, whether we admit it or not, we are constantly influencing and being influenced by clients anyway. Life is a network. The question is how much of the influence is done in awareness, for specific motives. Once faith and trust are present, the counselor wields quite a bit of power.

Several options for change exist. One possibility is making a direct suggestion. This is fraught with several perils:

1. We may undermine a client's sense of personal power and responsibility.
2. The suggestion may be "wrong" for the client who may act on it, and be unhappy.
3. The client may use the suggestion to sabotage counseling by carrying out the suggestion in such a way that failure or discomfort arises. Then the client can blame the counselor.
4. The client may play the "Yes, but" game with suggestions. Eric Berne and others have described the game he labelled "Yes, but" a trap for the unwary therapist who tries to give specific answers to a client. Each suggestion, no matter how reasonable, will be met with the response of: "Yes, but . . ." from the client, describing all the reasons the therapist's various ideas just won't work. For such reasons, many counselors avoid direct suggestions and turn to metaphors or stories.

There is another excellent reason for using metaphors. Much wisdom is not directly transmittable, but needs to be experienced or felt by the individual. Eastern traditions have long recognized this and are full of stories and parables Clients will often resist information and insights offered directly, while happily adopting insights they gain from metaphors. The indirect illumination gives clients a chance to be active, to construct their own meanings. It is more valuable in the end, because they live most of their lives that way anyway. The therapeutic goal is **not** to provide the "right" answer, but to provide an environment in which it is easier for clients to discover their own answers.

Milton Erickson was a past master at the use of stories. Many of his clients were "cured" by stories alone. Through careful use of intonation, pauses, phrasing and gestures, Erickson encouraged clients to identify with his stories. For example, he might tell a story about a flower in such a way that the client strongly identified with what happened to the flower. Clients who come seeking assistance are looking desperately for anything which might help them to cope. Thus, they are likely to "read meaning into" a variety of circumstances.

The astrological metaphor is quite useful here as well. Erickson liked metaphors partially because they allowed the client to identify unconsciously. The conscious mind might still resist. Clients come to astrologers with a mind set ready to consider statements about the planets and signs as actually statements about the client and significant people in his or her life. But having the identification even that one step removed from the person minimizes defensiveness. It is also enough of a slight shift of point of view to make it more likely the client can make other conceptual shifts, see other possibilities.

A variety of changes can be brought about indirectly. The counselor serves as a role model to the client. In behaviorist terms, the client is prone to imitating the actions and attitudes of the counselor. Thus, the counselor who is open, honest, responsible and self-examining is likely to encourage such qualities in clients. Neuro-Linguistic Programming puts a fair emphasis on change through nonverbal interactions. For example, if an NLP therapist determined that a client was primarily visual: reacted to how things **look**, the therapist might decide the client needed more kinesthetic awareness (how things **feel**) — perhaps to relate more easily with a partner. One technique is to mirror the client (use the predicates s/he uses, sit how s/he sits, breathe as s/he breathes, gesture as s/he gestures, etc.) This establishes nonverbal rapport. Then, the counselor can begin to **lead** the client. The counselor would gradually introduce more and more kinesthetic predicates (e.g., "Did that make sense to you? Did you feel good about that? Can you get a grasp on that idea?) The counselor would often glance down and to the right (the eye movements generally associated with kinesthetic reactions). S/he would use lots of gestures close to the body above the heart (also kinesthetic in the experience of NLP workers). If rapport is successfully established, the client will generally follow the lead of the therapist, often unconsciously (outside awareness) on the nonverbal level.

A major focus of skilled clinicians such as Erickson, Perls and (Virginia) Satir is turning liabilities into assets. A positive intent is assumed to everything. This is often a whole new way of perceiving for clients. Satir might suggest to a husband that his wife's constant questioning about his day is indicating her loving concern and desire for closeness. If he had been perceiving only jealousy and suspiciousness, he has the possibility of a wider viewpoint now. Satir might suggest to a wife that a husband's complaints about her activities showed a desire to spend more time together, not a need to restrict her and control her life.

A similar technique is used with a variety of problems. First, the issue is identified. Then, the client (with perhaps assistance from the counselor) determines the positive intent of (motivation behind) the problem behavior or situation. Next, the client can find a more fulfilling way in which to satisfy that intent. Zip Dobyns, I and other astrologers use these principles regularly. Psychosynthesis uses a similar procedure with the concept of subpersonalities. (All subpersonalities are useful and potentially good. We just have to find the appropriate time and place to express their natures.)

Consider, for example, a woman who had a strong freedom-closeness dilemma. This is very common in our culture: a need for intimacy, attachment, emotional warmth and commitment with a competing need for independence, freedom, space and individuality. People handle their freedom-closeness needs in different ways. Many will project one end, picking other people who overdo that side of life. Some will repress one of their needs, and eventually get ill. Some will swing from one end of the polarity to the other and back again, repeating the process endlessly.

This woman had identified with her needs for closeness, and was not aware of her needs for freedom and independence. She saw her family as self-centered, demanding, out for themselves. (Her family was living out the freedom side she denied in herself. Their "self-centeredness" was an excessive development of the self-assertion and independence she was not expressing.) Talking about the chart gave her the opportunity to realize that she had freedom needs. She saw that she had been creating space by distancing herself from the family through feeling critical and resentful. She changed her attitude. She began appreciating the closeness she did have, and took space directly when she needed it.

Since she changed, the entire family system changed as well. In this case, everyone else adjusted very happily, and the family life was much more comfortable and pleasing to all. Unfortunately, we cannot guarantee such happy endings. Sometimes people change, and find that the significant others in their life do not wish to change. When an individual changes, her relationships will be changed, because we are all interconnected and influence one another. But sometimes the change in relationships means the end of that relationship. If a spouse or partner is unhappy with the changes someone has made, the spouse may decide to get a new partner.

This is one of the risks people take in changing, and counselors must be aware of it. Major changes are upsetting to relationships. Everyone is used to behaving in a certain way. They are familiar with the rules. When the rules are altered (by one individual's changes), it comes as a shock to the rest of the system. If the others are totally unwilling to adapt to the changes, they will simply look for someone else with whom they can continue the old ways of relating.

Many people stay in unfulfilling relationships or situations because they understand, intuitively or logically, this very process. They would rather stay in an uncomfortable, but familiar, situation than risk the unknown. This saddens me because I think the risk is not as great as most people imagine. Patterns in relationships do seem to work. We attract other people from whom we can learn. But this also means that when we make changes, we can attract new people! If we alter so much that some of our significant others do not want to try our new direction, the odds are we will begin meeting other people who can teach us about this new direction and broaden our map of reality in this new territory!

The NLP idea of reframing involves a similar change process (turning liabilities into assets) as the astrological example given. A major difference is that NLP practitioners often work directly with the unconscious, "communicating" with "it" through bodily reactions. As an example, consider working with a phobia. The NLP approach would be to first identify the problem. Then, the unconscious mind is asked if it knows the motivation behind the problem. Any bodily reaction (e.g., tight stomach, tension between the eyes, twitching big toes) is considered an answer from the unconscious. The NLP therapist then asks the unconscious to repeat or intensify the bodily reaction if the answer is yes. Whatever the signal is becomes a "yes" and absence of it is treated as a "no" response.

Then, the therapist asks the unconscious if it would be willing to explain the motivation to the client. If willing, the client may get an image; or a feeling; or hear something. If not willing, the therapist simply works directly with the unconscious. The client is asked to access his or her "creative part" and a signal is worked out for that. The creative part and unconscious are requested to get together and brainstorm at least three new ways to handle the motivation, which will, hopefully, be more satisfying than the old (phobic) way. Again, the therapist asks for bodily signals to indicate that this program is being carried out.

If willing, the unconscious shares the solutions with the

conscious awareness. If not, the therapist requests the unconscious try out the new solutions for a few weeks to see if they are satisfactory. (Usually, they are.) The final step is to ask if there are any other objections. Again, bodily reactions are taken to be possible signals for discontent. Dialogue is established. Supposedly, eventually all "parts" of the individual are content, and the new solutions are put in motion, sometimes with the conscious awareness of the client still not involved in the decisions!

According to NLP resources, this technique works very well. Solutions tend to last and be much more satisfactory than the old ways of being. The pattern, however, is basically the same pattern described above, with specific techniques for handling the assumed unconscious mind. First, a problem is identified. The motivation(s) behind it are discovered. New solution(s) for meeting those motivations are generated, and put into action. Whether we do it within a framework of astrology, psychology, or something else, the overall process often seems to work.

Another important tool for change is humor. Like most techniques, this requires good empathy and a sense of timing for optimal use. There is a whole school of therapy, Provocative Therapy, which uses humor as a major catalyst for change. It is essential good rapport be established. Then the therapist can laugh at the client, and still get away with it, if done with sensitivity to the client's world. Frank Farrelly has written a book on the subject for anyone interested. Most humor rests on a shift in the frame of reference. That is, the punch line is usually a surprise; we look at the information in the joke from a different perspective all of a sudden. For that reason, humor can be very useful in helping people to change other frames of reference.

The healing potential of laughter is not to be underestimated. Norman Cousins discusses how he laughed himself to health in his book, *The Anatomy of an Illness*. A number of counselors note that being able to laugh at oneself is a very healthy sign. It takes clients temporarily out of their problems; everything seems less serious; the perspective lightens. The amount of humor one uses as a counselor will depend much on personal style.

The common theme in various techniques for change is an expansion of the client's choices and options. The client leaves the consultation with a wider world view than the one with which s/he entered. The client's frame of reference has shifted. Behavior is seen from a different perspective. Former problems become resources and assets. Karen Horney suggested this long ago when she said the role of the therapist is to take the clients' neuroses from in front of their faces, where they block sight and inhibit life, and put the neuroses behind, like an outboard motor, where they give added energy, zest and drive to the life.

Chapter 14

The Importance of Language

Language is one of the major tools which daily reinforces our world view. Thinking and speaking in a linear framework encourages us to continue to experience the world in a linear way. Words are potent. As Ms. Cameron-Bandler notes: "...words are attached to experience as are memories, and people truly experience much of what they are talking about" (12, p. 88). When we "Play it again, Sam!" we often feel the same heartache, joy, anger, or whatever, once more.

Paying attention to our language can aid greatly in the first step of counseling (establishing rapport). Avoiding jargon is important. Most clients will not know the specialized terms we use, and are likely to be bored or turned off. What does not make sense to them personally will not be attended to; they will "tune out." Jargon is best kept between professionals, who are familiar with this specialized form of communication. One astrologer can convey quite a bit of information to another with the comment: "She has Leo rising, with Pluto conjunct the Ascendant square her Sun and Mars in Taurus in the tenth." To the layperson, we might as well be speaking a foreign language. Similarly with psychological labels or any other kind of professional shorthand.

Listening to clients cannot be emphasized enough. If we listen, we will hear how they use words, and learn through their words important information about their world. NLP practitioners listen especially to predicates, and strive to phrase their responses to clients in the same representational mode (visual, auditory, kinesthetic) as that particular client uses the most. Kinesthetic clients "feel" understood when the counselor talks with them of sensing, grasping and getting in touch with things. Visual clients can really "see" what the counselor is saying, when using clear, image evoking words. And auditory types "hear" counselors best when the words in some way "ring" or "resonate" in their consciousness.

Using language too far removed from the experience of the client is likely to be distancing. For example, using multisyllabic words with clients of little education or literary background is counterproductive. We can also turn off clients by cutting off major parts of their world with our unguarded assumptions. Thus, if I discuss partners as if they are always marriage partners, (or always heterosexual), a number of clients will not relate to what I am saying. It does not "fit" into their world. My role as counselor is **not** to try to force clients into my world, but to find my way into theirs (and then expand it together).

Words can enhance or diminish responsibility. Knowing this helps us in our two steps of gathering information and changing paradigms. For example, the person who uses a lot of passive voice is usually avoiding personal responsibility, e.g., "It happened." Similarly, if the client seems to always be the reactor, never the actor, it is likely responsibility is an issue," e.g., "She made me . . ., "And so I had to . . ., "I couldn't do anything but . . .," "I had no choice . . . ."

There are a variety of techniques to aid awareness of responsibility. Fritz Perls stressed this highly in his work. Getting clients to change a "cannot" statement to a "will not" enhances responsibility. Clients can be encouraged to "own" their feelings, e.g., "I let her annoy me," rather than "She annoys me." Logotherapy, Haley, Provocative Therapy and other schools use a lot of paradoxes. For example, a patient who "cannot" lose weight is instructed to **gain** five pounds. If the patient resists, and loses weight instead, fine. S/he is moving towards a desired goal. If s/he does gain the weight, it graphically demonstrated that s/he has control of his/her weight!

Perls emphasized turning an "it" into an "I," e.g, "I did this," rather than, "It happened." He had people do a structured exercise involving the phrase, "I take responsibility for . . .," and filling in with whatever was going on — internal forces and behavior. Perls emphasized that responsibility includes "owning" all our feelings, even unpleasant ones which we would rather project onto others. He stressed how rich in experience we all would be if we would just take responsibility for every thought, feeling, action we make and shed responsibility for anyone else.

One therapist, Dr. Harry Ginsberg, handed out contracts for participants at marathons (72 hours of therapy) to sign which included the following points:

> 1. I will use the phrase "I can't" only to refer to situations where physical impossibility exists, e.g., "I can't leap over tall buildings." Where choice is any way possible, I will say "I won't; I choose not to," or a similar phrase in order to fully own my responsibility for my behavior.
>
> 2. I will not use the phrase "I don't know" to evade my responsibility or to stop interaction. Even when I cannot know absolutely, I always think, feel, believe in the Now.
>
> 3. I will relate in the "here and now" instead of in the "there and then." Story telling and reporting are useless, unless they relate directly to the present or to behavior I want to change.
>
> 4. When speaking of myself, I will say "I, me," etc. "You" does not refer to myself" (31).

The last point refers to such common statements as: "You make me angry." Therapists like Harry emphasize having the client take responsibility for her feelings: "I am angry."

This point of view means that another person does not "make" me angry, nor do I "make" them sad, etc. I **choose** to feel angry when that person acts in a certain way; she **chooses** to feel sad, etc. Choose is perhaps a tricky word here, because it implies conscious, thinking action. Often, we react emotionally before really thinking and examining. But our emotions are subject to much more control than we give ourselves credit for. John Grinder, a Neuro-Linguistic Programmer, noted that we are very culture bound in our ideas about emotions. According to Grinder, in other cultures, such as Tibet, they talk and accept the concept of changing emotions as quickly and easily as we conceptualize changing physical positions or changing clothes.

I think there is a danger in going to extremes here. Ellis' Rational Emotive Therapy (RET), in my reading of it, often seems to imply that we can control just about any reaction by thinking and being rational. However, a part of being human is not being rational always. I don't think total rationality is a desirable goal. The creative, impulsive, emotional side of our nature is very important. Life would be very dry and sterile without it. I think we need a blend of rationality and creative irrationality.

Another potential danger is in movements like est. I have known several people immensely improved through the Erhard Seminars Training. I also know several people whom I feel were worse after the experience. For example, the types who are already extremely assertive and inclined to go after what they want in the world, use the emphasis which est puts on responsibility as a cop out on compassion and relatedness. For example, "If you are totally responsible for your world, I can act like a ruthless, egotistical, insensitive clod, and it's your problem if it upsets you."

As usual, an extreme seems least healthy. Responsibility is a very important factor in psychological health, but clearly it is not absolute. We also have to recognize life's interconnectedness. We are a part of the universe, affecting and being affected by others. Adler recognized this in his formulations, which stress both personal responsibility and what he called *Gemeinschaftsgefuhl* which has been translated as social interest, or fellowship — the idea of cooperation with others and a valuing of other people.

Returning full circle, the new physics suggests a reality: "not a mechanical system made of separate objects, but rather as a complex web of relationships . . . an inseparable cosmic process, and these patterns are intrinsically dynamic, continually changing into one another, in a continuous dance of energy" (4, p. 30). The new physics emphasizes the fundamental interrelatedness and interdependence of everything. People seem to fit nicely into this framework. We are all interrelated. Behavior has meaning for everyone involved; we are all a part of it. We can share responsibility, and — hopefully — compassion and empathy.

"Why not?" is a very useful question. It reaffirms personal power and it throws world views up for grabs. "Does this have to be so?" It's amazing how often clients fail to question themselves and avoid being questioned by others. Corollaries include, "What would happen if you did (or didn't)?" When someone tells me that they had "no choice," I often respond, "I know of three choices off the top of my head." Most clients respond to the challenge by starting to think of choices of their own. (Incidentally, you had better have some options in mind, not to provide the client with answers, but to compare after the client comes up with some and says, "Now, what were yours?" It's okay if some were the same as what the client engenders.)

Many therapists make a point of challenging client statements that include such "necessity" phrases as: "cannot . . . ,have to . . . ,must . . . ," Typical challenges involve questions like: "Why not?" or, "What would happen if you did?" or, "Who is stopping you?"

Clients often have neglected the obvious. Questioning their assumptions may be fruitful. Kelly is one of the personality theorists who most fully recognized the importance of world views, and our construction of our world. His growing insight into this phenomenon began when he offered a few "preposterous" interpretations to clients, and they accepted them, and even got better! "My only criteria were that the explanation **account for the crucial facts as the client saw them,** and that it **carry implications for approaching the future in a different way.**" (56, p. 322) In other words, Kelly entered a client's world view, and made comments which allowed clients to envision a broader world view. When any of us, counselor or client, reexamines our automatic reactions, our "of courses," change and growth is possible.

Generalizations are another "red flag." Many generalizations lock a person into one way of looking at the world. Questioning the generalization or bringing it up as an issue can be a help in changing the paradigm. Ellis does this all the time in RET. One approach is to add qualifiers. People change statements such as "I am always...," to "I am often...," or, "I can never...," to "I seldom ...," and so on.

Another approach, used by Provocative Therapists and the like, is to exaggerate the generalization so it becomes even more absurd. If well done, this is like playing one end of a polarity. The client adopts the other end (to balance the seesaw). An example would be the client who says, "Men are such beasts." (The implication is that **all** men are beasts **all** the time.) A Provocative therapist might leap in with relish. "Yes, they certainly are. Why, men are **always** picking on women. They beat them. They discriminate against them. They refuse to hire them. They fire women first. They expect women to cook, clean, work and take care of the house as well as a job, and never help out. They demand that women do everything with the children, and never lift a finger. They always want sex, and never want to cuddle and be just loving. Why, I don't know one decent man myself. They are **all** rotten. My father, my brothers, my cousins, everyone...." This can go on. Usually, the client starts laughing. Or, the client may begin defending men, "Well, that's not true. I know **some** men who are okay." The Provocative Therapist may carry on the joke, just to be sure the point will be taken. "No, **really**? Tell me about this amazing man."

Another approach is to exaggerate the universality by adding even more universal qualifiers (and often upping the exaggeration through tone of voice and emphasis).

Client: "I'm never happy."

Counselor: "You have **absolutely never, at any time in your life,** been happy."

Or, **Client:** "People are always unkind to me."
Counselor: "Everyone in your entire life, from birth to this exact moment has been unkind to you." (Alternate: "There has not been even one solitary soul, in your entire life to date, who has shown you even a moment's kindness.")

Another form of generalization is when client make statements, usually judgments, as if they were statements of truth about the world, not realizing they are statements about the clients' models of the world. **Statement:** "That is a disgusting thing to eat." The subjectivity of this judgment may be revealed by asking, "Disgusting to whom or for whom?" **Statement:** "It is wrong to watch that much television." For whom is it wrong? How is it wrong? **Statement:** "This is the right way to live." Right for whom? The counselor may challenge the generalization through questioning, exaggerate it, or ask for further specifics.

Very often a simple question by the counselor is the first step to a client enlarging his or her model of the world. Such questions include: "About whom? About what? How, specifically? What would happen if you did?" The first necessary step may be to gather more information. Then, we can go on to assist in paradigm shifts. Note that the purpose in gathering information is not just for us, but also for clients — to become more aware of what they are saying and experiencing.

Examples:
Client: "I am afraid of her."
Counselor: "Whom or what are you afraid of?"
Client: "He's the best artist."
Counselor: "He's the best artist compared to whom, or in what way?"
Client: "I don't like that."
Counselor: "What about it don't you like?"
Client: "Nobody loves me."
Counselor: "Who, specifically, does not love you?"
Client: "That's too hard for me to do."
Counselor: "In what respect is it too hard?"
Client: "They forced me to ground them."
Counselor: "How, specifically, did they force you to ground them?"
Client: "My friend ignored me."
Counselor: "How did she ignore you? What did she do, or not do?"

Such questions will aid considerably what Carkhuff and Berenson refer to as concreteness. They will often help people realize the subjectivity of their viewpoints. For example, the person feeling ignored has the opportunity to discover that other people do not feel ignored when their friends pass them on the street without saying, "Hello."

NLP people point out another way we may limit our models of the world. It is called nominalization, and basically refers to turning a verb into a noun. When we do this, generally the sense of movement and change is lost. Verbs show process; nouns tend to be static, unmoving. The solution, suggest Bandler, Grinder, Cameron, Lankton and the like, is to return to the verb again.

"I don't get any attention!" (The client sounds passive and helpless.) "In what ways would you like to be attended to?" Or "How could people attend to you?" (Client has some power to make specific suggestions. Action and movement is possible now.)

"I shouldn't have made that decision." **Counselor:** "Is there anything stopping you from deciding to do it differently?"

Counselor can also change many "automatic" cause and effect statements made by clients. Such challenges help clients examine how they help create their reactions and feelings.   "I'm angry because he was early." **Counselor:** "How does his being early make you feel angry?"

"Her silliness bothers me." **Counselor:** "How does her being silly cause you to feel bothered?"   "You make me unhappy." **Counselor:** "How is it possible for me to make you unhappy?"

Fritz Perls criticized people often for trying to "mind read," acting as though they knew what other people were thinking and feeling. Many healers will challenge mind reading by clients.

"I know what she should do." **Counselor:** "How do you know what she should do?"

"Everyone thinks I talk too much." **Counselor:** "How do you know that everyone thinks you talk to much?" ("How do you know what everyone is thinking?")

"You know how I feel." **Counselor:** "How can you be sure that I know how you feel?"

I watch carefully in people's language for cues to self-esteem (how much someone likes him or herself). In my world view, high self esteem is very valuable. People with low self-esteem often have difficulties improving their situations because they feel, inside, they "don't deserve" any better. Thus, I am inclined to challenge people people when they make self-derogatory remarks. I will often ask a client to rephrase a statement, e.g., Client: (Laughing) "I sure am stupid." I might ask the client to say, "I'm very bright."

Some clients are heavily into putting themselves down. One option is for them to work on what Transactional Analysis calls retaping. This means working up a new set of messages to replace the ones they constantly play inside their heads. The client thinks of a list of supportive, self-affirming statements (short and simple is good) and writes them down, e.g., "I am smart. I am beautiful." Then the client reads the list aloud several times a day, preferably in front of a mirror, practicing accepting the statements, not fighting them and negating them simultaneously. Close friends may be given copies and asked to also feed in some supportive messages. Retaping assumes (like Ellis) that there is internal "self-talk" coded in auditory form. The list can also be done in second person, e.g., "Maritha, you are smart." T.A. suggests this because the theory assumes our earliest messages are from other people (e.g., parents) and in this form. The goal is to "erase" the old, negative messages by taping over them with new, positive ones.

Words can constrict or expand world views. When a counselor talks in terms of certainties, absolutes, "shoulds" and "oughts," she tends to cut off options for clients. Such imperatives encourage clients to see life as a one-choice-only proposition. The counselor's language is just as important as the client's. The above suggestions can be applied to the counselor's use of words just as well.

Words which leave options open, encourage choices and alternatives include such things as: "tends to, implies, suggests, might be, potential." One can mention "one of the possibilities" and "some of the options." The more flexible we are as counselors, the more truly open and unlimited our world view becomes, the more our language will reflect it, and vice versa. Our language helps keep us locked into various assumptions. Change the language; the assumptions are more likely to change. Change the assumptions; the language is more likely to reflect the new view.

Readers will note my avoidance of the generic use of "he" or "man" in this book. Research demonstrates that children, very early, learn the distinction between "man" and "woman." Having absorbed that, it is difficult to then think of both men **and** women when reading "man." The linguistic invisibility of women is another way in which we are encouraged to not include women as important in our thinking about the world. Since I am unwilling to continue this linguistic exclusion, I chose to use the admittedly awkward "him or her" at times. I hope readers will understand and forgive the inconvenience. (For references, see Joan K. Marshall and Casey Miller in the Bibliography.)

The Issue of Prediction

As astrologers, we have additional responsibilities regarding "predictions." Ample research demonstrates the power of the self-fulfilling prophecy. That is, people can help create events and occurrences by their expectations (beliefs). For this reason, astrologers need to exercise extreme care in any predictions they make. Most astrological organizations have provisions in their codes of ethics that forbid predicting death for this (and other) reasons.

Personally, I do not make specific predictions. That is my value judgment. I see specific predictions as limiting the clients' maps of reality, decreasing their options and choices. I prefer to increase their possibilities. I am not saying this is "right" for all astrologers. I do believe that concern for the human lives we mix in necessitates great care on the part of astrological predictions. I suggest astrologers consider carefully the possible impact of any statements they are considering making. For example, making a prediction of a negative event to an anxiety ridden (worrywart) client is likely to create even more fear and tension.

My major goal with any statements about the future is that my "predictions" give the client a sense of power, the ability to **do** something, and offer choices. This does **not** mean playing Pollyanna and burying my head in the sand. Tough configurations in the chart need to be confronted, but (Basic Assumption # 1) "There are always positive options."

Take as an example an individual who has a heavy Mars, Saturn, Uranus T-square being set off. I will **not** say: "Be careful, you might have an accident." Nor will I say, "Stay in bed to make sure you don't have an accident." I will say, "This shows an inner conflict between your need to be independent, free and go your own way versus your desire to follow the rules and work within the structure of society. If not handled, you could fight against the rules in any number of ways, e.g., with the boss, with father, fighting time or rebelling against social expectations. Or, you could overemphasize the rules in your own head, and stop yourself from some free and independent expression that is really okay. The key to any challenge aspect — which merely indicates inner ambivalence — is to find a way to do both (or all) sides of your nature. Here, it is necessary to find some avenue for your rebellious, free soul nature. You need to do something spontaneous, energetic, courageous or unconventional that is just for you. You also need to be aware of the context of the larger world, and work within the structure, rules and regulations that help protect others."

This astrological approach is **very** similar to the psychological approach Milton Erickson used with his metaphors. He would often talk in very general terms, or tell stories that seemed unrelated. But the clients would make the connections. It is really self-defeating to demand of myself that I always guess right in predicting exactly **which way** a client will express Martian needs to be spontaneous, courageous, active, assertive or solitary. If I explain the basic psychological tone, the client will make the connections. After all, it's his or her life. Our clients are the ones who know best how they fight against the limits, or how they block themselves by overemphasizing duty, responsibility, and following the rules.

For me, the bottom line is that prediction assumes that there is one, and only one, right answer. An interactive universe suggests that multiple answers exist, and the possibilities are constantly in flux and influencing one another. If I make a specific prediction and am right, I can feel omniscient, and the client is impressed. The client also loses feelings of personal power and responsibility because the assumption is: "She said it would happen. It did happen. Therefore it **had** to happen." If I make a prediction and am wrong, the client has still been given a world view that things **have** to happen a certain way. However, I and astrology look wrong every time I try to guess and miss.

If I talk in terms of psychological principles, my clients retain their personal power and responsibility. They make the connections, so I am usually "right" anyway. (I cannot deny it is an ego boost to be "right.") But clients are left with a picture of the world that is rich in a multitude of possibilities, and one in which they can choose from a myriad of specific options within a general framework of the emotional energy they have with which to work.

Astrology is another map of reality. It is a way of making sense of the universe, of organizing our experience. Each of the various schools of personality or psychotherapy is yet another model. Each has its own map, its own interpretation of how people function in the world. Thus, the T.A. (Transactional Analysis) model of human personality contains a Parent (blaming, nurturing, making judgments, opinions) part, an Adult (logical, problem-solving, dealing with consensual reality) part, and a Child (spontaneous, pleasure-seeking, impatient) part. The Psychosynthesis model includes a higher self (capable of intuitions, transcendence, mystical experiences) as well as a personal "I" (everyday self-awareness, consciousness of identity). The Gestalt image is of polarities within each of us, such as topdog (bossy, critical) and underdog (sneaky, whiny). There are some clients who have gotten major insights from each of these and many other models of human nature. The astrological model conceptualizes twelve basic motivational drives or ways of being in the world. This framework may turn out to be more useful to some people than the psychological theories. But it is **still** a model.

Research in psychology indicates that the specific details of the model used are not particularly important. What is most significant (and what clients remember best) is the kind of relationship established between counselor and clients. Effective counselors are similar to one another in their empathy, respect, caring for clients — even when their theories about the human personality are quite different.

Astrology gives us yet another way to conceptualize human nature. We can infer from the psychological research that astrological counselors will be most effective when we concentrate on the human relationship with our clients, rather than specific astrological details or knowledge.

My experience is that the astrological map of human nature is more complex and complete than any psychological systems. I feel astrology can encompass more people than any other personality theory. Partially that is because my approach is to keep options open. I use astrology as a model of human, psychological drives, but not of specific details: like broad brush strokes on a canvas with few fine points sketched in.

With this model, the client makes the connections. The astrologer provides an overview of possible feelings, conflicts, abilities, and so on. The client relates those general personality issues to her specific events, relationships and circumstances.

Take, as an example, a woman who has Saturn in the seventh house. The person interested in specifics would attempt to describe details in the life:
1. You are unmarried.
2. You are widowed (or will be).
3. You will marry late.
4. You will marry someone older than you.
Unless the astrologer is psychic as well, the chances of guessing right are not that great.

I would focus on the psychological issues. "Control, predictability, stability and power are concerns in your partnership area. If not handled, this could lead to fear of being dominated, controlled or criticized. Or, you might project the power and initially choose someone strong and controlling because s/he seemed strong, reassuring and secure. Or, you might play parent in relationships and carry too much of the load. The challenge is for both people in the relationship to trust, and to be strong and responsible. If that is accomplished, relationships tend to be stable, enduring, and built on a firm, steady foundation."

Notice that the specific details do follow logically from the generalist principles. Someone afraid of being dominated or controlled or criticized might very well avoid marriage altogether, or marry late (having delayed due to anxiety). If projecting the power, the individual could pick a strong, father figure type who could easily be older (and die first) and/or end up too strong and dominating. There is a whole additional theme here of facing the unfinished business we have with Dad through partners, which I will not pursue. This would be another case of possible face-painting or what I called cyclic projections. (First the power is projected onto Dad, then onto partners.)

My desire is, as much as possible, to recognize that the power and responsibility for their lives lie in my clients' own hands. I want to help them open up world views, not shut themselves in a closet.

Chapter 15
Similarities of Astrologers & other Counselors

I feel distinctions between astrological consultations and other forms of counseling are often overstated. There are two major differences most astrologers point to between what they do and what most counselors do. One is the time frame. Many astrologers see clients on a one time only basis or once a year for an update on progressions, transits, and so on. Most counselors see clients for more than one session and expect regular meetings at least a few times.

This distinction is becoming much less marked. The length of time needed for counseling is a hot issue now in psychology. Brief psychotherapies are enjoying a flurry of attention. A recent *Psychology Today* article (August 1981) looked at some variations. One therapist named Bloom specializes in one time only sessions. He tried one hour sessions, but found them too short. He now works with a two hour session. (A length of one to two hours is not uncommon for astrological consultations.) Bloom recently checked back with clients on the effectiveness of the one shot deal. Three to four months after therapy, 30 of the 32 clients considered the session had been of lasting help (32). Although there is no definite consensus in the field, the research to date shows brief (time limited) psychotherapies to be as helpful (or more so) as longer (open-ended) therapies. (Although one must remember that it is usually supporters of brief therapy doing the research.)

Supporters speculate that placing a time limit on counseling heightens motivation, and clients waste less time. Supporters also feel brief therapies lessen the likelihood of heavy dependency by clients and awkward transference or countertransference developments. And, of course, brief therapy is cheaper!

Bloom suggests that the first step is to identify a focal issue or problem, preferably "an interpretation that expands a patient's awareness of the issues underlying the problems he or she presents" (32, p. 63). This sounds an awful lot like getting the client to look at problems from a larger, more inclusive world view! The second step is to help clients initiate a problem solving sequence, according to Bloom.

Another point often forgotten by people in the helping professions is that about one third of those who consult a therapist in the United States go only once, not returning after the first visit. Therapists tend to regard such one time only sessions as failures and often believe the client was dissatisfied. This is not necessarily the case. One researcher called to ask clients who did not return why they did not. Two thirds of them said they felt they had already been helped! (32) Even if these figures are somewhat inflated, it seems likely that single session therapy can be powerful and effective.

I do not believe astrologers can count themselves out of the "people movers" ranks simply because they tend to be single session consultants. I also want to point out that a number of astrologers do **not** limit themselves to one session. They are available to clients to work on issues on a regular basis if it seems helpful.

A second difference I hear pointed out by a lot of astrologers is that they basically are "teachers." They provide information to the client; then it is up to the client to do anything. They do most of the talking; the client mostly listens. Such astrologers feel they just provide a neutral, objective view to the client.

In response to the above, I have several points (which I hope this book has helped to support):

1. Psychology and physics both suggest there is no such thing as an objective, neutral observer. Information is always provided within a context of values and judgments.
2. Regardless of how we label ourselves, we affect people and their lives. Our words have power and impact. Our interpretations influence people. I hope we will use that power as wisely as possible.
3. Carkhuff and Berenson studied teachers as well as therapists and found empathy, respect, congruence and concreteness vital in the educational environment as well. Students with

empathic, respectful teachers learned and retained more. So, if you want your clients to remember and learn from the information you provide, pay attention to the relationship between you.

4. Clients remember the quality of a relationship. They often forget specific verbal content and information.

5. Yalom found the imparting of information to be one of the least important therapeutic variables. Unless linked with meaning through experiencing hope, universality, or other factors, imparting information tended to be of minimal value.

The above can be summarized in that any interaction between two people is meaningful and has an impact (small or large) on both individuals. We cannot prevent ourselves from affecting, and being affected by, our clients. My goal is to make that influence as positive and enduring as possible. Research to date suggests that it is the quality of the relationship, not the quality of information given, that determines its impact. Clients need to feel a sense of hope; they flourish with acceptance and honesty. Empathic, respectful, congruent astrologers are most likely to get their messages across. Sensitive, self-examining, aware astrologers are most likely to grow and develop through their counseling relationships.

Chapter 16
Our Expanding Universe

The history of the human race is a history of breaking old limits. We have discovered new lands, plumbed the depths of the oceans and are reaching into outer space.

The frontiers of human consciousness are expanding as well. What once was labelled "impossible" is being done. People are curing themselves of dread diseases through therapy and their own visualization. People are managing severe pain through guided imagination. Yogis are observed and measured while stopping and starting their own hearts. Instances of telepathy and other forms of ESP abound.

Researchers are realizing that the limits of human potential are far beyond what we had believed in the past. Our old assumptions about what is real and possible served only to keep us in self-made prisons. As we unlock the chains on our minds and imaginations, an infinite universe stretches before us.

Physics is catching up with psychology and beginning to merge. It looks as though at least on one level of the universe, space and time (as we know them) do not exist. This makes sense out of telepathy, clairvoyance and the like. If there is a dimension or level of consciousness where we truly are **one** with the timeless cosmos, we could see "ahead" (clairvoyance) or behind, because "time" is not an issue on that level. We could know what "other" people are thinking because we are all connected (all one).

Physics shows us a totally interdependent universe. Psychology tells us a similar message. All interactions we have with clients —

or anyone else — are meaningful and have an impact on everyone involved.We are all influencing one another, constantly.

We often forget the interconnections of life because we are so busy filtering out the myriad signals we get from a complicated world. Our belief systems help us choose the perceptions we pay attention to, and those we ignore or deny. Our assumptions about the nature of the world are influenced by family and culture, which in the West have emphasized separateness.

As we come to grasp clearly the interdependence of life, we will pay greater heed to our connections with the people around us. When we look carefully, we find many subtle signals and exchanges just below our ordinary awareness. These cues can be a rich resource for the counselor in understanding clients and himself or herself.

Healers are rapidly discovering that the quality and kind of relationship that people have is what is most significant — not any particular exchange of information or specifics. Lover and beloved; counselor and client; parent and child; teacher and student: in any relationship we experience feelings, not just thoughts. We often convey our feelings through our bodies or try to disguise our reactions. But our psyches are wise and can exchange understanding on a deeper "unconscious" level.

We spend our lives instinctively attracting people who will give us the opportunity to become more of what we can be. We meet people living out our unactualized potential. We can choose to learn and grow from them (break another prison wall) or we can choose to judge and criticize and reject them (never seeing any message for us).

As long as we hug our assumptions tightly to us and are fearful to risk a change, we keep ourselves limited. If we refuse to see our power, are afraid to act on our responsibility, we stay in prison. If we remain flexible and open to multiple possibilities, we discover a world of fascinating people, all providing us endless chances to develop more fully. We open our senses and imagination to a universe vaster than most of us had dreamed.

The journey is here. The moment is now. Whether we experience our endless universe with blinders, earplugs, nose plugs and padded gloves, or with open hearts and minds is up to us. The view from where I am is incredibly exciting!

SECTION TWO

Applications

Preamble

The second half of this book will consist of step-by-step examples, exercises and checklists. It is my hope that illustrations will help clarify the theoretical material presented in the first half, and offer opportunities for readers to involve their imaginations and analytical processes.

The material here is **not** intended as a set of rules, or even suggested procedures, for counselors/astrologers to follow. It is intended to aid helper/healers in their examination and understanding of themselves and the counseling experience. I am hoping to spur your thinking and questioning in various areas. In simplified terms, this half is aimed at the **right brain** (global, intuitive) functions of the reader, where the first half was **left brain** (linear, logical) oriented. Some of the checklists given here will also serve as shorthand summaries of material presented elsewhere (and are very linear and left brain.)

A supervisor of mine once recommended that we learn all the techniques we could and compile a large "bag of tricks" in terms of counseling techniques. "Then," he said, "forget them all, and just **be** with the client. If you need a specific tool, it will come to you." That is what I hope readers will do with this book: read it and then give it to your unconscious. Your own inner wisdom will bring any useful ideas or techniques into your awareness when appropriate, if you simply relate to your clients as fully and honestly as you can.

The material here is set to follow, more or less, the order of chapters in the first half of the book.

Chapter 17
What Is Reality?

Different Views

"The world hath many centres, one for each created being,
and about each one lieth its own circle.
Thou standest but half an ell from me,
and yet about thee liest a universe whose centre I am not,
but thou art. ..."

Thomas Mann (49, pp. 180-181)

**Consider the pictures on this and the following page.
What do you see?**

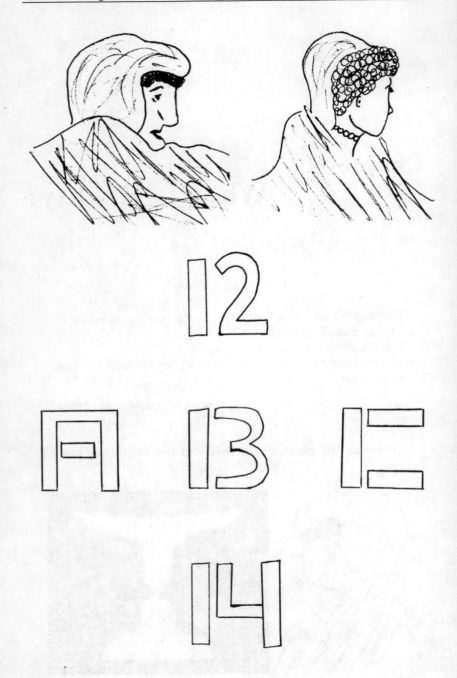

Chapter 18
The Question of Meaning

Introduction

"Truth is like a diamond.
One never sees the whole,
But each facet throws a gleam of light
That thrills the seeing soul.
Let's treasure the gleam that we see
And respect our neighbor's view,
Though he see another side than I
And I another than you.

* * * * *

"Truth is a golden nugget
With infinite patience panned.
Yet because I found a bit of gold
In a wilderness of sand
I need not stand on a hill and shout
'Only my gold is true.
If the gold you found is not just like mine,
You've let fool's gold make fools of you.' "

Zipporah Dobyns (66, p. 50 & 86)

Fill in the blank:

I believe _____.

The truth _____.

I trust _____.

The world _____.

My most important goal is _____.

I value _____most highly.

The meaning of life is _____.

People are _____.

Work _____.

Astrology _____.

Women _____.

Men _____.

Life _____.

Once you have completed the phrases, go back and look at what you have written. Does this give you a hint of some of your basic assumptions? Could you construct your theoretical model of life, people and reality?

Chapter 19
Theoretical Model

Following are examples of literature. One is a description of astrological services. The other is an introduction of services which Harry Ginsberg used in his therapy. These are not intended as ways one **must** do it, but as a stimulation to each of you working out your own theoretical model, view of what you want your consultations to include.

Description Of Astrological Services

Basic Natal Chart:
A discussion of the character: personality strengths, talents and abilities as well as potential challenges and weaknesses. Example talents might include artistic ability, mechanical skills, organizational flair, sales ability, etc. An example challenge might be the tendency to project certain qualities, that is, to find someone else to express our needs for freedom, intellectual stimulation or responsibility, and so on, rather than developing those qualities ourselves.

I assume the horoscope operates as a mirror — to help us see ourselves more clearly. The power and responsibility lie within the individual — **not** in the planets.

Current Patterns:
This includes progressions and transits — a look at what is going on now and future trends. The focus is on psychological states. I do **not** predict specific events. Our attitudes and beliefs come first; they

set up events. We can change what happens to us by altering our beliefs and attitudes.

The above two in combination constitute the usual single consultation: 1 to 1½ hours, depending on questions. Also available is: **Relationship Analysis:** Everyone in our lives is there for a reason. We have something to learn from all our relationships. Astrological analysis can help pinpoint areas of agreement and strength along with potential conflict areas. The horoscope also indicates how each individual tends to perceive the other (for we all live in our own subjective worlds). For example, each child in a family will see the mother differently. And their differing perceptions will encourage the mother to treat each of them differently. Each of us is indeed, in a sense, a "different person" depending on who we are with.

This service is particularly valuable for **parent to child** relationships; **partnerships** (business, marriage, living together . . .) and any associations of importance in your life.

The following is a copy of literature Harry Ginsberg gave to his clients, upon commencing therapy. Harry was a provocative, warm, involved, intense, committed, controversial figure in his life and practice. His wife, Mary Dell Ginsberg, has given permission for this to be printed. A small hint of the complexities of the man shows through in his words.

Introduction To Therapeutic Services
(By Harry Ginsberg, Ph.D.)

"This may be the beginning of a relationship wherein the issues in this statement, both philosophical and business, will affect us throughout the course of treatment. Therefore, rather than being surprised at a later date by anything not mutually agreed upon, I feel it is best to deal with the nature of our relationship at the beginning. The safest way to fly is with your eyes wide open.

The therapeutic relationship has a dual nature. During the course of therapy we may grow to be close as the patient learns to sustain intimate interpersonal relationships. On the other side of the coin, we have a business relationship. I am to take care of the patient's therapeutic needs and I expect that the patient will respect the financial and administrative issues I am raising herein, in order to take care of myself.

People have a variety of problems — both with other people

and within themselves. The therapeutic process makes available to each patient the opportunity of finding himself or herself. People may gradually come to know what they feel fully and without defensive distortion, to see reality clearly, to regain their personal integrity and potency, to gain in both cognitive and experiential awareness, and to assume responsibility for how they construct their lives — seeing clearly both the positive and negative consequences of their choices. It is largely through this process of finding oneself through direct interaction with the therapist and others that the patient may gain the internal strength and confidence to deal with his or her life situations.

The degree to which therapy may have a favorable outcome is to a large measure dependent upon the commitment of the patient in terms of his or her willingness to confront and deal with the fact that there may be continuing ambivalence through each step of the journey towards growth. People tend to view the therapeutic process in two ways:

1) Some patients are in pain and seek therapy to stop hurting. They may choose to stop therapy when they stop hurting. Patients who go this far may expect to obtain relief from their pain and a possible stabilization — managing their own lives in a less hurtful and more satisfying way. The danger here is the possibility of recurrence of the original symptoms if therapy is terminated prematurely.

2) Some patients may or may not begin therapy because they are hurting. They may be interested in expanding their human potential — moving along the road towards becoming all they can be in terms of their own personal power. Those patients may move far beyond the stabilization phase — they may explore areas of themselves which add greater meaning to their existence, as well as increased excitement, joy, and intimacy to their lives. They may experience what it means to come as close as they dare to being a fully alive and response-able human being. I shall fulfill my part of the contract as your therapist. The rest depends upon your commitment and courage.

The therapeutic process I am describing can be quite rewarding, quite demanding, and quite expensive, and has an average time span of between six months and three years. Of course there have been those who have gotten what they wanted for themselves in a shorter period of time and those who have continued longer. This depends upon the individual patient and the place in which he or she begins therapy.

Financial & Administrative Arrangements

1. My individual sessions are 45 minutes in length, although this is not inflexible. Sometimes we may finish our business a few minutes early, sometimes we may need an additional few minutes. If you are late, you may be cheating yourself of your full time with me. If I am late in starting, you will be given a full appointment
2. Patients will be charged for a broken or missed appointment unless a 24-hour notice is given and a rescheduling is arranged.
3. Unless we make other arrangements, fees will be collected at the beginning of each session. Patients will pay fees for the first session as well as for one session in advance at the first session. If a patient decides to discontinue therapy at the end of the first session, or if I decide that I don't want to work with a patient, he or she would only be financially responsible for the first session. If a decision is made to continue therapy at the end of the first session, there will be no refunds between the first and second sessions. Any issues that arise during that time will be considered part and parcel of the therapy process.
4. Insurance: For those patients covered by health insurance, I will do what I can to get you insurance reimbursement of your therapy expenses. I will collect directly from you.
5. Termination: In order to see that patients honestly confront themselves and their problem areas, I require that the issue of termination be dealt with in therapy for one full session before a final decision is reached. If this part of the therapeutic contract is not honored, patients will be charged for the session, whether attended or not" (30).

The above is offered as an example. Readers may agree or disagree with some of the basic assumptions, but raising the issues directly makes discussion and clarification easier. I highly recommend counselors put their expectations of the counseling process on paper — at least for their own understanding, even if they choose not to share anything in written form with clients. The clearer we are about our assumptions and agenda with people, the less likely we are to achieve them in "sneaky" (unconscious) ways.

Money

One of the issues a lot of healers have trouble with is money.

Money gets tied up with status and power in our society. It also is often connected to self-esteem. Yet, a part of some "spiritual" world views is that healers should never charge. Women have additional conflicts around money because they are encouraged to be volunteers and help people as a "natural" outgrowth of their maternal "instincts."

I advise astrological counselors (and others) to consider their feelings about money, and how much they want to charge. (Your friends may feel you ought to charge more than you do.) What feels fair to you? Sliding scales are one option. How do you judge when you are sufficiently professional to start charging? Do you put out direct, clear messages to your clients about money: fees, the expected manner and timing of payment, and so on? Harry used to say that money had replaced sex as the taboo subject in group therapy. Clear illumination makes it much less likely you or clients will be surprised or resentful at a later date.

Chapter 20
Negative Effects

How Will I Know If I Am Doing Harm?
A Checklist

Ask yourself periodically (especially with clients you see more than once) the following questions:

1. Does the client have more problems than when s/he first came?

2. Are the client's problems more severe than when s/he first came?

3. Is the client trying to do more than is possible at the moment, pursuing unrealistically high goals?

4. Is the client disillusioned with counseling and/or astrology?

5. Is the client using our consultations to:
    a. label a problem, and not change it?
    b. intellectualize?
    c. avoid living, saving up everything that happens to deal with when s/he sees me instead of living and reacting in the moment?

Any of these **could** be indicators of negative effects from counseling. The next step is self-examination. A common pitfall of counselors is what T.A. refers to as the Karpmann or Rescue Triangle (discussed earlier).

Possible Astrological Correlates
of Various Counseling Pitfalls

This is not offered as any kind of complete analysis, but to stimulate your thinking. If we consider the various factors which studies associate with negative effects, we can make some educated guesses about astrological configurations that might be prone to some of those errors.

For example, counselors prone to be into rescuing or doing too much for their clients, are most likely to have strong earth and water. Water indicates compassion, wanting to help people; earth indicates practicality and willingness to do something. Such people are often the "mothers, fathers, saviors of the world," in Zip Dobyns' terms. The trouble is, they may overdo it. (Then she terms it the **Atlas Syndrome** — carrying the world on your back!)

Strupp et al. warn that goals must be mutually reached, agreed on, not too high or expected too quickly. People with strong mutables often have conflicts in goals. They may be unclear about goals. They may have conflicting goals (head versus heart goals). They may have unrealistically high expectations. Sagittarius, especially, may want too much, too fast. (As in the Dobyns system, I use the alphabet system of astrology. The theme symbolized by Sagittarius is also symbolized by Jupiter and the ninth house. See diagram on page 147 for brief summary. See *Encounter Astrology* or one of Zip Dobyns' books for a more thorough explanation.)

Overintellectualization is a common defense of people with a lot of air, and also with mostly air and earth. Those are the rational, logical elements. People with too much air (and earth) may avoid the emotional part of life.

Playing the perfect healer role — omniscient and omnipotent — is most likely when the individual has a strong power drive and need for control. The sides of life most oriented towards power are 5 (Sun, Leo, fifth house), 8 (Pluto, Scorpio, eighth house) and 10 (Saturn, Capricorn, and tenth house). The more they interact with one another (e.g., planets in each others' signs and houses, strong aspects between power planets), the stronger the power drive is likely to be.

Overly intense therapy is warned against. The intense emotional elements are fire and water. Strong fire and water people are very warm and loving and extremely intense. They are often ambivalent about how much to express their emotion outwardly, in the world, and how much to hold back and keep inside.

The Astrological Alphabet of Zipporah Dobyns

PLANET	SIGN	HOUSE	ELEMENT	QUALITY
Mars ♂	Aries ♈	1	Fire	Cardinal
Venus ♀	Taurus ♉	2	Earth	Fixed
Mercury ☿	Gemini ♊	3	Air	Mutable
Moon ☽	Cancer ♋	4	Water	Cardinal
Sun ☉	Leo ♌	5	Fire	Fixed
Mercury ☿ Ceres ⚷ Vesta ⚶	Virgo ♍	6	Earth	Mutable
Venus ♀ Pallas ⚴ Juno ⚵	Libra ♎	7	Air	Cardinal
Pluto ♇	Scorpio ♏	8	Water	Fixed
Jupiter ♃ Chiron ⚷	Sagittarius ♐	9	Fire	Mutable
Saturn ♄	Capricorn ♑	10	Earth	Cardinal
Uranus ♅	Aquarius ♒	11	Air	Fixed
Neptune ♆	Pisces ♓	12	Water	Mutable

Rigidity is another potential danger. Generally, earth and water tend to be more conservative, on the side of the *status quo*, but one cannot depend on it. Also, any of the fixed letters (2,5,8,11) may appear (and be) rigid, because they change **only** on their own terms. Any part of the chart or psyche which is overemphasized can lead to rigidity. The tendency is to do that part of life **a lot**, and perhaps too much. It's as if people feel, "I know how to do this, so I'll do it all the time" (even when inappropriate). You can see this at times with major stelliums.

Strupp et al. warn against an excessive internal or excessive external focus. Speaking again in generalities, air and water tend to be internal. Earth and fire tend to be external (acting in the world).

A number of personality traits are listed as negative in a counselor. Coldness we would associate probably with little fire or water. Obsessiveness is most often indicated by letters 6 (Virgo, sixth house, Vesta, Ceres), 8 (Pluto, Scorpio, eighth house) and 10 (Saturn, Capricorn, tenth house). Pessimism may be linked to underdeveloped fire. Fire is generally the most positive and optimistic element; air after that.

Narcissism is **one** (of many) possibilities with an emphasis on the first three signs, houses, and rulers thereof. These parts of the zodiac refer to personal needs, and our ability to get what we want in the world. An overdevelopment here could go into narcissism among other things.

Greed we would associate with a strong emphasis on earth and water (needing security), especially 2 (Venus, Taurus, second house) and 8 (Pluto, Scorpio, eighth house) which are very concerned with money and material possessions.

I could go on, but want to remind the reader that these are all only **possibilities**. Part of my basic world view is the assumption that everything in the horoscope and personality can be manifested in a positive manner. Thus, the above configurations and patterns would only be problems if the individual did not find a positive channel for the drives suggested. I am **not** saying that these are the only possible astrological correlates for the various issues. I am also **not** saying that these placements **must** lead to negative effects. That is contrary to my basic belief system.

Helpful counseling, like all of life, needs **all twelve** sides, all twelve ways of being in the world to be most effective. We need the warmth, enthusiasm and confidence of fire; the practicality and willingness to work of earth; the intellectual capacity, desire to communicate and detachment of air; and the sensitivity, the caring and empathy of water. And so on, for the various signs and houses. Each one has a positive, useful energy to contribute in living life and doing counseling!

We can see this very clearly if we look to the other side of the coin. For example, we know from the research that certain personality characteristics are associated with positive outcomes in therapy. What might we expect for them, astrologically?

Empathy is a highly desirable characteristic. Water in general is assumed to be empathic, suggesting the ability to feel with another person, to be sensitive to their needs and experience. Pluto, Scorpio and the eighth house in particular are associated with depth psychotherapy as well as self-analysis and self-control. Letter 7 (Libra, seventh house, Juno, Pallas) also often manifests as an ability to put one's self in the place of the other.

Positive regard for others is helpful in counseling. The ability to form close attachments to other people is especially characteristic of letters 4, 5, 7 and 8.

Concreteness, or getting down to the nitty-gritty is necessary at times. We would expect some earth in the chart for this capacity. Earth tends to be practical and focused. If we listed everything, we would end up needing all the twelve signs, houses and their rulers. The question remains how the individual client or counselor is expressing those various qualities. Any basic energy can be manifested in a variety of ways. It is up to us to find the most positive and fulfilling of channels!

Checklist — Factors To Avoid
(Which Can Contribute To Negative Effects)

1. Inadequate training and/or preparation.

2. Discomfort with and/or lack of skill in dealing with people.

3. Trying to do too much in a session.

4. Trying to be too powerful (or too helpful).

5. Setting unrealistic goals for clients.

6. Not discussing goals with clients.

7. Not reaching **mutually** agreed upon goals with clients.

8. Expecting clients to reach goals too quickly.

9. Too much internal focus (personality dynamics of individual).

10. Too much external focus (the outside world).

11. Rigidity.

12. Overly intense consultations.

13. Too much rapport.

14. Too little rapport.

15. Countertransference (not confronting and dealing with one's own conflicts).

16. Failure to maintain proper distance, especially sexual involvement with clients.

17. Unhelpful personality traits, including coldness, willingness to exploit people, voyeurism, pessimism, self-centeredness, obsessiveness, hostility, and lack of self-examination.

Enjoying The World

A special issue for many people concerned with spiritual growth is sensuality and sexuality. My personal feeling is that growth means enrichment, never diminishment. Thus I cannot agree with those schools which preach true "spirituality" as a total denial of the physical side of life. I believe we are on the physical plane in order to master it as well as the spiritual.

My values include moderation: being able to have ethics, dreams, goals, ideals, being able to feel one with humanity, to be concerned with the pain of others, but also being able to earn a living, and enjoy the sense world without overindulging.

I am concerned with a kind of puritanism that sometimes appears in "mystical" circles. I see it as a limiting view: cutting off a natural part of life (and part of the 12-Letter Astrological Alphabet). I suspect the reasons are many: misplaced idealism; envy ('If I can't enjoy it, neither can you!'); remnants of Puritan ideas of "sin;'and avoidance of intimacy are all possibilities.

Please note that I am **not** addressing the life-style individual astrologers choose for themselves. I am taking issue with astrologers who put out as a value that "truly spiritual" people are not physical, and — subtly or not so subtly — try to talk clients into a life of sensual and sexual renunciation. Personally, I want my clients (and myself) to have the **option** of experiencing all the myriad joys and potentials available in this incredible universe on **all** planes of existence!

Ethics

Since counseling affects human beings and their lives, healers face a number of ethical issues. Value judgments are not subject to any absolute, but a consensual standard of ethics does exist among counselors. Most questions can be resolved by applying the golden rule: treat others as you would like to be treated.

Following is a list of rights of the client and responsibilities of the counselor which psychologists recognize (81). I think counseling astrologers need also to be aware of these rights:

1. The right to be fully informed as to your qualifications to practice, including years of experience, any degrees or other credentials, training, background, etc.

2. The right to ask questions and receive considered answers regarding issues that are relevant in your consultation(s), e.g., your values, attitudes, beliefs, background, and so on.

3. The right to full information regarding your limitations and areas of specialization as a counselor/astrologer. The right to a referral if your expertise/experience is not appropriate.

4. The right to know the limits of confidentiality. In what circumstances, and with whom, might you discuss their case, their horoscope?

5. The right to be fully informed about your fees and how you expect them to make payment.

6. The right to be fully informed of your policies on missed appointments, emergencies, hours of availability, and so on.

7. The right to ask questions at any time.

8. The right to know how much of their sessions are taped or recorded in written files and how accessible those records are.

9. The right to give or refuse their permission for you to use their case (or portions of it) for a presentation or publication.

10. The right to refuse to answer any questions.

11. The right to solicit assistance from the ethics committee of the appropriate organization if they have any complaints or doubts about your conduct.

12. The right to know the code of ethics which you follow.

13. The right to leave at any time.

14. If you are not immediately available, the right to know how long the wait will be.

15. The right to work out goals and expectations for your session(s) together, and reassess these goals as needed.
(The following are more applicable for clients we see over a period of time):

16. The right to be informed of your estimate of the time needed to meet the goals you and the client have agreed upon.

17. The right to be told of specific treatment strategies you intend to use.

18. The right to get a written contract (if desired) covering the conditions of your consultations.

19. The right to refuse any intervention or treatment (or suggestion or interpretation).

20. The right to consult with another professional regarding your procedures.

21. The right to be given, if requested, written summaries of files you are keeping.

Following is a possible sample contract. Usually, such contracts are oral rather than written, but occasionally a client, especially one you will be seeing regularly for a time, may request a written contract. This example is modeled on one offered by a handbook written to help guide women in choosing (or not) psychotherapy (81). Ideally, counselor and client work out together the goals, expectations they have for one another, and their mutual responsibilities.

Sample Contract

I, _____
agree to join with, _____
every _____ for a period of _____
minutes. We will meet at
_____.

We will mutually work toward the following goals:
1.
2.
3.
4.
   I will pay _____ for his/her services as an astrological consultant. Payment will be made
_____.

   If I am not satisfied with progress toward our goals, I will discuss the matter with _____. If conditions do not improve, I will cancel our work together, giving at least _____ hours notice. In that case, I will not be held financially accountable for any missed sessions. Otherwise, I will be responsible for sessions missed without _____ hours warning.

   At the end of _____ sessions, my astrologer and I will renegotiate this contract. We may change some goals. I am aware that this contract does not guarantee me reaching these goals. It is merely _____offer of his or her resources in good faith toward those goals.

This contract will be available to both of us as desired, but not to anyone else without written consent by both of us.

Any information I impart during our work together will be kept confidential by _____.

I _____ give _____ my permission to tape record our sessions together. S/he will not publish, talk about, or in any way disclose information from our sessions, without my written consent.

Date: _____

Client's Signature: _____

Astrologer's Signature: _____

Post Session Questions

After a session, put yourself in your client's place and try to imagine how s/he feels after a consultation with you. This can help us tap into rights and responsibilities that are emotional rather than concrete. A client concerned about the value of a consultation will be asking questions like the following after the session:

1. Do I feel positive towards this person (the counselor)? Can I trust this individual?

2. Did we have honest dialogue? Was the healer direct or evasive? Am I satisfied with the counselor's answers to my questions?

3. Was I comfortable in the setting (office, home . . .) where the consultation took place?

4. Was I treated seriously and with respect?

5. Does this person seem to understand me? (Tying into the need for empathy by counselors.)

6. Does this person basically like me, despite my faults? (Tying into need for positive regard.)

7. Do I understand this person? Is s/he clear?

8. Does this person send out mixed messages (incongruent) or does s/he seem in agreement on all levels: mind, emotions and body?

9. Do our goals for our session(s) together seem compatible?

One way to approach this is to ask yourself these questions. Feelings of liking, respect and understanding tend to be mutual. If you feel positive regard and respect for your client, odds are the client feels similarly towards you.

Chapter 21
Positive Outcomes

I indicated in the theoretical section that the above qualities tend to be associated with positive outcomes in teaching and counseling when the teacher or counselor has them in high degree. Following are some concrete examples to illustrate the qualities, and some ideas and suggestions for exercises and activities to further develop them in one's self.

Examples Of High, Medium & Low Level Empathy & Respect

Client: "I'm concerned about my relationships. I don't seem to be meeting the kinds of people I need. Somehow they don't find me." (Body language: posture drawn inward, slight twitching of hands, little eye contact.)

Low Level
Astrologer: "What you need to do is stop this running around and get married!"*Or*

"This is not a good time to pursue relationships. Wait six months until Venus finishes its square to Mars." *Or*

"You poor dear! Let me give you the phone number of this wonderful man/woman I know."

Adequate Or Average Level
Astrologer: "It sounds like you are unhappy about your lack of present relationships and are not sure what to do." *Or*

"I guess you would really like a satisfactory relationship and are hoping I can help. " *Or*

"I hear that getting a good relationship is very important to you and a place for us to focus in our time together."

High Level
Astrologer: "Must one wait until relationships come to us? (Also possible: "How have you gotten into relationships in the past?") Basically, this client is putting the responsibility on the other person to arrange a relationship. The use of language ("...they don't find me") is passive. Questions may help the client challenge her limited view of relationships (i.e.,"They find me") and perhaps change it. *Or*

"How do you feel right now in your body?" Client is saying s/he wants relationships, but avoiding relating to me right now in this room (little eye contact, drawn inward with body). There appears to be ambivalence. Each counselor has her own style of confronting a client's incongruity — some more gently, others more directly. That is an individual decision we make, based on personal feelings, the client and the situation concerned. *Or*

"Would you be willing to try a little experiment? I want you to lean forward, look me right in the eyes and tell me what kind of people you want to relate to." This is another gentle confrontation. I am asking for **action** to change unfulfilling patterns of behavior. Often action, even a very small one, can do more than a thousand insights. I am also placing her in the active role with my language. She is to do the relating.

Of course, there are many other possibilities. Each astrologer can find the one(s) most personally appealing.

Examples of Genuineness or Congruence

Low Level
Astrologer: "I'm very happy to meet you." (Bored tone of voice, no eye contact) *Or*

"No, I don't mind questions." (Looks at watch, sighs, answers questions hurriedly or with irritated tone of voice) *Or*

"Of course you can do it if you really want to!" (Pats client on the head like a child. Voice condescending. Implication is you will never want **hard** enough.)

Adequate Level
Same words. Voice is excited, but body droops. *Or*
Same words. Does not look at watch. Voice is matter-of-fact. Handles questions very rapidly or withdraws slightly each time a question is asked. *Or*
Same words. Voice a bit too hearty. Astrologer appears trying to convince self as much as client.

High Level
Same words. Voice a bit louder than usual. Tone excited. Body has a forward tilt. Eyes are bright and making good contact with client.
Same words. Friendly smile also. Relaxed, unhurried demeanor. Each question is received with pleasure and answered completely, without rush or irritation. Manner and posture open, inviting reactions from client. *Or*
"Of course you can do it!" or "Yes, you can do it!" Eliminate qualifiers. In that context, they are often a subtle put-down of ability. Tone of voice is emphatic, definite. Demeanor is confident. Body is energetic, outgoing.

Examples Of Concreteness

Client: I am really interested in people.

Low Level
Astrologer: "Obviously, you are a person of wide interpersonal concerns." *Or*
"People will always be a source of great involvement and energy in your life." *Or*
"Humanity is of major importance to you."

Adequate Level
"You seem to want to know a lot about people. Are you interested in working with people?" *Or*
"It sounds as though the people you associate with are very important to you. Is that correct?" *Or*
"Interest in people might lead to humanitarian causes. How do you feel about that?"

High Level

"Are you particularly interested in the people close to you? If so, what one relationship would you like to explore first?" *Or*

"Are you saying you would like to indulge your curiosity about people in a professional way? If so, what careers have you considered?" *Or*

"Your interest in people might lead to crusades on their behalf. Are you drawn to any particular political or social causes?"

Empathy Exercises

One of the best sources for exercises in empathy training is the literature on Psychodrama. A couple of ideas are offered here for your use as well.

Probably the most basic and useful tool in strengthening and fine tuning one's empathic ability is role plays. A role play can be done at almost any time, alone or with others. Alone, we simply imagine ourselves as another person (animal, object) Moreno, the originator of Psychodrama, developed a whole exercise around this which he called the "directed fantasy double." In it, people choose an animal, person or object, and then imagine **becoming** that animal, person or object. Then they try to feel what it is like. They envision their past. They imagine their future. They describe their appearance. And so on. The more one does this, the easier getting "inside" someone else becomes.

Another exercise involving role plays is secret pooling. A group of people writes down secrets. Preferably, each person writes a secret s/he has never before shared. The secrets are dropped into a hat, and each person draws one. If you draw your own, some people toss it back and try again. Others just work with it. One by one, each person reads the secret and talks about it as if it were her own secret. S/he identifies with the information and makes more intuitions and guesses about the situation and life experience. S/he talks about what the secret means to him or her. This is all an extended role play. The basic idea is, "How would I feel having a secret like this? How might it have begun? What are my fears, anxieties around this secret? How has it affected my life?"

Another possibility is to have people pair up, each with pencil and paper. Then each person writes down three qualities (physical or emotional or mental or spiritual) about himself or herself which s/he likes, and three which s/he dislikes. Then the two people trade lists. Each reads the other's list. Then one begins to talk. The idea is to make extrapolations about the other person, to guess, to generate hypotheses.

The person talking bases his or her guesses on the little bit of information s/he does have, but tries to extend it. For example, "You wrote down that you like your caring. I would imagine you are a very loving person. Perhaps you are very affectionate and like to hug people. You are probably generous as well. I imagine you do a lot for your friends. Perhaps you do too much sometimes, and then feel resentful, or unappreciated."

The idea of the exercise is not whether or not you are "right," but how much you can allow yourself to **brainstorm,** to make associations and educated guesses. The principle is to ask yourself: "If I had these qualities, how would I feel? What would I be like? What might my life be?"

After one person has finished his or her guesses, the other person takes his or her turn. Then, at the end, they can compare notes, if desired. Each can share with the other what s/he found accurate in terms of the guesses. This may also give clues to the guessers about projection. Qualities with which the other person does not identify at all are probably issues we have to look at within ourselves.

Genuineness Exercises

One of the best ways to find out how you are coming across is to ask friends to observe you and let you know when you send out mixed messages. They can give you specifics about what you tend to say in words, in gestures, voice tone, posture, and so on. You may find patterns. For example, my irritation shows clearly in my voice, even when I don't want to admit it (including to myself). My fear and anxiety tend to show most clearly in my body language (drawing inward, making myself "smaller").

People who tend to feel conflicted around certain strong emotions (and thus are prone to sending mixed messages) can practice congruence. One potential exercise (in a group or with one other partner) is to construct simple sentences expressing feelings and say them to your partner (or group member), e.g., "I am **really** angry." The other person observes your body, gestures, tone of voice, as well as words, and responds truthfully either, "I believe you," or "I don't believe you." If the other person is not convinced, you try again, until that person feels you are in agreement on all levels of your being.

Concreteness Exercises

It is very helpful to occasionally ask: "What am I assuming?" This may lead to questioning information which we thought was clear and complete, e.g., the client says, "My wife is always nagging me." Most of us have an immediate reaction and idea of what is happening. Asking for more specifics, however, seldom hurts. "What exactly does she do or not do?" The additional information may indeed confirm the image we had. Or, it may turn up surprising information, e.g., the wife is always nagging about the husband smoking and the wife has emphysema. (Smoking around a wife with lung problems seems to indicate some hostility!)

Other helpful questions include:
1. What specific people have we discussed?
2. What specific conflicts have we clarified?
3. Does the client have some actions at his or her disposal now?
4. Have we looked at and made any helpful changes in the life circumstances of the client?
5. Can we list any attitudes or beliefs we have altered?
6. If I asked the client, "In what concrete way has this session been helpful to you?" would s/he be able to give me a satisfactory response?

Successful Counseling Environment — A Checklist

1. Hope
2. Universality
3. Acceptance by and of Other People
4. Catharsis
5. Personal Responsibility and Power
6. Identification & Imitation of Others
7. Gaining Information and Insight
8. Family Reenactment (Cyclic Projections)
9. Interpersonal Learning
10. Focus On Strengths More Than Weaknesses

Chapter 22

Projection

My Favorite Client

One important issue to look at before (and during and after) the client is there, is our own projections. Here's one way to do it. Compile an imaginary description of your favorite client. Then analyze it. Such an experience will often point out portions of your assumptive world that are significant in your interactions with people, that you may have never questioned or examined.

Example

1. **My ideal client would be female.**
   Assumptions: I find women easier to get along with than men. I find most women talk more easily about feelings than men, are more supportive, emotional, understanding and willing to compromise. More of my friends are women than men.

2. **She would be young.**
   Assumptions: My fantasy is that a much older woman would consider me "too young" to be helpful, or not sufficiently knowledgeable or experienced. With much younger women, I fear there would be some generation gap to work through, e.g., my feelings about drugs and sex are probably more conservative than the younger generation (here in California). My ideal client would be probably not more than 10 to 15 years younger than me, nor 20-30 years older.

Note: this fantasy of mine is already diminishing as I get older. Now that I am approaching 30, I have much fewer qualms about how older people will feel about me as a counselor, than I had at age 25. Also, paying attention to others' responses helps. I have not had any older clients say, or even imply, they felt I was "too young" to understand or help.

3. She would be bright.

I am impatient with my own "stupidity," and with "stupid" people. I do not like making "mistakes," and I sometimes feel not very bright if people do not immediately understand what I am saying or communicating. Note: all of this **assumes** that "brightness" or "stupidity" is something that can be objectively measured. How many of us have said or done something "really stupid" that turned out later to be "absolutely right?"

4. She would be working or contributing to society in some way.

I have trouble accepting my lazy side, and would likely feel critical towards someone who I felt was totally unproductive or a "parasite" on society. (I have **assumptions** about what "counts" as productive and what does not.)

5. She would be flexible and capable of progress.

I get very angry at myself when I get into a stuck position, and this is reflected in my feelings about others also. I am committed to a world view that is optimistic, that believes progress is possible. Thus, I tend to feel inadequate or threatened when dealing with clients who do not seem to improve. (They threaten my **assumptions** that progress occurs normally.)

Again, none of this is intended to be a role model. I'm not defending my values. They are mine; other people will have their own. I'm suggesting this exercise as a way to get in touch with some of our values, so as to be more aware of them, and possibly decide when they are useful, and when they are counterproductive in the counseling situation. Realizing that I tend to see women as more likable than men can help me avoid falling into the trap of "automatically" liking a female client, and adopting a "show me" or "wait and see" attitude with a male client. Once we are aware of our tendencies, we can choose to act (or not to act) on them. If we don't examine our opinions, prejudices and values, we will continue to put them out on clients, with no knowledge of the harm we may be doing.

Taking a good look at ourselves usually reveals a multitude of answers. Like the Chinese puzzle boxes, we often discover motivations inside motivations inside motivations. For example, I have a strong tendency to fall into an Earth Mother role (Cancer rising; Moon conjunct Jupiter and Ceres). I could just excuse my tendency to be overly nurturing. Digging a little deeper, I realize that playing Earth Mother is disrespectful to others. (This assumes, "They cannot or will not do it for themselves." Or, perhaps, "They will do it incorrectly.") It is also arrogant. ("I will do it correctly.") There may also be self-esteem issues, e.g., "The way to get people to like me is to nurture them; they may not like me unless I do things for them." And, of course, control issues are probably a part of the picture. If I am the Great Earth Mother, I'm in charge. The point is that most of us do what we do for many reasons. (There is not just one right answer!)

My Least Favorite Client

You could also do the exercise in reverse, of course.

1. **Victims.** I find perpetual victims boring, and they hook into my omniscient healer and Great Earth Mother fantasies. Unless I am careful, I get caught trying to take care of everything. Then they feel ripped off when I am only human, or I feel resentful when they do not improve.

2. **Violent people.** I have a lot of unresolved feelings about physical/ emotional/verbal violence. It is difficult for me to imagine times when violence is appropriate or helpful. I do not like to acknowledge my violent side.

3. **Self-centered people.** These also hook into my sacrificial, Great Earth Mother role, and I come to resent it. I do not resent them regularly. When they bother me, it's a good clue that I've been denying myself something I would really like to have or do on the grounds that it would be "selfish," or I haven't "earned it."

4. **Great Stone Faces.** I will often decline to see people who are trying to "prove or disprove the validity of astrology." I am susceptible to getting into power plays, and really don't need that game. If I take the hook from these kinds of people, I get into my desire to be "right" (omniscient) and my zeal to "do something" for astrology (savior). Belief systems are not usually changed by logical analysis. Generally, I save myself the agony by not getting involved.

5. **Blabbermouths.** I stop myself from chitchatting easily

through perfectionistic standards, self-consciousness, lack of practice and defensive snobbery ("That's not important."). So, I can get caught feeling contemptuous of people who talk a lot. They are doing what I do not allow myself to do.

The point of all of this is to be able to utilize this information. By facing and confronting my assumptions and prejudices, I have the opportunity to change them. This will not only help my clients, it will help and improve me. This listing can be a good place to start, but like most pencil and paper exercises, it is too cerebral. Our best clues, remember, are in the here and now reactions with others. When we have strong feelings, we are most involved. Pay attention. We can go back later and analyze what might have been going on, and work to deal with conflicts, ambivalences and limiting ideas which show up.

Go back and look at the fill in the blank statements that you made for the Meaning Section. Consider them in light of any possible projections.

Projection Through The Horoscope — Abbreviated

Remember the possibilities of projection shown by the chart. Anything (planet, sign) in the following houses **might** be projected. This also fits for planets and signs, e.g., a planet in Libra might be projected onto a partner. A client might let Daddy express all of his or her power, responsibility, stability and practicality, (Saturn side), never learning to do it him or herself.

First: Physical body.

Second: Money, possessions.

Third: Siblings, collateral relatives, neighbors, people in the early environment, including early schooling.

Fourth: Parent (more commonly Mom, but can be Dad).

Fifth: Lovers and children.

Sixth: Colleagues and co-workers, or even the job itself ("My job is so nitpicking!" Who chose that job?)

Seventh: Partners, open enemies, any close, regular peer relationships including counseling and close friendships.

Eighth: People with whom we share an intimate physical relationship or with whom we deal sexually or over the issue of money and other resources.

Ninth: God, ideals, nature, science, etc. (e.g., "Science is so rational and cold," may show our discomfort with our own cold and calculating side.)

Tenth: Parent (usually Dad but may be Mom) and other authority figures including boss, society, the establishment, the social system, the economic system ("I can't do anything. Society has all the power.")

Eleventh: Friends, causes, groups and other associations.

Twelfth: Our own unconscious, secret enemies, the cosmos, everything (cosmic glue).

Chapter 23

Displacement & Repression

Displacement — Checklist

Remember, this is simply doing something potentially good in an inappropriate time, place or amount. Any mixtures can be displaced. Here are a few common ones (in terms of the astrological alphabet):

1-9 or 1-12: *Mixing identity with search for God or an ultimate.* "I am God. (I can do as I please.) I should be God. (I'm nothing if I'm not perfect.) My goal is to continually seek the truth and search for God."

1-6 or 1-10: *Mixing identity with work.* "I am what I do. My identity is to be productive. I am always judging my performance. My job is to look for the flaws in myself."

4 or 10 with 7 or 8: *Parents mixed with partners.* "My parents will be my partner(s) forever. My parents will allow me to be an equal. I will seek partners I can parent (nurture or be responsible for). I will seek partners to parent me (nurture or be responsible for)."

1,9, or 11 with 4: *Freedom with Closeness in the warm, attached domestic, home sense.* "My home must always be changing, moving, active or coming and going. I will take my home into the world. I will bring the world into my home. I will leave my home constantly. I will create instability in my home environment."

There are lots more possible displacements, and lots of possibilities with each displacement. The point is to find an appropriate time and place and amount for each of the motivations involved in the combination.

Repression — Checklist

Letter One: Issues around anger, free self-expression, freedom, space, independence, a sense of identity. Possible problems: *cuts, burns, accidents, headaches, colds, surgery, violence.*

Letter Two: Issues around pleasure and comfort. Possible problems: *throat, handling sugar in body.*

Letter Three: Issues around early peer relationships, communication, learning and thinking. Possible problems: *hands, arms, shoulders, lungs, allergies.*

Letter Four: Issues around nurturance and dependency. Possible problems: *stomach. Getting ill to be taken care of.*

Letter Five: Issues around power, ego, pride, self-esteem and creativity, including children. Possible problems: *heart.*

Letter Six: Issues around efficient functioning, including general bodily health. Need to do a good job somewhere. Possible problems: *intestines, and health as a whole.*

Letter Seven: Issues around equality, sharing with a partner, comfort and pleasure in a balanced relationship. Possible problems: *kidneys, sugar balance in body, craving for sweets.*

Letter Eight: Issues around sharing the material, sensual world with another individual. Being able to love and let go. Knowing when to stop. Possible problems: *bowels, bladder, sexual organs.*

Letter Nine: Faith, ultimate beliefs, ethics, moral principles a focus. What do we trust? Possible problems: *liver.*

Letter Ten: Responsibility, practicality, working within the limits of the structures of society and life. Following the rules. Possible problems: *back, premature crystallization (e.g., gout, arthritis), bones, teeth.*

Letter Eleven: Freedom, uniqueness, ability to rebel, urge for the new, different and unconventional. Desire for unbonded relationships. Possible problems: *ankles, possibly tied to nervous system and electrical system in the body, accidents.*

Letter Twelve: Search for ultimate love and beauty through artistic, healing or victim routes. Yearning for connection to the universe, cosmic consciousness. Possible problems: *dissolving ailments, poisons in the body, infections, mysterious ailments, feet.*

Remember, the point is to go from the problems to the motivation behind it, in order to find solutions. How can we satisfy that need in a more appropriate way?

Of course, we can have physical problems from overdoing parts of life as well. It is not just repression. For example, overindulgence in food leads to overweight. Usually, however, if we overdo one area, we are underdoing another, e.g., if we overeat, we still do not gain weight if we exercise enough. (Letter One balances out Letter Two.) In cases of excess, we can look for other areas to increase. We can also find ways to spread out the overdeveloped area. For example, Letter Two craves physical comfort, pleasure from possessions, beauty, sensuality. If we are doing too much indulgence in alcohol, food or smoking, we might start getting more back rubs, spending money on a few possessions we can cherish, creating some beautiful things, etc. The more varied our expression, the less likelihood of severely overdoing in one area.

Exercise

Go back in your mind to the last time you were sick. What part(s) of your body were involved? What were your life circumstances at the time? What pressures were you under? Were you feeling deprived in any particular way? What resulted from you not being well (e.g., didn't go to work, friends paid attention, friends were upset, had to give up on a commitment)?

Can you make any sense of your experience in terms of the above model?

Chapter 24
Responsibility & Free Will

Introduction

"How many envy a neighbor's flowers
When a crop of thorns is their own?
But the law of life has distributed both.
We reap what we have sown."

Zipporah Dobyns (66, p. 56)

Checklist — Common Tactics to Avoid Responsibility

1. Compulsivity.

2. Giving away the power (to parents, planets, society or others)

3. "Losing control" (but getting rewards for it).

4. Dependency.

5. "Innocent Victim" routine.

As a counselor, I am striving to change equations in clients' minds:

from: **Responsibility Equals Guilt**

to: **Responsibility Equals Power**

Chapter 25
The Issue Of Power

"Counseling is a fifty:fifty proposition. The minute I give more than fifty percent, counseling stops and rescuing begins."

Harry Ginsberg

Fantasy

If you can, set up a tape recorder and talk during this fantasy, so you have a record to go back and check. Let your mind wander. Try not to censor your thoughts. Let whatever comes to you flow out into words, no matter how grand or small, "significant" or "petty."

You Are Now Dictator of the World. You can use your powers to create peace, freedom from hunger, equality, etc. You can amass riches and help your friends. You can do whatever you please. Play out a number of options in your mind. Do not hesitate to get down to specific programs, e.g., "In order to deal with overpopulation problems, I will initiate sterilization of anyone who has had more than two children. Would-be parents will be screened for suitability and required to take training in order to cut down on abuse."

* * * * * *

Once you have completed this fantasy, which can be done several times to get a flavor of the different actions you might in terms of what is important to you. Look at the assumptions behind any programs you would make, e.g., training and education will lessen child abuse. What is radical for you? What is logical and makes sense?

It is unlikely any of us will live out most of these fantasies, but they can help us get a flavor of some of our inner drives and dreams. Fantasies we might judge as power-hungry or dominating are still useful information. If we are aware of our drives, we have choices about how we channel the energy. If we are not in touch with our potential for destruction, we may wreak havoc unknowingly.

Checklist On Power

1. Remember the rescue triangle.

2. Stay in touch with your omniscient, omnipotent fantasies. (We all have them, at least occasionally.)

3. How directive do you choose to be with each client?

4. Know thy Shadow. (Pay attention to your enemies and what disgusts you most.)

5. Know your values and how to put them out clearly without forcing them on clients. Give clients room to disagree and have other opinions.

6. Be willing not to be "right." Being wrong is the best way to learn. Always being right means no growth. Mistakes are how we evolve.

7. Pay attention to client signals (e.g., withdrawals may indicate we are coming on too strong; clients getting weaker instead of stronger suggest we may be doing too much).

Chapter 26
Establishing Rapport

Checklist: Establishing Rapport

1. Avoid jargon.

2. Use client's language and meanings for words as much as possible.

3. Mirror client's posture, eye movements, body language and visual, auditory, kinesthetic predicates.

4. Maintain good eye contact and a relaxed, receptive demeanor.

5. Listen to your feelings. Use your feelings to help understand client.

6. Be honest.

7. Be respectful, empathic, congruent, concrete, flexible, and stay in the here and now when possible.

Consider the following scenarios:

Scenario # 1

The telephone rings. An astrologer answers. Her voice is very gentle, and sometimes difficult to hear.
Astrologer: Hello?
Client: Hello. Is this Ms. Windameer, the astrologer?

A: Yes (Very softly)
C: I'd like to make an appointment.
A: How lovely. Let me find my book. (Long pause) I seem to have misplaced it. When would you like to come?
C: How about next Tuesday, perhaps eight o'clock?
A: That will be wonderful. What is your name, my dear?
C: Mary Mistonick.
A: What a beautiful name. Your parents must have loved you very much. When were you born, Mary?
C: May 21, 1952 at 7:36 AM in Tucson, Arizona.
A: I'm looking forward so much to seeing you, Mary (caressingly). . . . Oh dear, I just remembered. Tuesday is impossible. Our meditation group meets then. Could you possibly come at 8 on Wednesday?
C: Okay. What is your address?
A: 838 Fifth Avenue. We are just a few blocks past the Vons grocery store and just up from the Shell station.
C: I'll check my map. You have everything you need now?
A: Yes, 7:36 in the evening on May 21, 1952 in Tucson, Arizona.
C: No, 7:36 AM, **not** PM.
A: Oh, thank you. I'm so glad the cosmos led you to ask. I'll be so happy to see you on Wednesday, Mary.

* * * * *

Wednesday Evening. The doorbell chimes gracefully. Ms. Windameer answers the door. She is dressed in a multilayered chiffon dress, with long, flowing sleeves, and seems a bit preoccupied. She has long, blond hair which appears to flow haphazardly with her dress. She is not wearing a watch.
Astrologer: (Softly) Yes?
Client: I'm Mary Mistonick. I have an eight o'clock appointment with Ms. Windameer.
A: (a bit taken aback): Oh! Oh, yes. I'm **so** sorry. A friend and I got swept away remembering our Atlantean lives. Do come in.

She ushers Mary Mistonick into another room. It looks much like an artist's studio. There are two chairs, constructed of cushions, very low to the ground. A variety of prints, sketches and paintings adorn the walls and are scattered about on the floor. Most are in soft pastel colors, with delicate figures, or abstract canvases full of color with little form.

Ms. Windameer sweeps some books and papers and sketches to one side and softly says, "Please make yourself comfortable. I must say good-bye to my friend. May I get you some juice or herb tea?'' Mary Mistonick declines any refreshment.

Ms. Windameer returns shortly, smiling winsomely. "Now, as soon as I find your chart...,'' she remarks, leafing through a pile of papers. ...

Scenario # 2

A phone rings. A recorded message goes on: "You have reached the answering service of Ms. Blentnor. If you wish to make an appointment, please leave your name, phone number and birth data. I will return your call as soon as possible.'' The voice is crisp, businesslike and firm. The words are not exactly rushed, but the pace is quite brisk.

Another phone rings.

Client: Hello?

Astrologer: This is Margaret Blentnor returning your call. You wished to make an appointment?

C: Yes, I'm concerned about my job. You see. ...

A: (Interrupting): Excuse me, but it would be best if we made the appointment now and discussed the situation in person. (The voice is firm)

C: Yes, of course.

A: My machine recorded your birth data as May 21, 1952 at 7:36 AM in Tucson, Arizona. Is that correct?

C: Yes.

A: You requested an evening appointment this week, if possible. I can see you Tuesday at 7; Wednesday at 8 or Friday at 6 PM

C: Wednesday, please.

A: Fine. My fee is $150. Consultations are for one hour. If you run over that time, you will be charged accordingly.

* * * * *

Wednesday Evening. Ms. Blentnor answers the door. She is dressed in a dark blue tailored suit with a light blue blouse. Her hair is brown, in a short, stylish cut which obviously requires little more than a blow dry and a comb out. Her makeup is sparing and subdued in coloring.

She leads the client into what looks like an office. There is lots of dark wood paneling. The walls have orderly bookshelves on one side and certificates and plaques on the other. Ms. Blentnor seats herself behind a large immaculate desk which has a single horoscope in the exact center.

She gestures for Ms. Mistonick to seat herself in a firm, straight backed chair near the desk. Ms. Blentnor glances at her watch, and waits for 30 seconds. She then picks up the horoscope, and announces: "Now we can begin. Perhaps you can give me a **brief** summary of the situation."

* * * * *

These scenarios are (hopefully) exaggerated examples, but do serve to illustrate how much unintended information healers sometimes provide their clients. If I gave the reader a list of personality traits for Ms. Windameer and Ms. Blentnor, I'm sure you would feel secure checking off a number of items, e.g., "businesslike, scattered, organized, forgetful, cold, good intentions, artistic, conservative," for each astrologer.

Checklist: The Counseling Setting

Where in town do I practice?
Where do I advertise?
Who refers clients to me?
What literature do I distribute, including color, tone, wording?
What feelings and information do my stationery and business cards convey, including color, design, wording?
Where is my consulting room: home, office?
Do I have a receptionist or secretary?
An answering machine?
What is the state of my furniture?
Color scheme?
Degree of neatness?
Order versus chaos?
What is my personal appearance, including: hair, clothes, makeup, colors?
Voice analysis?
Nonverbal visual analysis, including: nervous habits, eye contact, gestures, etc.?

Chapter 27
Gathering Evidence

Introduction

"Is your mind as clean as your house is,
Or is it cluttered with junk?
Frittered on flippant fancies,
Or plain and simple bunk? . . .

"Though we spend our lives cleaning
cupboards
And vacuuming the rug,
It's a good idea now and then
To give our minds a scrub."

Zipporah Dobyns (66, p. 111)

Checklist: What Do I Already Know?

Before a client comes, I already have information and some tentative hypotheses. It may be helpful to review them systematically. Remember, the goal is to generate hypotheses, but not get attached to them. We must be ready to discard any impressions that do not fit the client in person or further information which we obtain.

Hogie Wycoff on "banal scripts" for men and women. Her essay is in her book, *Solving Women's Problems*, and also in *Scripts People Live*, by Claude Steiner. She mentions such common roles as The Woman Behind the Man, Plastic Woman, Creeping Beauty, Poor Little Me, Nurse, and Mother Hubbard for women; plus Big Daddy, Playboy, Jock, The Man In Front of The Woman, the Intellectual and Woman Hater for men.

2. Age.

Here, it is helpful to be familiar with the psychological research on life cycles. The most recent work is by Daniel Levinson, et al., but focuses on the male life cycle. Gail Sheehy has done some work with women. And Ms. Sheehy has also researched people that are able to dramatically change, and weather crises well. She calls them path finders in her book by the same title. Erik Erikson's formulations are still prevalent in the literature, and, of course, Freud's. It is also useful to bear in mind the astrological transit cycles.

The following tables are condensations of the work of Erik Erikson (see *Childhood and Society*) and Daniel Levinson (see *The Seasons of a Man's Life*). I am not suggesting them as any final answer, but to spark people's thinking in the area.

Stage #1 (Ages 0 - 1-1/2) Basic Trust Versus Mistrust

Tasks include developing attachment (parents to child and child to parents). Basic issue of world view is trust ('The world is nourishing') versus mistrust ('The world is hostile'). Oral needs a focus.

Stage # 2 (Ages 1-1/2 - 4) Autonomy Versus Shame & Doubt

Learning to assert one's self and say "**No.**" without fighting the whole world and doubting one's own worth. Anal needs and toilet training a focus.

Stage # 3 (Ages 4-7) Initiative Versus Guilt

Going into the wider world. Exploring options, including sexuality, without loss of self-esteem.

Stage # 4 (Ages 7-11) Industry Versus Inferiority

Learning to be productive without falling into either overdrive ("I have to do it all") or self-blocking ("I'll never do anything right").

Stage #5 (Ages 11-18+) Identity Versus Role Diffusion

Finding out "Who am I?" and "How do I fit in (or not) with my peer group and society?" Avoiding excessive conformity and excessive rebellion.

Stage #6 (20's & 30's) Intimacy Versus Isolation

Learning to establish a long-term, committed relationship.

Stage #7 (40's & 50's) Generativity Versus Stagnation

Being able to involve one's self creatively with the younger generation, to pass on valuable experiences, to learn new perspectives. The mentoring relationship.

Stage #8 (60 and up) Ego Integrity Versus Despair

Renunciating material goals and gains for spiritual ones. "Healthy children will not fear life if their elders have integrity enough to not fear death" (23, p. 269).

In Daniel Levinson's framework, (see p. 182) **bold lettering** indicates what he and his colleagues called "transition periods." They are generally four to five years. During them, people reappraise their lives, leave the old, begin the new. Sometimes, the necessary changes are far-reaching.

The other periods within each large division Levinson et al. called "stable periods," ranging usually six to seven years, up to a maximum of ten years. People build life structures in their stable periods, elaborating the foundation already set.

According to this theory, we would expect alterations in world views (paradigm shifts) to be more likely during the **transition** or "crisis" periods. Of these, Levinson stressed the "Age Thirty" and "Mid-Life" transitions as most universally experienced by people. These correlate with major transits. Everyone has transiting Saturn conjunct their natal Saturn around ages 28 to 30. The midlife crisis includes Neptune square Neptune, Saturn opposite Saturn and Uranus opposite Uranus. (And, for some of us, Pluto will square Pluto about then — early forties — as well.) Levinson also found the "Age Fifty Crisis" very prevalent.

The roman numerals on the following page indicate the divisions Levinson made of the life cycle into large eras, usually about twenty to twenty-five years each. There are particular life tasks to be faced each era.

Of course, these patterns are generalizations, and there are always exceptions. Levinson noted some pattern breakers, usually highly unique, possibly eccentric individuals. One man in his sample did not go through the cycles the other men did. He is a homosexual poet living on the West Coast. It is possible that the people who most dramatically break the generalized patterns will be highly unique, inventive or rebellious. And Levinson's work, as indicated in the title, is with men only.

I. Childhood & Adolescence (Years 0-22)
   Early Childhood Transition (0-3)
   Middle Childhood (5-11)
   Adolescence (12-18)
   Early Adult Transition (17-22)

II. Early Adulthood (17-45)
   Entering the Adult World (22-28)
   Age Thirty Transition (28-33)
   "Settling Down" Stage (33-40)
   Midlife Transition (40-45)

III. Middle Adulthood (40-65)
   Entering Middle Adulthood (45-49)
   Age Fifty Transition (50-55)
   Culmination of Middle Adulthood (55-60)
   Late Adult Transition (60-65)

IV. Late Adulthood (?65-85?)
   . . .
   Transition to Late, Late Adulthood (80-85)

V. Late, Late Adulthood (80 and up)

3. Cultural Background
If we already know a client belongs to and identifies with an ethnic, religious or cultural group, that is valuable information. Again, we must be wary of stereotyping, but know that certain patterns are possible. For example, trust is likely to be a bigger issue for a black person in our society (especially if coming to a white counselor or astrologer) because blacks have been discriminated against and treated in ways that discourage trusting (particularly trusting whites).

4. Astrological Information
This is a two-edged sword. Of course, we can use any horoscope we have to further our insight into the individual. But any diagnostic

tool is only as good as our interpretive powers. If we lock ourselves into a certain view of the horoscope, we may miss significant aspects of the client entirely. I've known astrologers fearful to meet a client because: "His Saturn is on my Sun," or some other traditionally "bad" contact. If we assume something is going to be negative, we can help create that negativity.

5. Other Background Information

Too often I find astrologers, particularly, are reluctant to get any kind of case history. Astrologers caught in the role of omniscient mystic are afraid to ask questions such as, "Are you married?" lest the client respond, "Can't you tell from the chart?" That is one reason I dislike the omniscient role!

It is not essential we have masses of background data, but some items are useful. I may not request them in advance. They often come up naturally in a session. And, if not, I can always ask. We are social animals who operate in a context of other people, influencing and being influenced by them. It helps as a healer to know some of the significant people in our clients' lives.

Background information which is almost always useful includes:

1. Partnership situation, e.g. married, divorced, separated, widowed, living together, living alone and enjoying it (or not).
2. Any children, including experiences with repeated miscarriages or infertility.
3. Parental situation of the client, e.g., a two parent family; a one parent family; level of discipline; level of affection; values.
4. Siblings and birth orders.

Other information may be useful in some cases. That tends to come up in the consultation, e.g., special health problems; unique work history; handicaps; particular religious or ethical beliefs.

6. Presenting Problem or Question.

Many people will mention a particular question, issue or problem, something they wish to focus on during the consultation. That will give additional clues as to what is important to this particular client.

Checklist: When The Client Arrives

1. Colors selected (often a clue to mood).

2. Style of dress.

3. Overall neatness (or not) in appearance.

4. Stylishness (clues to a sense of fashion, conformist needs).

5. Hairstyle (casual, easy to care for, elaborate, "fussy").

6. Makeup (e.g., if especially elaborate and painstaking, perhaps the client is overly concerned with the "face" s/he presents to the world).

7. Degree of nervousness or ease indicated in voice, gestures, body language.

8. Ethnic or cultural group important?

9. Body language cues.

10. Voice cues.

11. Body size, if significantly different from norm, e.g., very overweight people often have self-esteem and security issues to name two. Very short men often have power issues.

Notes on Visual, Auditory & Kinesthetic Types

NLP assumes that people take in and put out information primarily in three channels: visual, auditory and kinesthetic (feeling and sensing). Often, people experience difficulties because they are not receiving information (which is being sent on a different input channel than the one to which they are accustomed). Or, people — including counselor and client — may miscommunicate because they are sending information in different ways.

The following are generalized descriptions. There will be lots of exceptions. Try to consider each individual in his or her own context.

Visual Types

Use lots of visual predicates, e.g., "I can see that. Is that clear? That doesn't look right." Such people tend to use a majority of upward eye movements. Their gestures are more often sweeping, and wide, as if painting a mural. They do not like people to stand very near to them because they experience life almost as if there were a movie screen in front of them. People standing too close get in the middle of the picture!

Auditory Types

Language focuses on hearing. "That rings a bell with me. Can you hear me? You're coming in loud and clear." Their eye movements tend to be down and to the left.

Strong auditory types are rare — supposedly only about ten percent of the population has audition as their primary input mode. Visual is the most common.

Kinesthetic Types

Language centers on feelings. "I can't get a handle on what you're saying. It just doesn't feel right. I am trying to make sense of it." Their eye movements tend to be down and to the right. Gestures tend to be short and center around the heart. They often gesture inward and touch themselves in the middle of the chest.

Mirroring the client is helpful in establishing rapport. If the client is visual, use images; paint pictures. Once rapport is established, you can begin leading clients. They will often unconsciously mirror you, once you have established the initial rapport in rhythm with them. Changing systems, e.g., visual to kinesthetic, can often help change attitudes and paradigms (models) of the situation.

Nonverbal Exercises

Talk with someone for ten minutes, without words. You can use letters or numbers, e.g. "One, one, one, **Three!**" It is cheating to spell. This will help you tune in to how you use your voice: inflection, tone, volume, to convey information. You will be able to analyze where you are gaining information from the other person nonverbally: posture, gestures, voice, and so on.

We can practice our nonverbal information gathering at almost any time. Observe people at airports, parties, restaurants, and so on. Try to guess the tone of their interactions. Are they angry, sad, happy, worried, rushed?

Another useful exercise is to have two people sit behind a closed door and carry on a conversation, perhaps simulate a counseling session. Take notes on what you observe. Even though you cannot hear any words, you probably can guess when one is pushing the other for a reaction; when one or the other is concerned, upset, relieved or frustrated.

Paying Attention to Client Feedback: Checklist

The term feedback refers to all communications given by another person — verbal and nonverbal. Nonverbal feedback has general trends, but much individual variation. Check out your impressions with each client; things may not be what they appear!

Watch and Listen and Feel

Facial Expressions: e.g. frown, smile. Generally, there is a subtle drawing in and tightening up of the face when we are threatened, anxious, fearful. The face tends to loosen with pleasure.

Body posture: e.g. leaning forward (usually involved, attentive); leaning backward (may be relaxed, disinterested, turned off). Much crossing of arms, legs across the body can be putting up walls. "Seductive" postures may be come-ons, hooks for attention, insecurity. Rigidity often tension, overly intellectual.

Nodding or Shaking Head: (Often very slight movements) — usually agreement or disagreement.

Eyes: Eyes tend to be more open and look "softer" with pleasure; close up and get "harder" with discomfort, anxiety. Pupils also dilate with pleasure.

Physical proximity: tend to sit, stand closer to those we care for; more distant to those we do not care for. Appropriate distances very culturally relative.

Yawning, sleepiness: and other signs suggest disinvolvement. Non-participation in groups.

Staring: could be surprise, hostility, lack of understanding.

Preoccupation with writing, doodling, taking notes: may indicate compulsivity, fear of involvement, refusal to relate, anxiety.

Tone of voice: very loud or very soft often control (power play) issues. Insecurity.

Tempo of speech: verbal diarrhea often a sign of anxiety — a sign of anxiety — a distracting mechanism used to create distance. Overly slow speech may indicate overweening self-importance or someone who fears s/he will stutter or make a mistake if speaking at a normal pace.

Sounds: what do grunts and other non-words suggest? Note tone, timing.

Touching: generally we touch people we like, but some touches feel hostile. Also, people who initiate the contact tend to feel "superior" to the one they touch, e.g., boss pats employee on shoulder.

Physical relationships: e.g., in a circle, does one person sit outside — fear of involvement, feeling above the group, alienated? With family therapy, do **not** set up the seating arrangement so that you seem on one side or another of various family alliances.

Word selection: what feelings, concepts, images are important to this individual based on the words s/he selects, especially repeated words and/or phrases.

Eye contact: more contact generally associated with comfort and intimacy; less with anxiety and withdrawal. What is lots for one person may be little for another.

Gait and carriage: graceful, at ease, loose, flexible, careful, rigid?

Pulse: may be discernable in neck; helps indicate excitement, anxiety, stress.

Generating Hypotheses

In gathering information about clients, counselors constantly make hypotheses. Brainstorming, coming up with a number of different possibilities for any given situation, is an excellent first step in problem solving. The initial goal is just to list as many ideas as possible, no matter how "wild" or "crazy" they are. Step two is to go back and check out the ideas; see what is most functional under the circumstances.

You can set up your own brainstorming situations. Sit with pencil and paper, or a blackboard and create a scenario. Then see how many different ideas and possible motivations you can originate.

For Example: A client arrives fifteen minutes late, exclaiming, "I finally made it!"

My Hypotheses:

1.   My directions were inadequate. (Note that if this is your first impulse, you may have some unspoken assumptions about your efficacy and some self-esteem issues to deal with.)

2.   This client gets lost often.

2(A).   The client avoids being prepared (by not looking at maps, not adjusting for traffic). S/he is into a "confusion racket" in T.A. terms. The payoff is bad feelings; these could be feeling inadequate, getting anger or blame from other people, feeling stupid.

2(B).   Client is careless and unobservant, so misses turns. How might this lack of care and failure to pay attention affect other areas in the client's life?

2(C).   Client is preoccupied, thinking about too many things. Client tends to be overextended, doing too many things at once, so none of them gets done well. (This is one form of the mutable dilemma in astrology, so I would see if the chart supports this hypothesis in any way.)

2(D).   Client has no sense of direction (literally and metaphorically). S/he is not sure or does not know where s/he wants to go or is going in life. Goals and directions are unclear. (This is another form of the astrological mutable dilemma. Again, I would check the chart. Of course, the ultimate check is always with the client and his or her life. Any interpretation is subject to error.)

3.   Arriving late is a pattern this client has developed as a means to get attention.

4.   The client is ambivalent about seeing me (or an astro-counselor), so agonizes over the decision, and eventually arrives late.

Again, the first step is simply to come up with a number of different ideas. Then we can see if any of them fit for this client. If not, we go back to step one and start generating new hypotheses. Thus, it is clients whom we first "bomb out" on who teach us the most! If we guess correctly right away, we haven't had to stretch ourselves or learn much new. If we miss and have to look further, we are more likely to expand our world view, to start considering options we do not normally examine. This can be very growth enhancing for us as well as clients.

Chapter 28
Changing Paradigms

Checklist

1. Turn liabilities into assets:
   a. Identify the problem.
   b. Find the motivation(s) behind the problem.
   c. Discover more satisfying ways to fulfill the motivation(s).
2. Use history as a resource. When has the client handled these issues positively in the past? (For example, perhaps the client becomes nervous and insecure when asking a boss for a raise, but feels calm and assured when asking a friend to help him or her move.) Focus in on the positive experience, and role play the worrisome situation, constantly returning to the images and feelings of the positive situation. (This is another idea from Neuro-Linguistic Programming.)
3. Metaphors are powerful tools for change.
4. Humor is useful.
5. The counselor is an effective role model — in actions, even more than words.
6. If we change one person, we change his or her interpersonal relationships. Some significant others may change as well. Some will choose to end the relationship. This is threatening to some people. They may need support and reassurance to stay with the changes and find new people with which to relate.

Postscript: One model which can be useful in working for changes, is the concept that many people suffer because there is a large discrepancy between their self-image (how they believe they are) and their ideal image (how they believe they should be).

In working for change, one can go in both directions: to raise the self-image (through concentrating on strengths, which the client often is ignoring or minimizing) and/or to lower the ideal image (which often has perfectionistic expectations, e.g. "I should always be loving and kind").

Language: Introduction

"I set my thoughts in order
And feel my way through words,
And try to pin on paper
Those fluttering concept-birds.
Swiftly they flit within me
Striving to get away,
Elusive, alluring intangibles
As I reach to make them stay.
Till I catch them here on the paper
And they settle down with a sigh.
Giving some of their beauty and freedom
To answer a human cry."

Zipporah Dobyns (66, p. 13)

Checklist on Language

1. Listen:
2. Responsibility enhancement:
   a. Change "I cannot," to "I will not," or "I choose not to."
   b. Change "You annoy me," to "I feel annoyed."
   c. Change "It happened," to "I did it."
   d. Stay in the **here and now** more, *there and then* less.
3. Words and questions to expand world views:
   a. Why not?
   b. What would happen if you did (or didn't)?
   c. Possibly, might, may, potential, can, likely, somewhat, could be, might be, tend to, imply, suggest, lean in the direction of, a number of, seems, appears, often.
4. May be helpful to challenge:
   a. Words which tend to limit world views: must, have to, cannot, necessary, absolute(ly), final, of course, obvious(ly), no choice, inevitabl(y), without fail, it is.

b. Generalizations (always, never . . .).

c. Subjective judgments which are stated as facts.

d. Mind reading (e.g., "You know how I feel," or "I know what you're thinking").

5. Return nominalizations to verb form to restore possibility of movement and change.

6. Confront self put-downs.

Postscript: There is a wonderful book called *The Kin of Ata* which includes an island society that truly understands how words label, condense, and constrict a multicolored, complex reality; when we have a label, we often believe we understand completely. In this society, the word for "**word**" is "**lie**." (11)

Finding the
Message Behind the Words

Consider the client who arrives and immediately begins to tell you one catastrophe after another that has happened to her. What is implied by her words and actions? Is there a message **behind** the message? What might she be wanting from you as a counselor?

Sometimes a client may want sympathy. She may want a literal (or metaphorical) shoulder to cry on, someone to commiserate with her about how awful it must have been. She may also desire reassurance, that it will not go on, or that she will survive and be okay, or that it is not her fault, that she does not really deserve these awful happenings.

Some clients may be "wanting" criticism. If being put down is a usual or familiar position for them, they may recite disasters as proof of their inadequacies. They are likely to eagerly grasp any suggestions of their responsibility as further indications of their guilt.

Some clients may be seeking attention. Their history has demonstrated that arousing sympathy or horror is the best way to remain center stage. Clients' harrowing experiences may also be used as a tactic to gain and maintain control. If they can continue to determine what is discussed, they will not be obliged to risk being vulnerable or discussing issues that they find threatening.

Being human, we are inclined to have a number of fairly "automatic" responses, e.g., I tend to instinctively offer sympathy when I hear of catastrophes. As counselors, we need to question our automatic responses. If we can go outside our usual framework, we will be more likely to help clients go outside their usual assumptions about life.

Messages are often sent by people's body language or behavior. Someone who is sending one message in words, and another with their bodies is called **incongruent**. The messages are mixed. It is not usually helpful to assume that one message is "true" and the other is "false." Generally, both are relevant to the person. For example, the person who says, "I care about you very much," in a tone of voice full of feeling, but with a rigid, withdrawing body, is not necessarily "lying" with her words. One possibility is that she may be feeling very deeply, and is simultaneously threatened by the depth of her response. Or, she may be sincerely touched, but embarrassed because other people are around and she has qualms about expressing strong emotions in public. Or, prior history with the person she is expressing her caring to may have taught her to expect her verbalizations to evoke sexual overtures. She may wish to express caring feelings, but want to avoid sexual involvement. Carrying an image of a multilayered reality can be very helpful to counselors.

People will often make "statements" with their behavior which are in conflict with their words, e.g., the person who commits suicide and leaves a note addressed to an individual which says in effect: "Dear Someone, don't blame yourself for this. I just couldn't take it anymore." The words say do not feel guilty. But the action of choosing to write a note, and addressing it to one specific party points a definite finger of blame. (Suicides and suicide attempts often have a revenge motive as part of the picture.) A counselor might ask a would-be suicide: "Who would you be suiciding against (be punishing)?"

People will give away a tremendous amount of information, if we just pay attention. Take the client who tells you his life story. In it, you hear a saga of ingratitude and abuse. Everyone in his life has deserted him, mistreated him, does not appreciate him. Even his own children will never do what he wants them to, will not help out. One message behind all of this is: "Beware, ye would-be helper. I will find some way to make you desert me. I will find fault with whatever you do. I will be impossible to please."

Listen for the messages below the surface.

Chapter 29
Putting It All Together With Cosmic Glue

Summary Checklist

1. Reality is vaster than we imagine.

2. Our brains filter out huge amounts of potential information

3. Our beliefs and attitudes, influenced by family and culture, determine that filtering: what we perceive, what we accept as possible and impossible.

4. Limiting beliefs and attitudes lead to limited lives.

5. Human beings have an urge to be all that they are capable of being (self-actualization).

6. Human beings have a competing urge for stability, in order to feel a sense of control over their world.

7. Self-actualization drives pull us up to learn, understand, perceive more. Stability drives pull us toward the past, to understand the present in the model of the past.

8. Being human entails making maps of the world, our best guesses about people and what is going on.

9. Maps, by definition, condense, generalize, oversimplify a complex reality. The map can become a trap.

10. Astrologers, scientists and all human beings filter and interpret their perceptions based on past experience, present desires and

future hopes. There is no such thing as an objective observer.

11. Astrology offers one map or model, visualizing people with twelve different ways of being in the world, intermixed and inter-mingled in unique combinations in each of us.

12. Psychology offers a number of other maps of human nature.

13. Research in psychology suggests the most important element in counseling is the relationship between counselor and client, not the map, theory or techniques of the practitioner.

14. Successful counseling correlates with a warm, caring relationship between counselor and client.

15. Skilled clinicians exhibit empathy, respect, concreteness, congruence, spontaneity, confrontation (of assets more than liabilities), honesty and flexibility.

16. Positive counseling experiences include at least some of the following: hope, catharsis, universality, acceptance, responsibility, identification, information, family reenactment and interpersonal learning.

17. The major tool of counselors is their own body and mind: feelings, reactions, impressions.

18. The counseling interaction affects both counselor and client.

19. Client will mirror our own issues, often in exaggerated fashion.

20. We will sometimes react to clients in inappropriate ways because we are hooking into our own inner conflicts and am-bivalence (countertransference). Being aware, honest, flexible, and watching client reactions are the best tools for minimizing counter-transference.

21. Clients (and all humans) relate to people within a framework of beliefs and attitudes about the world, and often repeat old (nonuseful) patterns of interaction. They may reenact family situations with partners counselors, etc. (Transference, cyclic projections)

22. The counseling experience can be divided into three steps: establishing rapport; gathering information; changing models of the world.

23. Establishing rapport needs to be done nonverbally as well as verbally. Effective rapport is mutual.

24. Gathering information is a process of generating hypotheses, testing them, throwing out the nonviable ones and finding new ones. Nonverbal cues, the horoscope, the motivation behind clients' words, as well as what they tell us are all sources of data (about the client and about us).

25. Changing the paradigm involves helping the client to envision a broader world view. Often this means a shift in how they interpret situations, events, turning liabilities (problems) into assets and resources.

26. Language is a major way in which we lock ourselves into certain assumptions about the world.

27. Humor can be effective in shifting the frame of reference, helping people see alternatives.

28. An unconscious part of each of us collects information which we filter out of consciousness. This is a valuable resource for change, for finding other options.

29. The effective counselor will be broadening his or her world view along with clients' world views.

30. The concepts of projection (attracting people to express sides of our own nature we are not manifesting); repression (denying a part of ourselves; pushing it into the unconscious) and displacement (expressing a useful and necessary part of life in an inappropriate time, place or amount) can be helpful in our growth and the development of our clients.

31. Astrologers have special issues with clients around responsibility (and free will) and power. Astrological clients are even more inclined to give away power over their lives to the planets, society, etc.

32. The astrologer's belief (or nonbelief) around personal responsibility and power to alter one's life will affect his or her clients. Successful counseling is associated with increased feelings of personal power and personal responsibility by clients.

33. All counselors need to confront their own omniscient, omnipotent fantasies, lest they do harm with clients.

34. Counselors can aid the societal *status quo* or work against it. Our attitudes and values will either support current standards and stereotypes about people, or conflict with them.

35. We live in an interconnected universe. What we do affects others; what they do affects us.

36. Accepting that we interpret reality in terms of beliefs which may be outmoded and no longer useful; accepting other people as mirrors to aid our growth and transcendence; trusting our own power and responsibility; and searching continually for the positive alternatives are likely to result in continued growth and transcendence for client and counselor.

Effective counseling occurs when both client and counselor are able to expand their world views.

SECTION THREE

Demonstration

Preamble

Following is a portion of an example consultation: a transcript from an actual recorded session with a client who gave her permission to use and publish the material. I am including large sections to help give readers a flavor of our interaction. I have removed a few "ands," but basically the text is as the words were spoken by us. This includes run-on sentences, incomplete sentences, and bad grammar for which I apologize. For space reasons, I will not include the entire session. Also, because certain themes and issues came up repeatedly and were addressed more than once, I will summarize some areas. My brackets — [ ] — will indicate where material was deleted. But I believe the feeling of our consultation still comes through the transcript.

I am not suggesting that the way I handled this consultation is optimal. I believe we have **many** opportunities as counselors to improve our skills. I know, in any given session, there are many times when I could have said something differently, been more empathic, listened better, been clearer or more concise, gone in a different direction. And so on. One of the shifts I am working on in my counseling style, is to be less concerned with "getting everything in." I am working towards being less focused on covering everything in the chart, and more able to center on a few vital areas, and cover them in depth with clients. (Obviously, the clients' desires also affect this. Some clients want the total overview. And, having a tape, they can listen over and over again to the basic information.)

I am including this example in the hopes that readers will peruse it looking for other possibilities. What else might you have said? How might you have worded a point differently? Where might you have pushed a client more, or been less confrontational? What might you have done? What issues would you have stressed? What other questions would you have asked?

Naturally, one does not have a "perfect" session. Many times, there are a variety of ways to go, and more than one path can still take us in a growth enhancing direction. I want to stress looking for alternatives, because the more options we can see, hear and be in touch with, the more we can convey that sense of open vistas and a rich reality to our clients.

I will point out in the text a few moments where I was aware of having choices as to a direction to go. Many others exist. Within an interview, we constantly choose (mostly intuitively) our focus and direction. I encourage readers to consider a wide variety of other possibilities.

Of course, in an actual consultation, it is a challenge to relate to the client, keep the horoscope in mind and still keep a part of one's mind searching for alternative choices in the interview. It is much easier to analyze on paper. But we need to start there. The more one practices, the greater the level of skill. Once we are comfortable with multiple options on paper, the searching and seeking process can be almost automatic when with clients.

Background Information

This client made the first contact by phone, having been referred by another client. We made an appointment about two weeks later than when she called. I had at that time just the birth information, and her phone voice. Her speech is fairly quick, and there is often a hint of laughter in her voice. Her voice sounded forceful; I had the impression that she had strong opinions and feelings.

The hour of the appointment, she did not show. After a half hour, I called the number she had left, which was a work number. She had already left. She did not appear at all. The next day, she appeared at the appointed hour. I had already made plans, so it was not convenient to see her. She was highly apologetic, and felt she had probably written the wrong day down on her calendar. (She had remembered being surprised when she saw Friday, as she normally does not makes plans for Fridays, other than fun things.) We made a later appointment at that time.

She is a very pretty, vivacious appearing woman in her early thirties. She could easily pass for younger. Her appearance is very attractive: fashionable clothes, some makeup (not overdone), a good figure, short, but well-styled hair. She made a joke about going home and "beating the children" when she left, so I knew she had children and possibly (?) some ambivalent feelings around the nurturing role.

She also gave the impression of an active social life, not wanting to make plans for Fridays or the weekends.

Since I had called her work, I knew she worked in a law office.

My client, whom I will call Lynn, arrived on time, and apologized again for the previous mix-up. I showed her into the study, and asked her to select a chair. I seated myself, and we exchanged a few sentences. (I generally chat a tiny bit beforehand, to help clients settle in. We can discuss the weather and whether they had any trouble finding my house, and so on.) Then, I tested the tape recorder, to be sure it was functioning properly.

I asked Lynn if she knew anything about astrology, and she said she is interested, and has studied some. So, I told her I would include more of the astrological references than I normally did. I asked her to feel free to comment or ask questions at any time, that I would be happy to hear anything she wanted to say. Then I began the recording. "M" shall refer to Maritha (the astrologer), and "L" to Lynn (the client).

The horoscopes referred to in this consultation appear on pages 228 and 229.

Chapter 30
An Example Consultation

M: This is a horoscope recording for Lynn done in Los Angeles in February 1982. . . .I do like to have my basic world view on the tape, which is that the planets aren't doing anything; that they are just like mirrors put up there for us to understand ourselves better. I don't think they are **causing** anything to happen; they are just reflections of our own personality, character tendencies and traits. I do believe that the power and the responsibility is inside: that in any given astrological configuration, there are a variety of options and different ways that we can handle what is being symbolized there. It is up to us to choose the more positive ways to express our needs.

As you know, you have Capricorn rising, and we do use four asteroids that not all of the astrologers use, and one of them, which we call Juno, is closely conjunct the Ascendant. Juno is the asteroid of marriage. This puts a very strong Libran theme there, despite the Capricorn rising: that it is important for you to share the world with someone else, to have a partner. That there is a natural cooperativeness and a spirit of wanting someone else in your life. At the same time, there is a bit of conflict because of your strong Aries stellium which includes Mercury, Mars, Venus and also one of the other asteroids, Ceres, which all say, "I'm identified with being a loner, with doing it myself, with going my own way, with making my own rules and roles and not having to answer to anybody else, and being able to go my way."

And then the Capricorn rising, which is naturally square that Aries, which says, "No, I'm really responsible for taking care of everything." Capricorn rising is identified with working, with doing a good job, with being productive, with being responsible, all of the puritan virtue kinds of things. There is a strong sense of, "I need to take care of things; I need to do it because either I'll feel guilty if I'm not doing it, or because others are going to blow it, so I have to do it to make sure that it gets done right.'

So there are three different keys to the basic sense of identity, and they are pulling — in a sense — in three different directions. Where the Aries side of the nature is saying, "Go off, be a pioneer, do it your own way and don't get involved with anybody else, just be a loner because that's the way to travel, the best way, to be alone. You travel fastest that way and you have the most fun." And then there is the Juno thing, "But I really want a partnership; I really want somebody to share my life with, to have a close, committed relationship with." And then there is the Capricorn side, "No, what is really important is my responsibility, my role in the world, my career, things that amount to something and functioning in a productive manner in society.'

So, when we have a mixture, an ambivalence like that in the chart, it is just saying that all three of them are important. That you are not someone who can do any one of them to the **exclusion** of any of the others. That it is important for you to have a career. Whenever Capricorn or Virgo is a basic part of the identity, a person needs to work. They can feel a little bit guilty when they are not working, like they **should be** contributing, being productive and so on. So that's a part of them feeling good about themselves and happy with themselves. At the same time, you need to have some area in your life when you are very much that Aries free soul type person: not answering to anybody else, going your own way, your own hobbies or interests or things that you can do **just** for yourself and not having to worry about anyone else. [Note: I went off into another issue, and did not repeat the Juno needs.]

A lot of that is likely to come out in the mental world, because most of that area is centered in the third house. Which is like the person who says, "I think for myself and nobody else tells me how to think. I have my own ideas about how everything is." It is also a very quick mind, because any fire connected, like Mercury in Aries, to the mind quickens the thinking. A person who can think on their feet, is often very good at things like debating and it's also the potential of using words like a weapon. Being able to be assertive with words: biting, ironic, sarcastic. It's the quick-witted kind of sense.

The Capricorn rising will hold back a little bit on **saying** it, because of feelings of responsibility and also a little bit of self-criticism with Capricorn rising. There tends to be a little bit of constantly looking at yourself, "Do I measure up?" and so on, that can sometimes hold back on spontaneous expression. But a lot of sense of humor and sense of fun and natural quick-wittedness and expressiveness with all that Aries in the third house. A good flair for language and for thinking, and a natural rebelliousness in terms of really wanting to think your own way. Sometimes this is a problem in early schooling where the person does not want to particularly follow the rules and learn it the way other people are learning it.

L: Sometimes, I think the Capricorn is not doing its job lately. (Laughs)

M (Laughing): Well, maybe because you were too good when you were little, it's saying, "Now is the time to come out.'

L: Unfortunately, that's not the case. Capricorn can't seem to get out there.

M: There's some of both, but it's certainly saying that that strong Aries needs an outlet some place where you can be spontaneous and let it all hang out and not worry about what people think, or where it fits in, or having to follow the rules, because Aries is the natural free spirit of being able to do what you want to do, and go your own way.

Now the Sun in Taurus does add to the earth function in the chart, and the need to work and be productive. The earth element is into, "Let's do a good job, let's add something to the world, let's make a living, let's handle it," and so on. It's very widely conjunct Vesta, another of the asteroids, which we call the **workaholic** asteroid. It's like a super Virgo asteroid, "Doing a good job," not for money, or glory, or anything like that, but a sense of, "I did that well. I did that in the manner it should be done," good craftsman type of ethic. So putting Vesta on the Sun, even though it is wide, is another count like the Capricorn rising, for the need to work, to be productive, to feel a sense of, "I'm contributing to the world." Some of that, however, can be done through the home and family because it is in the fourth house which is like the domestic scene. And that shows that some of the careful thoroughness is put into your role as wife/mother/homemaker kinds of things in the fourth. "I really want to do a **good job** about building a home, making a place that is important." And with Taurus, that looks comfortable, where people are comfortable, and very often some of the artistic feeling of this chart will come out there, making it beautiful as well, because Taurus is one of the signs that has a feeling for beauty, for things that are attractive.

L: That was very true when I was married.

M: And you really did it, didn't you?

L: That's very true. When I was married, homemaking/family/children was everything. I like to do a good job, of course, but there are only so many quilts you can make and pies you can bake...a real workaholic.

M: Well, as long as you can take off, because that Aries side is always going to say, "Let me loose, let me loose," and unless you have some channel, that is a lot of nervous energy, because all of fire needs to be doing something physically. Fire is naturally physically active, so a lot of stuff in Aries says you do need to do something with your body as well. You cannot just work all the time, nose to the grindstone kind of thing. So, it can be things like sports. It can also be active, artistic things, like dancing, figure skating, and so on, are very good where there is that grace and movement and beauty imparted through the physical action.

L: I try to work as hard as I play and play as hard as I work. I think that's good for everyone. Sports are a major part of my life right now.

M: Right.

L: It's a nice balance.

M: It sounds like you have a really good balance and that you are doing both, which is all that the chart is asking — that there be room for both.

And it is a bit of a question in terms of the work, because the Scorpio in the tenth, even though it is a Libran Midheaven, there is Scorpio there, with Chiron, one of the other asteroids there. Scorpio is very good at being compulsive and thorough and organized and detailed and handling everything. On the other hand, the day to day details of the work, you have Uranus in the sixth in Gemini, and Mercury, the ruler, is back in Aries which are very, very variety oriented, and also very intellectual. It is important that the work involve your **mind**. It should be with ideas and people because they're both air planets. So communication and something that involves working with your mind and the need for an intellectual challenge from the work.

Both Mercury and Uranus say that the work should involve some variety and change so that it is not the same thing over and over again, but there is a sense of being able to do something new and different. Changing of scene, changing of people, changing the details. And yet the Chiron in Scorpio and the Moon in Virgo say you are very able — and the Capricorn rising — to be thorough, to be organized, to be careful, to be detailed, to put everything in order and to have everything in its place. So, it's like the organizational skill is there, but the desire for work that involves a fair amount of variety and change is also important.

L: When I was married it was very difficult to apply all of that, so I was constantly trying to create something to do at home. I would get really frustrated with pent up nervous energy. So, at that time, I began breeding and showing horses again. A physical outlet.

M: Oh, that's great!

L: Well, you know, with two little kids, you can't go out too much. . . . It's only been in the last six years, that I've been able to apply both those things, and I've been **very** happy. I have my job, and I do a good job, and then I organize [confidential] for [confidential], and things like that. So, I feel really balanced now. [**Note:** This is the second or third time she has mentioned being balanced. Sounds like Juno (Libran) on the Ascendant, doesn't it? Also notice I begin to use some of her language, e.g., "balanced.']

M: That's wonderful! So you are really doing two jobs. One job is the more mundane organized job and then, when you do things like with the horses and with the [confidential] that there are a lot of different people and variety and changes of scene, which satisfies that need that both Uranus and Mercury are saying, "Stir things up, make it different, let's go off and do something new.'

L: Until I began organizing these [confidential], putting the whole thing together, I never really realized how self-satisfying it was. I was able to utilize all the qualities I didn't really believe I had! You don't know you have them until you do it. ..Being a housewife, I could just never cut it.

M: With Capricorn rising, you needed to work. Being a housewife is important, because anyone with Sun Taurus in the fourth, that's part of your ego needs. To be proud of your ability to create a home and to create a loving domestic environment. But there are enough of the career needs in your chart, that you couldn't **just** do that, you couldn't just stay at home. At the same time, it is typical with Capricorn rising and Virgo Moon, because there is some self-criticism, or at least some self-**doubt** there — for the person not to really believe they can do something until they have actually done it. And once they have done it, it's like: "Oh, wow, well, that wasn't so tough after all!'

L: That's what happened.

M: Right. So there is that real sense of once it's done, once it's physical, once it's real, once it's happened, then you trust it, and will keep on doing it. But that little bit of self doubt will say, 'Well, what if I don't make it this time?" But usually with people with Capricorn and Virgo like that, the more they do, the more they realize they can do. So it's a matter of first getting started, and then the first successes, they will just build on that and do more and more and more. And then the thing you have to watch out for is your tendency to feel like, "I should be responsible," and taking on **too** much.

L: That's what I did last year.

M: Yes, it gets into, "Now that I know I can do it, and I want it done right," there is a tendency to feel, "I have to do it to be sure it gets done right," or feel, "Someone won't do it as well or properly or just the way I want it." Then you do have to beware of taking too much on your own shoulders. Know when to delegate the authority, when to say, "I don't have to do it.'

L: I can't say no. Last year, I knew I was coming up against just that, and I told my friends, "No, I can't do that. I have too many projects right now, and I won't be able to do a good job." So, after three weeks of, "We need you!' 's I just went, "O.K." (Sigh)

And it was really difficult for me turning down people. I really wanted to help. These are my friends!

M: Right, and you don't want to let them down.

L: I did it anyway, but I really had a tremendous cast. They did all the work, and I was just like top man. I'd go around and ask, "Did you do your job?" But that's difficult for me. I'm a better Indian than I am a chief.

M: Well, you also do a lot of things well when you know what needs to be done and just do it. Go off and do it. Because that Aries quality is very good with that loner thing, although there is a lot of need for people [indicated by the Juno, seventh house, etc.] In terms of figuring things out, "If things need taking care of, I can go take care of them."

It is good practice for you in saying "No." because that is part of getting more in touch with the free side, the Aries side of your nature. With the Juno on the ascendant, like Libra, it constantly is saying, "What will other people think, will they like me, will they be happy, how can I please them, how can I keep them comfortable?" And it's the Aries that is able to say, "No, I don't have the space, I don't have the time," to assert your own needs: "Lynn has priority at this time," when it is really important.

L: I try. But it's usually, "Okay, okay, I'll do it!"

M: Yeah.

L: I do have that real problem that if you want it done right, do it yourself and I'm always. ...

M: Wanting to get your fingers in there. Sure, it's a natural response for somebody that is very competent, and it's a matter of reminding yourself that they can handle it, that it is their job, that it is not really your responsibility. And it does not sound like it is really that serious of a thing.

L: Uh huh.

M: You're basically pretty balanced.

L: Yeah. The paranoia was pretty bad when I was young. "My God, what will they think?" It got to the point where it was just ridiculous in my late teens.

M: It's fairly typical, particularly for women that have any of that type of concern for other people, and wanting to please them, to project some of the power when they are younger, because societal roles encourage that, and to worry about what other people think and constantly try to please. Usually with maturity, even given the sex roles, women do grow out of that and realize that is is not that big of a deal. "Suppose someone doesn't like me this time. So what?'

L: Women my age have a very big problem with that anyway: their role identity. But with me, I took it way to an extreme — much more so than most women my age. It was, "I will be exactly what he expects me to be." Therefore, I lost my whole identity. Of course, I didn't particularly like me anyway, so it was easy to give up. But due to my marriage. . .it was really beneficial, even though it was a difficult marriage. It was beneficial because I found out I could like me. And I didn't really give a damn what anyone else thought of me.

But it was very difficult, and I talk to a lot of women my age and older, and have just a lot of **empathy**. Not so much with younger women, they don't seem to have the same problems we did. But my friends, now that we're all in our thirties, we've got to get it **then**!

M: That's usually when the shift comes along, and people start balancing it out. But with both Saturn and Pluto in your partnership houses, your seventh and eighth, which are particularly marriage, long term committed type relationships where we live with them, where it's on a regular basis. Those are two of the power planets that are into dominance, control, being in charge, and so on. These are saying that this is the energy you were looking for in a relationship and if you weren't comfortable with your own strong dominant side, you would pick somebody who did it for you, who lived that out, who tried to say, "This is how you should be." That you would pick someone to tell you how to do it, rather than being in touch with your own strength and power yourself.

But, obviously, that doesn't last forever because nobody can continue to express something that is our own need. Eventually they get carried away, they do too much of it, then we come to terms with: "I want to do some of that myself." Then the relationship breaks down. Either both people change and the relationship changes, or one person changes, and the relationship stops because the other person is not willing to change in the same way. But it does say that your partnership relationships are where you are coming to terms with the power archetype, with the question of, "Who's in control; who's in charge; whose life is it anyway?" kind of questions. It is very important to you to be able to have that sense of you being an equal partner, you sharing the power in your relationships. The danger with Saturn and Pluto is either extreme. It is very common, particularly with women in our culture, to first go into the first extreme, where they pick a partner that is like a father figure who is in some way stronger, more controlling. They give away all the power, and they try to please the other person and live up to their expectations.

But it is unfortunately very common that a lot of women get out of that. They realize what they have done; they are not going to do that again, and then the big danger is going to the opposite extreme without realizing that they have gone to the opposite extreme. They feel, "I'm never going to do **that** again." so they pick somebody that is much weaker than them the next time around. Then they end up being the father figure, being the one who is responsible, to carry the whole load, who ends up being in charge of everything. They have the strength. They have gotten their power back into their own hands, but it is still not an equal relationship. The power is still an issue in the partnership.

L: That is basically what happened to my marriage. As I became a more competent individual myself, the marriage got worse and worse.

Then he ended up marrying another woman who was exactly like me when we got married. And he's very happy. She's still that way, and he's still that way, and **very** happy.

M: And if she never changes, they will stay happy.

L: I don't think she will. She's a very . . . subservient type of woman. . . . But, I do find that I'm attracted to men that are not as **tough** as me. And I just shy away from those relationships. Because, I can get real pushy, and if I get away with it, I just get worse. . . . Therefore, I don't have any relationships. (Laughs)

M: Well, that can be an interim possibility, certainly, and yet relationships are very important to you. Anybody with Juno on their Ascendant, it's important to have a long term relationship, and to **some** extent, friends can substitute for that and things like what you are doing, organizing groups and social things to be together, and working with people can be very helpful where you get some of your closeness needs met through the job and associations.

At the same time, with Saturn being a ruler of your Ascendant and in the seventh, having a partnership relationship is an important part of your identity and something that you really **do** want. You want to share that one to one equality with other people. . . . So, if you can figure out a way to make more of a place for it in your life. . . .

All of these things are only a priority if we decide to make them. Like the person that says, "I really want to get married." If they really wanted to get married, they would be married, because they would have made it an absolute priority. Yet, the chart suggests that that is something important to you, that you would like to have. But it is necessary to pick somebody as strong as you are. The attraction is to a relationship where the power is an issue, and that the only way it is going to be an equal partnership is if you are both very strong people, because you're a strong person. So it has to be somebody that is as strong and powerful as you are. And anybody that has Capricorn rising and a lot of Aries as you is **pretty** strong!

L: I have been single for ten years, and never had a close relationship. I do substitute a lot. My children are. . .someone with whom I can express love and affection. . .and my friends. Between the combination of my friends and my kids, I figure I've come up with one man!

I run with a tremendously large group of people, and am a big star with them, the [confidential] and all. And I know it's just a big substitute. Because, I know, I couldn't, I can't **deal** with relationships. (Voice gets tense)

That's my problem that I admit, and will not deal with. I go, "Well, you sit over here for awhile, and I'll get to you when I have to."

M: And if it is not bothering you in any major kind of sense, you don't have to deal with it yet. When the issues are really fundamental, our psyche forces us to face them one way or another.

So, if you are not having any major problems with it, I think you're getting enough substitutions from other things. Your chart does say it is important to have a close, committed relationship, but if you have found that your friends and children have substituted enough, then it is not a problem.

It may be that when your children get older and leave home, then it may become important enough to you to do something about it at that time. [**Note:** This was a decision point. I could have pushed harder for ways in which she might not be facing this issue. There was obviously discomfort in her voice and body language. I chose to defuse the issue. Other options were available.]

L: Well, that's one of my other, very **reasonable** excuses, that it is very difficult to start a relationship when you have teenaged kids. . . I enjoy them and they enjoy me. . . . And it's only a matter of time until it all catches up to me, anyway. You can only **postpone** things for so long. [We postponed the issue until later in the session.] . . . Before they manifest in some other way. . . . But I figure I'll postpone it a little longer. (Laughs)

M (Laughs): Yeah, as long as you're not having any serious problems around it, I wouldn't worry about it. Because you are aware of it, it is not like you are pushing it into your unconscious or not working at it. When the time is a little more appropriate, I think you will find a way to do something about it.

L: I can't understand why the men that I 'm very attracted to are never attracted to me, and the men that are attracted to me, I'm not attracted to. For instance, I'll be attracted to someone and he won't to me, but we will become good friends. And my impression is that a lot of these men are very weak. I'll think they're strong at first, but after some time, maybe a year, I'll realize that they are not as strong as I thought, and I'm much better off! I haven't quite figured that one out. . . .

[I could have pursued the freedom closeness issue. If we always pick people who are not interested in us, we retain our freedom. Power was a possible issue. (Who's in control; whose choice will be the decisive one?) Dad was another issue. I went with Dad.]

M: How did you feel about your father when you were growing up?

L: That he's a jerk, but I love him! He's a very immature, childish man, but **heart**! He'd do anything for his kids. He's a Virgo: **horribly** jealous of my mother, that kind of thing. A workaholic, but he'd give us kids the shirt off his back. If it was his last dollar, he'd give it to us.

But at the same time, he was very childish. And I love him anyway. I don't like him so much, but I really love him. . . .

My sister and brother didn't have much trouble with him. I — we had a real poor home life, so I kind of detached myself very young, from the whole thing. Mom and the sister were just real close, and Dad and the brother were real close and I was the youngest. . . .

M: Sounds like you were the odd person out.

L: Yeah, and I just went. . . I swallowed myself up in my horses. That became my family, so to speak. I still am quite detached from my whole family. I love them, but they're just there.

[Vesta in the fourth can be feelings of alienation in home environment, among other possibilities.]

M: The reason I asked is that very often with Saturn in the seventh, the relationship with the father in some way is a key to later love relationships.

L: He did influence me a lot, because he was a liar. He messed around with anything that moved. But he, to this day, would **swear** that he never, ever, touched another woman. It's baloney. My mom and I have read his diary. We know. Everybody knew, but he was actually a pathological liar. He actually believed it.

And I know that had a tremendous influence on me, because I **detest** cheating of that kind. And lying. I mean honesty, I don't care if it hurts; they have to be honest! So that had a very positive effect on me [encouraging honesty].

I always kind of felt sorry for him.

M: So in some ways you did see him as fairly weak also?

L: Yeah, well, he is. . . . I mean, a **hard** worker, still is: a triple Virgo I think . . . but, you know it's hard to say because it's your father, but I always felt so sorry for him, because he could never put it together.

M: Well, it's something that when you do want to get into the partnership thing, you might think about your feelings about him because usually with that Saturn placement, the person in some way is playing out unfinished business with the father in their later partnerships. It's like a role model relationship. They face the same kinds of questions in the partnership as they had with their father. So, whether that might be a key to use. . . . You know, finding out that these other men end up being weak, where you have to take care of them, feel sorry for them, at some level, like your father.

I don't know if the honesty thing fits in there or not. Certainly it is very important to you personally with Aries in the third. Aries is terribly forthright, tell it like it is particularly with Mercury there. The whole communication style is blunt, honest and to the point. Or, it's like: "That's it; there's no reason to tell it any other way."

But it just may be that there is something that you can work through. Not necessarily with father *per se*, but it's like your feelings about that early living situation and early relationship sometimes continue to influence present relationships.

L: Well, that really makes sense because my ex-husband wasn't **anything** like what my father was at all, not remotely like him.

M: So you tried to get the exact opposite.

L: Yeah. But, well, he did lie to me. He did play around. . . . Not as blatantly, not to the same extent. . . . He's Sagittarian. Moon in Aquarius and Libra rising. That's just the way he was — still is. Good man, you know. He only lied to me because he didn't want to tell me he was fooling around. But it was an **extremely** important issue in my marriage. I mean, he could have done **anything**, but that! Because it went back to what my dad was. At that time, I was sure that anyone I became involved with was sure to fool around and would not be honest, and inevitably, that's exactly what happened.

M: It seems to be a truism in life that when we feel really, really strongly about an issue, when we make an absolute, we are really in danger of getting disappointed. If we make anything into: "This is the most important thing, it **has** to be this way!" then the odds are something is going to go wrong.

L: Well, that's the main reason I avoid relationships.

M: Yeah. If it is still really, really imperative to you that there be that kind of faithfulness, there is a good chance that you would end up disappointed.

L: I don't know if I'm pessimistic or that untrusting or what. Because I just sort of figure that it's going to happen, regardless of the person, over a **long**-term relationship — it's kind of a problem that rises its head. **honesty** is the big thing. **absolute** honesty.

M: How would you feel if they had an affair, but told you about it?

L: Better. My ex-husband was having an affair at the end of our relationship, and I knew what was happening. We talked about it right out front, and I told him, "If you're going to continue in this relationship, just tell me, and don't do it on my time." And we tried to work with it. But all during that time, he continued his affair, while telling me he wasn't. So that was even more disillusioning — to find out we couldn't even work it out honestly — when I was **prepared** to handle it.

It is a very big issue, and that's basically why I don't get involved with **anybody** is that fear. It's really tremendous, so I just figure, "I can deal with that someday."

M: Yeah, eventually you will have to deal with it. The fear and anxiety thing is typical with the Saturn which says, "If I keep far enough away, I won't get hurt; I won't be disappointed; I won't be let down." That's why some books associate Saturn in the seventh with never getting married. It's the person who chooses the option of: "This is my way of remaining safe, of not being disappointed, of not getting something I won't like." But there are all sorts of other ways to handle it! The basic thing that Saturn is saying is: "Pick someone who is equally responsible, equally strong as you so that you can each trust and accept one another."

The other thing about the honesty issue is that most of us have some mixture; very few of us are totally one way. It is like, if we have something in our nature, we have the opposite there, at least in a small potential kernel. So even though you are really, really strongly identified with being forthright and honest and that's the only way to be, there is a little small part of your nature that can consider the white lie, that there are times when it's appropriate, and to save somebody's feelings, and so on and so forth.

L: Uh huh.

M: So, we all have some of both sides. And it's typical when we deny one part in ourselves really really strongly by identifying with one part, like the honesty, to unconsciously attract other people who are doing the opposite.

So that's why I feel that if you stay really, really strongly identified with the honesty and that's the most important thing — because the psyche tends to balance out and create a wholeness there — you will tend to attract people who are doing the other extreme. Which is the white lie, the dishonesty, and so on.

So, if you can find ways to moderate your position a little bit... Find and focus on, "Okay, there are some times when it's okay to not tell the whole truth or to tone something down, or to be tactful." And, as you moderate your position, it is more likely that you will get involved with and attract people that are more moderate in their position. Because when we are at one extreme, we tend to attract unconsciously people at the opposite extreme.

L: I do find more introverted type people are attracted to me and me to them. [She is changing the frame of reference slightly. We have shifted from the honesty/dishonesty (and tact) polarity to the introversion/extroversion polarity.]

M: Because you are exactly what they are looking for. You do all the fun and lively things that they won't let themselves do, so you are living out the fun and the wittiness and charm and charisma that they would like to do, but are insecure about. And they are living out the inward introspection that has attraction for you, but right now you're doing the social and outward side.

L: Well, I stay away from them too! As soon as I find myself becoming attracted, I just immediately go, "Come on, Lynn, forget it. This is ridiculous!"

M: Right now, that's not what you need in your life. You need to stay active. This is a very lively, active chart. That's part of what makes you a fun person to be around, because you're naturally someone who is going to stir things up and keep things active and keep things happening.

L: That's for sure.

M: People will never be bored around you! (Laughs)

L: And I'll create something outrageous if things are going slow.

I mean, I apparently do it in a . . . good way, in a productive way, because everyone reacts pleasantly. I haven't been hit in the mouth yet! (Laughs)

M (Laughs): No, I think you have enough sense of social mores, and values to do it with consideration for other people, but there is that natural sense of fun and the need for excitement which is very strong in your chart.

L: I am starting to become more attractive to people that are more like me: just as energetic, just as outgoing, and a lot of fun.

M: Good.

L: I don't want to be in competition with anybody, but I know better than to get involved with someone who is not as active as me. I mean, that did seem to be the case of opposites, but **too** opposite. I mean, I wouldn't go up to a lady and tell her, "Wow, what an ugly dress." I'd say, "What a **beautiful** dress." But I do take my honesty very seriously, to the point where it keeps me single and unattached. I don't even date. If I want to go out, I just call up my "buddies" and we can go out.

M: Yeah. Well, I think the main thing is whether it works for you. And if it works for you, that's fine.

L: Well, I don't think it's very healthy, but it has been working so far. But someday, I know I'll have to deal with it properly.

M: Yeah, yeah. . . . It will come, I'm sure, eventually. . . . [I edited out some material concerning her children here.]

L: . . . [Talking about her children] They both get almost straight A's with practically no effort and I had to really work at it.

M: I suspect that having to work hard may have been because you were not very secure in your self-image at that time. The chart suggests you are very bright, and I think that perhaps when you were younger you didn't give yourself enough credit and you were afraid. And possibly the anxiety made it more difficult for you to realize how much you knew. I bet if you, like took training for your job or other things right now, you would pick up things pretty fast.

L: I do find that. But in school . . . I hated school.

M: Yes, the Aries in you got bored. It was too routine and it was too much other people telling you what to do.

L:: I would study. I'd do my homework, but I couldn't concentrate.

M: Aries in the third learns best from doing it yourself and on your own and does not do so well in a structured environment. School is not a good place for you to learn. Things that you can pick up on your own, or talk with people, like a private tutoring situation or something that is very open and flexible is ideal and particularly experiential kinds of things where you can **do** it. Learn by doing is the best. But there is a lot of really high intelligence in your chart, so I think that was just the situation you were in at that time.

L: I definitely was not what you would call a model child. I hated school. (Laughs) They hated me too.

M (Laughs): I'm sure you were not an easy child to deal with in that respect.

L: Oh, I was awful. (Laughs)

M (Laughs): Well, it's good for teachers to be shaken up occasionally, too. . . . And there is also that sense of the nodes across Gemini/Sag as the perpetual student: the person who is learning all the time, whether they're in school or not. The person who has an open and curious mind and is always exploring other ideas and new things, and asking "How does that work, what's going on?" That sense of real insatiable curiosity and wanting to know more is like an ongoing part of your chart. You are always going to be learning things throughout your life. It's also a good combination for constant travel. The person who wants to expand the horizons physically as well as mentally, always, "What's over the next hill? Where will that be?" That is a part of learning for you — travelling and seeing other places and reading other people and so on.

L: I travel constantly. If I stay in town for more than two weeks, I get nervous.

M: And that satisfies a lot of the need for activity too, because you need to be active in doing things with this kind of a chart and not too settled. Particularly if you have a somewhat settled job, it is all the more important that you satisfy that restless side of your nature through other kinds of things.

L: If I don't have anything going, I will go someplace close just for the afternoon.

M: Yes, that's typical.

L: [Asks about the nodes. Then gets into children again. From children we went to current patterns.]

M: [After a short description of the theory of secondary progression and transits, we went into the patterns.] You have had Venus going over Vesta, and that is a typical placement for this feeling of alienation in personal relationships, which you have been doing for about ten years. Now, the aspect has not been there that long. It's been there for about the last year, maybe a year and a half. It's going to be out of orb in another half year to a year. It's going, maybe about ¾ of a year, because it's going fairly fast. Venus being a key to the love relationships and Vesta the workaholic asteroid operates like Virgo. Very often there is a sense of critical assessment and judgment, looking for the flaws. There is often a feeling of personal alienation where Vesta is involved with emotional parts of life. It is very good in the work area, where doing a good job and focusing and so on. In the personal relationship area, it tends to be this attitude of looking for the flaws, "What could go wrong here and what could be the problem? . . .

So I think that [feeling] has added to your reluctance to be involved in any kind of relationship. Like saying, "Well, there are all these possible problems and possible flaws," you could make it difficult. So I think that that aspect, which is going to be out of orb in about 3/4 of a year, leaving is one of the possibilities of things opening up a bit more in that area, of you being more willing to consider, "Well, maybe it wouldn't be so bad, maybe under certain circumstances. . . ."

L: Would it make me more critical of things in general?

M: Particularly of people that you were thinking about getting close to, but people in general — the tendency to be aware of the flaws, and mistakes, the shortcomings.

L: My attitude for the past several months has been very negative, which isn't like me.

M: You're naturally an optimist. . . .

L: If somebody messes up, I think, "It figures!" which isn't my natural thought, and it is really starting to bother me.

M: I think that has been part of this aspect and it is going to be out of orb soon. But it is that real critical judgment side of you looking at things and saying, "Well, okay, where are all the mistakes and problems and so on?" And kind of expecting the worse.

L: I don't like it at all.

M: Venus will be out of orb in about 3/4 of a year. In the meantime, just being aware of it, you do not have to fall into it, even if you feel that way. You can make allowances.

L: Well, I'll have some of these thoughts and I'll think, "Oh, my God, what's the matter with me." This has gone on for quite a while now. So it's a matter of getting my act together and kind of thinking properly. You know, erase the bad thoughts and put in the good ones.

M: Yes, reprogram it. [I wish now I had addressed her put downs of herself here.]

[We went into the progressed Moon on the Ascendant and discussed issues with her children. They may be leaving home with that aspect. Or she may travel.]

[We discussed the need for more change with Mercury on the

Descendant and transiting Uranus conjunct and opposing the nodes of the Moon: possibly more travel, and/or studies — mental stimulation.]

M: Another key to your current feeling critical, particularly at work is transiting Saturn going over your midheaven. It's right on your midheaven, which is the key to career and status and reputation — what you do in the world. And because it's retrograde, it's moving fairly slowly, so it inches up a bit and then inches back a bit and goes over again. It's been there for a couple of months and will be going back and forth into the fall.

That is an increased sense of responsibility, you know: "Let's do it right," and, "Other people are going to blow it." and that whole feeling of judgment, and wanting things to be done the **right** way. The main thing is just to be realistic with a strong Saturn, because you can get into being too judgmental with it. The two main dangers are taking on too much, on your own shoulders. "I have to do it, nobody else can do it right. I'd better take care of it." Which is more a problem with your chart. The other danger is where some people who are under a Saturn aspect will say, "I can't do it. I'd just fail or fall short." So they give up. With your kind of chart, there is the natural confidence in your ability to do something. It's more of saying, "Okay, I'll take care of it; I'll do it; I'll do everything that needs to be done." And be overly responsible and carrying too much of that load.

But particularly be aware that there is a tendency, and it's likely to continue for a few more months, and be able to say, "Okay, that's not my job; that's not my responsibility; I don't have to worry about that."

If we handle the [symbolism of the] Saturn aspect, it is a very good time for making strides in your career, in terms of your efforts being recognized. Getting some compensation for your hard work and efforts that you have put in, and so on, but you should be aware of the dangers of taking too much on. You know, in terms of . . . to let go of it. Saying, "Okay, enough is enough already," and moving on from here.

L: I am always taking on too much, particularly now.

M: It's very easy to do, particularly since that Saturn is the key to your ascendant, to say, "Okay. I'll do it!"

L: That happened last October when I was talked into running the [*confidential*] and I was already in charge of [*confidential*] beginning in November. It was too much, especially when I had just gotten out of the hospital. I know they are going to want me to do it again this year, and I have a desire to, but I've already started making plans of how to handle it through assistants rather than doing it myself.

M: Good!

L: I was so saturated by the second [*confidential*], I didn't know if it was them or me who was irritable. I've run these [*confidential*] for three years, but this last year everybody seemed to be complaining and bitching about the smallest things. I had 350 people ask me some of the dumbest questions- they could have asked someone else.

M: It was probably a combination of both — and also your increased sense of responsibility would draw those people to you. Because you would be feeling that it was your responsibility, so the people would sense that and intuitively pick you to complain to rather than someone else. If you were feeling the sense of "I'm in charge; I'm running it; I'm responsible," what happens then is people would be more likely to seek you out to complain to and tell you, "This is what's wrong."

L: That's what happened.

M: The more you can let up your own feelings of responsibility and having to worry about everything and make sure it all goes right, the more that will be distributed among a variety of people. It may be you got more than your share of the bitches because of your extra share of responsibilities.

L: I started doing this because it was such a good program and I wanted everyone to have a good time, but these last two times, I felt more like a hostess and a baby-sitter.

M: Taking care of everything and making them all happy and pleasing them. . . .

L: Never again.

M: Somehow you won't do it next time!

L: No, I won't.

[I mentioned a number of aspects stressing restlessness, which had to be integrated with the Saturnian need for accomplishment and practicality, including taking reasonable care of ourselves, warning that one possible outcome of trying to do too much is ill health, when the body forces us to slow down.

We also discussed possible career options in terms of integrating her flair for organization with her needs for variety and stimulation. The travel business is one real possibility.

Then I asked if she had any questions.]

L: Well, the last six months have just been ridiculous! (Frustrated tone of voice) Seven years ago it was the same thing: **nothing** went right. Financial problems, physical problems, to the point where — you just get to a point where you're just **saturated**.

And, I don't know, somewhere I got the idea, in the back of my head, that after the first of the year, all this stuff was going to be fine. And, the first of the year, the kids blew up the television; they blew up the clutch I'd just finished putting in — a $500 brake job on the van $1000 dollars — I had a mastectomy last July — I went into the hospital in October to be rebuilt and the insurance company hit me with a $1000 dollar bill telling me it was cosmetic surgery! I'm going, "Just hold it! I've decided after the first of the year, I'm not going to have these problems anymore. My battle with the obstacles is done." It was harder to handle because I had somewhere in the back of my mind that this was all going to quit at the first of the year. So I thought, "I must be sitting on some kind of a nasty influence! And I want to find out when it's going to leave!'

M: Well, I think part of that is the real heavy responsibility. If the kids messed up the clutch, were they careless? Is it something they could have avoided?

L: They had a party and one of the kids poured a drink down my television and it blew up!

M: And who's paying for it?

L: They are!

M: Good!

L: I mean, I paid for it but I'm not giving them any allowance until it's paid for.

M: And the clutch in the car?

L: The clutch just blew and Jason (her son) fixed it for me. He didn't have a very good summer either. . . .[details]

[List of things breaking down and financial difficulties.]
It was a constant besiege of **problems**. . . . Plus there were all these projects that I had already gotten myself into. I got out of the hospital and went down and ran this [*confidential*] show. As soon as I finished that, I had to put this camp together, which was immediately followed with another one. And I didn't have any money. It was just kind of on and on and on. . . .

M: I think part of it is the real heavy sense of responsibility and you taking care of everything. I personally believe that there are emotional roots with illness, that there is an emotional component as well as a physical component.

In terms of a mastectomy, that is related to the Cancerian quality which is our ability to nurture and be nurtured. It really sounds like right now in your life, you're the one who is being responsible. You're the one who is taking care of things, and there isn't anyone around that really nurtures you. There isn't anybody that you feel safe to lean on and depend on and be like a little girl. And that is part of the Cancerian need, to be like a child where somebody just takes care of us and we don't have to do anything. That's a part of life too.

And it sounds like in your life right now, the way you have structured it, you don't have a partner that can do that for you, that you can lean on sometimes. And the way things are with your kids right now, you don't really get that from them; they're not supportive in that way because they are into asserting their independence and finding their own lives and so on.

I think part of it was your body really crying out, you know, "Who is going to take care of me? Who is going to nurture me? Who is going to nourish me?" and the stress finally just piled up in the sense that you had all these responsibilities, all these things that you were supposed to be doing and it was all on you.

I think it is even more imperative that you really, really be careful about what you take responsibility for. And look around among your friends. Is there anybody you would feel comfortable, even in a little way, depending on, leaning on?

The way to change a long-term patterns is not to make any big shifts, because they won't last. If we try to make a major shift, usually we just flip. You know, we just flip to the other extreme, and then we flip back. But if you can make little, small changes, like asking for a tiny favor that you wouldn't normally ask for. Lean on them a little bit more than you normally would. Let the other person do a little bit more for you, accept that favor that you normally don't accept. Those kinds of little things to be more the receiving person, and not always be the person who is putting out, who is doing, who is organizing, who is taking care of, who is being the star.

It is hard because again that Capricorn rising says, "I have to be strong, I have to do it myself." So, it's saying [instead]: "I will let other people do some of it for me," and really allowing that. Which would be a hard emotional shift to make, and part of that does go back to your early environment in the sense that you didn't really receive that kind of support, that kind of nurturing and taking care of when you were little. So, it's harder to trust now that other people would be willing to do it because you don't have an early environment to go back to and say, "Well, it's happened before."

So it's like rewriting your history in that sense. "Okay, I didn't get it from my family, but that doesn't mean I can't get it from other people now." It doesn't have to be the same kind of thing. Being willing to risk the dependency, being willing to risk the vulnerability, because it is vulnerable to lean on other people, to depend on somebody. And that is why I say it's real important, if you are going to make the change, to start out very, very small, because it would be a huge threat to all of a sudden bring somebody into your life, "Okay, I'm going to be dependent!" Of course, you wouldn't. But if you can do it in some little ways — and be real careful of those responsibilities that you take on your shoulders.

L: Because when I found out I had cancer, that was — people just came unglued. I couldn't believe the reactions. And that was very, very difficult because of all the love that was sent to me, and I'm sitting over here with my — with my...my affection is done in jest. And there was this tremendous **outpouring** of letters and cards and flowers and people crying, and I'm going, "**Hey**! I'm okay. I'm **all right**. Don't cry."

It was very difficult for me because of the **affection** that I was getting. I'm not used to — I'm used to keeping affection at arms length.

And I'm thinking, "Oh, my God, all these people really care about you and you've let so many times go by when you didn't tell them how much you cared too."

That was basically the hard part of it — not the cancer. It was their reaction.

M: At the same time, we do everything for a reason, so on some level there was a part of you that wanted the illness so that you would get that — be taken care of — from other people. [I missed an opportunity to emphasize that she was still depriving herself of that nurturing — reassuring her friends, instead of accepting their love and support and caring for her.]

L: That's what I thought too. It was some way to get me to break loose on an affectionate level. Because basically I shouldn't have had cancer — not by the stats. I knew that just because the physical cancer was cured, there was something wrong spiritually. So, after all the surgery and the reconstruction and everything was cleared up, I had a physical reading from a really good man in Taos. He is pretty much like Cayce. So I asked the question of what the karmic issue was. Cancer is one thing that has a lot more to it. And his answer was deprivation. I still haven't quite figured that one out. It seems too simple.

M: And I don't think it's ever just one thing, just one reason. In other words, I do think you were putting a lot of physical and emotional stress on your body, literally, by doing all of those things, because stress is hard on your body. By having all those responsibilities, all the things you had to take care of, you knew you were trying to handle, and there was a sense of "Gee, can I do it all? Can I keep it all together?"

And at the same time, I think one of the reasons was that a part of you **does** feel deprived; a part of your being that needs somebody to nurture, somebody to lean on; that needs to express that dependence which wasn't being met. That side of your nature wasn't being satisfied, so it was feeling deprived. And this is one way to get some of that satisfaction.

Because, that part of your nature, that little girl, is the hardest to integrate with all your Aries and Capricorn rising. Because the Aries says, "I don't need anybody," and the Capricorn rising says, "I can do it myself." And so does the Moon in Virgo. So that little girl side is easy to push down into the unconscious, where you are not really in touch with it. So, you do the "I don't need anyone; I can take care of myself," and so on.

And the longer we sit on a part of our own nature, the more it works from underground and illness is one underground way of doing it.

L: Yeah. Everybody was pretty surprised when I got cancer. But I thought, "Somebody is trying to tell me something." And I've got to figure out the answer because I'll just get it again — in three or four years. I'll have **bone** cancer or something.

M: If we don't change, **If** we continue to do it in the same serious degree, because we have to have been doing it either very very **seriously** or for a long time, to get something as serious as cancer.

L: Yeah. Well, it's been ten years. I **know** it's because of the way I feel about personal relationships. I've just always put it off as long as I could and figured someday I'd have to deal with it.

M: Well, if you got cancer, I'd say it's time to deal with it. [I wish I'd mixed in a little more sympathy here.]

L: Well, medically I'm cured, but spiritually I'm not, therefore I'm not cured at all.

M: Yes, if the emotional habit patterns are still there, then you've got to do something about it.

L: Well, there's certain aspects — I mean I understand it all — but there's certain aspects I don't understand; I guess I don't want to understand yet, but there's certain key things missing within that knowledge that keep me from fully understanding and acting on it.

M: Do you have any pets or plants that you take care of?

L: I have lots of plants, but my last pet had to be put to sleep last summer and that's the **last** pet I'm going to have!

M: How long was it between when you put your pet to sleep and when you found out about the cancer?

L: Months after. It was after I got out of the hospital the second time, in October after the reconstruction. I loved that old dog.

M: Because that's another way to meet some of those needs for closeness. Those nurturance and dependency needs. Having a pet that is dependent on you still could satisfy some of that need for real intense closeness where there is that little dog that really cares about you, and you're kind of the center of their universe kind of thing. Some people can get some of those feelings of satisfaction from plants, but there is not near the emotional component.

L: I don't get it from plants. I used to breed horses and that was life and breath...and then I finally just sold all of them. And then Linda (her daughter) wanted a dog and I said, "**No**! When...[her dog] is gone, that's the last pet I'm going to have."

But yet I did have — I was more fond of my animals than I was of people. I've really enjoyed them — a lot of **real** communication...I still miss my mare; I go see her once in a while.

But...it's just another thing to be responsible for if I am traveling a lot.

[The freedom-closeness struggle comes even with pets: wanting the closeness, but not wanting to be tied down.]

M: Yeah, it is hard when you travel. You might think about how you can satisfy those needs in some other ways that would fit into your life, because there is obviously a part of your nature that needs to be taking care of a pet or having someone that you can lean on and cry on their shoulders sometimes, and let them do things for you and be there and be warm and affectionate and caring.

L: **That's** what I have to work on because I haven't ever been able to do that. When I first got married that was **everything**: to be **in love**! But it was just a wash. After so many years with the constant rejection of any kind of affection, it just aggravated the whole problem.

M: So you decided, "Well, I'm never going to get it, so I'll give up," on some level.

L: Yeah. "Adios, buddy! I can handle it myself!" kind of attitude.

M: Which is understandable and a large part of your nature doesn't need it. But, there is a part that very much needs that closeness, that attachment, that commitment and that's what you have to deal with. How are you going to incorporate some of it, which is like the first part of lie, you went overboard and you gave away all your power by needing love so much, and now you've gone overboard the other way by saying, "Well, I don't need it at all." ...

[She brought up several issues which we discussed in turn: the hope that she would open more up to relationships after her kids left home (another delaying tactic); the concern that getting too close to her friends would ruin the friendships (seeing the situation as polarized — where the closeness would be suffocating, rather than having some freedom and some closeness); the contributions of her background: an emotionally nonsupportive home environment, a husband she felt rejected by. She also recalled a similar situation years before when she had received a lot of support from friends.]

L: And it happened, oh years before, when I was miserable, at the bottom of the pit and all my friends were **right there** and I promised myself: "I'll never **ever** take advantage of my friends again and not express to them that I do care for them as being my **friends**.

And found myself doing exactly the same thing. There I sat last summer, going, "Oh, God! I did it again!"

M: Well, we all do; we repeat patterns, and that's how we come to recognize them. At some point, we say, "Gee, that looks familiar!"

L: Basically everything we have talked about just now is exactly what I needed to hear out loud. The only thing that is driving me absolutely crazy is my financial problems. I can . . . Iimagine I could still get to Canada if I really wanted to. I'm afraid to leave the kids all alone in the house again. They would probably burn it down! (Laughs) [Still taking all the responsibility.]

M: That's again where you have to look at the Saturn principle and be very realistic about what are your options, using the money that you do or don't have, what can you realistically expect to do? And also in terms of the kids. If they really are responsible for the television then they have to pay for it, and if they act in irresponsible ways, they have to take the consequences. I think you are basically handling it.

[Another short discussion of various problems and her feelings of irritation with people, which I reassured her were natural and quite understandable under the circumstances. I encouraged her to continue expressing her anger, not bottling it up.]

M: . . . It is very frustrating to have all these things go wrong and feel like you have to take care of it all. It is good that Jason would do some of the car work. It would be nice to have other people that would at least support emotionally, even if nobody else is going to step in financially to help out. The sense of, "I don't have to carry the whole load, somebody else can sometimes do something and contribute, be there for me to cry on their shoulder." That's important.

L: Probably would be a good idea. I tend to shut everybody out, go home and when no one is there, I talk to myself, all about it, pat myself on the back and say, "I'm all done; now let's go!'

M: It sounds like you know yourself pretty well, and it's just a matter of doing it. Any change is hard, but you certainly have the insight and the self-discipline to be able to do it because it does take work and you have the willingness to hang in there and do what needs to be done!

L: If I just get the courage to try it!

One thing that I heard, isn't there one particular planet that is considered the ruling planet of the chart. . .?

[From here, we went into some specifically astrological questions, about general astrology and her chart in particular. A friend had interpreted her chart years before and she had some questions regarding that. We also got into activities where I live, including a delineation group she may begin attending. We wound down into social chitchat, and I turned off the tape.]

As she left, my parting words were asking her to have a good time, and let go of some of her responsibilities.

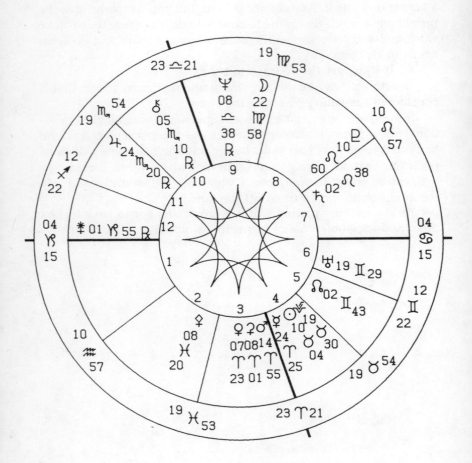

LYNN
4 30 1947 22h46m 0s PST
PLACIDUS 34N 3 118W15

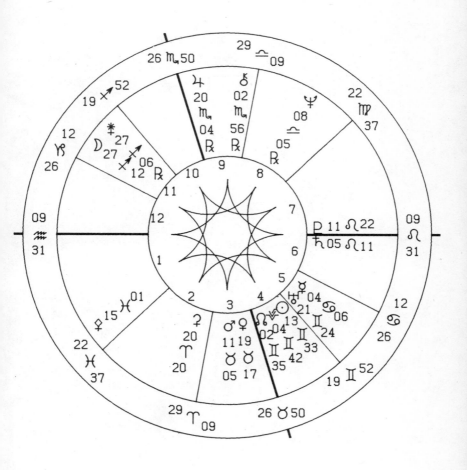

PROGRESSD TO FEB 4 1982

LYNN

4 30 1947 22h46m 0s PST
PLACIDUS 34N 3 118W15

Bibliography

1. Assagioli, Roberto, M.D., *Psychosynthesis* (New York: The Viking Press, 1965).
2. Bandler, Richard and John Grinder, *Patterns of the Hypnotic Techniques of Milton H. Erickson, M.D. Vol. I* (Cupertino, California: Meta Publications, 1975).
3. Bandler, Richard and John Grinder, *The Structure of Magic, Vol. I* (Palo Alto, California: Science and Behavior Books, Inc., 1975).
4. Bandler, Richard and John Grinder, *The Structure of Magic, Vol. II* (Palo Alto, California: Science and Behavior Books, Inc., 1976).
5. Bergin, A.E., "Some Implications of Psychotherapy Research for Therapeutic Practice," *Journal of Abnormal Psychology* 71:235-246 (1966).
6. Bergin, A.E., "The Deterioration Effect: a Reply to Braucht," *Journal of Abnormal Psychology* 75:300-302 (1970).
7. Berne, Eric, *Games People Play* (New York: Ballantine 1973).
8. Blatner, Howard A., M.D., *Acting In; Practical Applications of Psychodramatic Methods* (New York: Springer Publishing Co., Inc., 1973).
9. Broverman, Inge K. et al., "Sex Role Stereotypes: A Current Appraisal," *Journal of Social Issues*, 28:2 (1972) pp. 59-78.
10. Bruner, Jerome and Leo Postman, "On the Perception of Incongruity: A Paradigm," *Journal of Personality* XVIII:206-223 (1949).
11. Bryant, Dorothy, *The Kin of Ata* (New York: Random House, 1971).

12. Cameron-Bandler, Leslie, *They Lived Happily Ever After* (Cupertino, California: Meta Publications, 1978).

13. Capra, Fritjof, *The Tao of Physics* (Berkeley, California: Shambala, 1975).

14. Capra, Fritjof, "The Turning Point: A New Vision of Reality," *New Age*, 7:7 (February 1982) pp. 28-31; 53.

15. Carkhuff, Robert and Bernard Berenson, *Beyond Counseling and Therapy* (New York: Holt, Rinehart and Winston, Inc., 1967).

16. Cassirer, Ernst, *The Logic of the Humanities* (New York: Harper and Brothers, 1946).

17. Collingwood T.R. and I. Renz, "The Effects of Client Confrontations Upon Levels of Immediacy Offered by High and Low Functioning Counselors," *Journal of Clinical Psychology* 25:221-226 (1969).

18. Corsini, Raymond J., Editor, *Current Psychotherapies* (Itasca, Illinois: Peacock Publishing, 1977).

19. Cousins, Norman, *Anatomy of an Illness* (Boston: G.K.Hall, 1980).

20. Dobyns, Zipporah, *Finding the Person in the Horoscope* (Los Angeles: Tia Publications, 1973).

21. Ellis, Albert Ph.D. and Robert A. Harper Ph.D., *A New Guide to Rational Living* (North Hollywood, California: Wilshire Book Company, 1977).

22. *Encyclopaedia Britannica, Macropaedia* (Chicago, Illinois: Helen Hemingway Benton Publisher, 1975) Vol. 7, 15th Edition.

23. Erikson, Erik H., *Childhood and Society* (New York: W.W. Norton and Co., Inc., 1963).

24. Fabry, Joseph, et al., Editors, *Logotherapy in Action* (New York: Jason Aronson, 1979).

25. Fabry, Joseph B., *The Pursuit of Meaning* (San Francisco: Harper and Row, publishers, 1980).

26. Farrelly, Frank and Jeff Brandsma, *Provocative Therapy* (San Francisco, California: Shields Publishing Co., Inc., 1974).

27. Ferguson, Marilyn, *The Aquarian Conspiracy; Personal and Social Transformation in the 1980's* (Los Angeles: J.P. Tarcher, Inc., 1980).

28. Foulds, M.L., "Self Actualization and the Communication of Facilitative Conditions During Counseling," *Counseling Psychologist* 16:132-136 (1969).

29. Frank, Jerome, *Persuasion and Healing; a Comparative Study of Psychotherapy* (New York: Schocken, 1973).

30. Ginsberg, Harry, personal communication.

31. Ginsburg, Herbert and Sylvia Opper, *Piaget's Theory of Intellectual Development; An Introduction* (Englewood Cliffs, N.J.: Prentice-Hall, Inc., 1969).

32. Goleman, Daniel "Deadline for Change: Therapy in the Age of Reaganomics," *Psychology Today* 15:8 (August 1981) pp. 60-69.

33. Goulding, Robert M.D. and Mary McClure M.S.W., *The Power Is In The Patient* (San Francisco: TA Press, 1978).

34. Guggenbuhl-Craig, Adolf, *Power in the Helping Professions* (Irving, Texas: Spring Publications, Inc., 1979).

35. Haley, Jay, *Strategies of Psychotherapy* (New York: Grune & Stratton, Inc., 1963).

36. Hand, Robert, personal communication.

37. Hastorf, Albert, et al., *Person Perception* (Reading, Mass.: Addison-Wesley Co., 1970).

38. Hoffer, Eric, *The True Believer* (New York: Harper & Row, Publishers, 1966).

39. Horowitz, Laurence and Victor Daniels, *Being and Caring* (Palo Alto, California: Mayfield Publishing Co., 1976).

40. James, Muriel and Dorothy Jongeward, *Born to Win* (Reading, Mass: Addison-Wesley Publishing Co., 1976).

41. James, William, *Varieties Of Religious Experience* (New York, Random House, 1929).

42. Japenga, Ann, "For Women Hooked on Legal Drugs," *Los Angeles Times*, February 18, 1982, pp. 1, 11.

43. Jourard, Sidney, *Disclosing Man To Himself* (New York: D. Van Nostrand Company 1968).

44. Kopp, Sheldon, *If You Meet The Buddha On The Road, Kill Him!* (New York: Bantam Books, 1972).

45. Kuhn, Thomas S., *The Structure Of Scientific Revolutions* (Chicago, Illinois: University of Chicago Press, 1970).

46. Lankton, Steve A.C.S.W., *Practical Magic: A Translation Of Basic Neuro-linguistic Programming Into Clinical Psychotherapy* (Cupertino, California: Meta Publications, 1980).

47. Latner, Joel, *The Gestalt Therapy Book* (New York: Bantam Books, 1974).

48. Leeper, R., "The Role of Motivation in Learning: a Study of the Phenomenon of Differential Motivation Control of the Utilization of Habits" *Journal Of Genetic Psychology* 46:3-40 (1935).

49. Leshan, Lawrence, *Alternate Realities; The Search For The Full Human Being* (New York: Ballantine Books, 1976).

50. Leshan, Lawrence, *The Medium, The Mystic And The Physicist* (New York: Ballantine Books, 1975).

51. Levinson, Daniel J. et al., *The Seasons Of A Man's Life* (New York: Ballantine Books, 1978).

52. Marshall, Joan K., *On Equal Terms; A Thesaurus For Nonsexist Indexing And Cataloging* (New York: Neal-schuman Publishers, 1977).

53. May, Rollo *The Art Of Counseling* (Nashville, Tenn: Abingdon, 1980).

54. Miller, Casey and Kate Swift, *The Handbook Of Nonsexist Writing* (New York: Lippincott and Crowell, 1980).

55. Miller, Jean Baker, M.D., *Toward A New Psychology Of Women* (Boston: Beacon Press, 1976).

56. Monte, Christopher, *Beneath The Mask; An Introduction To Theories Of Personality* (New York: Praeger Publishers, 1977).

57. Newman, Mildred and Bernard Berkowitz, *How To Be Your Own Best Friend* (New York: Ballantine Books, 1971).

58. Oppenheimer, Robert, *Science And Common Understanding* (New York: Simon and Schuster, 1966).

59. Ornstein, Robert E., *The Psychology Of Consciousness* (New York: Penguin Books, 1972).

60. Palazzoli, Mara Selvini et al., *Paradox And Counter Paradox* (New York: Jason Aronson, 1978).

61. Partnow, Elaine, Ed., *The Quotable Woman*, Vol II (Los Angeles: Pinnacle Books, 1977).

62. Perls, Frederick M.D., Ph.D., *In And Out Of The Garbage Pail* (Lafayette, California: Real People Press, 1969).

63. Pottenger, Maritha *Encounter Astrology* (Los Angeles, California: Tia Publications, 1978).

64. Pottenger, Maritha, "House Foundations," *The Mutable Dilemma* 3:2 (Pisces 1980) pp. 5-19.

65. Pottenger, Maritha "Maritha on Counseling," *The Mutable Dilemma* Issues: Virgo 1978; Sagittarius 1979; Gemini 1980; Virgo 1980 and Sagittarius 1980.

66. Pottenger, Zipporah (Dobyns), *God's World* (Chicago, Illinois: Inner Creations, Inc., 1957).

67. Pribram, Karl, communication during Conference on the Healing Brain, Los Angeles, October 1981.

68. Progoff, Ira, *The Death And Rebirth Of Psychology* (New York: Julian Press, Inc., 1956).

69. Progoff, Ira, *The Symbolic And The Real* (New York: Mcgraw-hill Book Co., 1973).

70. Rogers, Carl R., Ph.D., *Carl Rogers On Personal Power* (New York: Delacorte Press, 1977).
71. Rotter, Julian, "Generalized expectancies for internal versus external control of reinforcement," *Psychological Monographs*, 80:1 (1966) Whole No. 609, p. 25.
72. Satir, Virginia, *Conjoint Family Therapy* (Palo Alto, California: Science and Behavior Books, Inc., 1967).
73. *Scientific American* "50 and 100 Years Ago Scientific American," 246:1 (January 1982) p. 8.
74. Sheehy, Gail, *Passages* (New York: Bantam Books, 1977).
75. Singer, Erwin, *Key Concepts In Psychotherapy* (New York: Basic Books, Inc., 1970).
76. Steiner, Claude, *Scripts People Live* (New York: Grove Press, Inc., 1975).
77. Strupp, Hans H., et al., *Psychotherapy For Better Or Worse; The Problem Of Negative Effects* (New York: Jason Aronson, Inc., 1977).
78. *Symposium On Consciousness, Presented at the annual meeting of the American Association for the Advancement of Science, February 1974,* (New York: The Viking Press, 1976).
79. Wilson, Robert Anton, "The Science of the Impossible," *Oui* 8:3 (March 1979) pp. 81-84; 130-132.
80. Wolf, Sidney, "An investigation of counseling type, client type, level of facilitative conditions and client outcome," doctoral dissertation, The Catholic University of America, 1970 (Ann Arbor, Michigan: Dissertation Abstracts International, University Microfilm, No. 70-22,093).
81. *Women And Psychotherapy: A Consumer Handbook* (Washington, D.C.: Federation of Organizations for Professional Women, 1981).
82. Woolridge, Dean E., *The Mechanical Man* (New York: Mcgraw-hill, 1968).
83. Wycoff, Hogie, *Solving Women's Problems* (New York: Grove Press, Inc., 1977).
84. Yalom, Irvin D., *Existential Psychotherapy* (New York: Basic Books, 1980).
85. Yalom, Irvin D., *The Theory And Practice Of Group Psychotherapy* (New York: Basic Books, 1970).
86. Zeig, Jeffrey K., Ph.D., *A Teaching Seminar With Milton H. Erickson* (New York: Brunner/Mazel, Publishers, 1980).

Index

Where alternate forms exist, the general form was used, e.g. science, scientists, and scientific would all fall under science. Some ideas are mentioned by page, even if that particular phrase (e.g. cultural conditioning) does not appear.

A

Acceptance, by others, vi, vii, 13, 39, 49-50, 127, 160, 194, 196
Adler, Alfred, 11, 13-14, 27, 39, 73, 100
A.F.A. (American Federation of Astrologers), 68
Age, vi, vii, 6, 97, 100, 101, 161, 180, 209
Air (element), 60, 146-148, 206
Alcoholics Anonymous (A.A.), 45, 47, 104
Altruism, 43, 46-47
Ambivalences, iv, 41, 46, 55, 58, 72, 80, 95, 104, 121, 141, 146, 156, 164, 188, 194, 200, 204
Anger, 34, 65, 67, 95, 105, 168, 233
Anomaly, 4
Anxiety, 9, 44, 51, 76, 81, 121-122, 216
Appelbaum, Ann, 37
Aquarius, 213
Aries, 59, 61, 147, 164, 203-206, 208, 211, 213, 216, 224
Arteriosclerosis, 67
Ascendant, 113, 203, 207-208, 210-211, 218
Assagioli, Roberto, 13, 22-23, 72
Assumptions, 4-7, 12, 14-15, 21, 24-30, 32-33, 38, 44, 78, 94, 99, 114, 116, 129-130, 138, 142, 161-164
Asteroids, 203
   See also Individual Asteroids, e.g. Juno
Astro-Counseling (Astrological Counseling), 31, 50, 54, 125-127
Astrologer, 12, 23, 32, 41, 44-45, 76, 80, 102, 113, 125-127, 145-148, 152, 175-178, 183, 193-195
   See also Astro-counseling
Astrological correlates to illness, 67-69

Audition, 91, 114, 175, 185

B

Bandler, Richard, 14, 25
   See also Grinder, John
   See also Neuro-Linguistic Programming
Bandura, 72
Bannister, Roger, 74
Basic mistakes according to Adler, 13-14
Bateson, Gregory, 17
Behaviorism, 71-72, 107
Beliefs, vii, 3, 13, 193
   See also Assumptions
Bell, John, 16, 29
Berenson Bernard: *See* Carkhuff, Robert
Bergin, A. E., 30, 38
Berne, Eric, 11, 14, 74, 77, 106
Blaine, 39
Bloom, 125-126
Body language, 28, 91-95, 100-102, 155, 184-187, 192, 211
Broverman et al, 37
Bruner and Postman, 4

C

Cameron-Bandler, Leslie, 52, 85, 101, 113
   See also Neuro-Linguistic Programming
Cancer (the illness), 6, 223-224
Cancer (the sign), 61, 68, 99, 163; 221-222
Cannon, 39
Capra, Fritjof, 16,
Capricorn, 60-61, 146-147, 203-207, 211, 222, 224

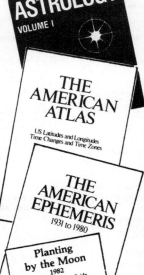

We calculate. . .You delineate!

CHART ANALYSIS

Natal Chart wheel with planet/sign glyphs. Choice of house system: Placidus (standard), Equal, Koch, Campanus, Meridian, Porphyry, or Regiomontanus. Choice of tropical (standard) or sidereal zodiac. Aspects, elements planetary nodes, declinations, midpoints, etc 2.00

Arabic Parts All traditional parts and more 1.00

Asteroids Ceres, Pallas, Juno and Vesta. Included in natal wheel + major planet aspects/midpoints .50

Astrodynes Power, harmony and discord with summaries for easy comparison 2.00

Chiron or Transpluto (not both) in wheel . . . . .N/C

Fixed Stars Robson's 110 fixed stars with aspects to natal chart 50

Graphic Midpoint Sort Proportional spacing highlights midpt. groupings. **Specify integer divisions of 360⁰** (1 = 360⁰, 4 = 90⁰, etc.) 1.00

Harmonic Chart John Addey-type. Wheel format, harmonic asc eq. houses. **Specify harmonic number** 1.00

Harmonic Positions 30 consecutive sets of positions **Specify start harmonic number** 1.00

Heliocentric Chart Sun-centered positions 2.00

House Systems Comparison for 7 systems 50

Local Space planet compass directions (azimuth & altitude) plus Campanus Mundoscope 50

Locality Map World map showing rise, upper & lower culmination and set lines for each planet 5.00

Midpoint Structures Midpoint aspects + midpoints in 45⁰ and 90⁰ sequence 50

Parans Meridian and horizon co-transits 1.00

Rectification Assist 10 same-day charts **Specify starting time, time increment, i.e. 6 am, 20 minutes** 10.00

Relocation Chart for current location **Specify original birth data and new location** 2.00

Uranian Planets in wheel + half-sums 2.00

HUMAN RELATIONSHIPS

Comparison Chart (Synastry) All aspects between the two sets of planets plus house positions of one in the other 1.50

Composite Chart Rob Hand-type. Created from midpoints between 2 charts. **Specify location** . . .1.00

Relationship Chart Chart erected for space-time mid-point between two births 2.00

CONCENTRIC WHEELS

Concentric Wheels Any 3 charts available in wheel format may be combined into concentric wheels. . . . . .3.00 Deduct $1.00 for each chart ordered as a separate wheel.

COLOR CHARTS

Color Wheel any chart we offer in new, aesthetic format with color coded aspect lines 2.00

Local Space Map 4-color on 360⁰ circle 2.00

PROGRESSIONS & DIRECTIONS

Progress Chart secondary, in wheel format. **Specify progressed day, month and year** 2.00

Secondary Progressions Day-by-day progressed aspects to natal and progressed planets, ingresses and parallels by month, day and year. **Specify starting year, MC by solar arc (standard) or RA of mean Sun.** . . . . .5 years 3.00
10 years 5.00
85 years 15.00

Minor Progressions Minor based on lunar-month-for-a-year, tertiary on day-for-a-lunar-month. **Specify zodiacal (standard) or synodical lunar month, year, MC by solar arc (standard) or RA of mean sun** . . . . .Minor 1 year 2.00
Tertiary 1 year 2.00

Progressed Lifetime Lunation Cycle The 8 Moon phases a la Dane Rudhyar 5.00

Primary Arc Directions Includes speculum. **Specify time measure: solar arc (standard), birthday arc, mean solar arc or degree/year. Specify starting year.** . . . . .1st 5 years 1.50
Each add'l 5 years .50

Solar Arc Directions Day-by-day solar arc directed aspects to the natal planets, house and sign ingresses by month, day and year. **Specify staring year. Specify time measure—same options as primary arcs.** Asc and vertex arc directions available for same prices. . . . . . .1st 5 years 1.00
Each add'l 5 years .50

TRANSITS

Transits by all planets except Moon. Date and time of transiting aspects/ingresses to natal chart. **Specify starting month.** Moon-only transits available for same prices. . . . . .6 mos. 7.00
12 mos. 12.00

Outer Planet Transits Jupiter thru Pluto 12 mos. . .3.00

RETURNS

Returns in wheel format. All returns can be precession corrected. **Specify place, Sun-return year, Moon-return month, planet-return approximate date.**
Solar, Lunar or Planet 2.00
13 Lunar 15.00

POTPOURRI

Transparency (B/W) of any chart or map $1.00

Custom House Cusps Table For each minute of sidereal time. **Specify latitude ⁰ ′ ″** 10.00

Fertility Chart The Jonas method with Sun/Moon squares/oppositions to the planets, for 1 year. **Specify starting month** 3.00

Same-day service
Lamination of 1 or 2 pages $1.00
Handling charge $1.00 per order

ASTRO COMPUTING SERVICES
P.O. BOX 16430
SAN DIEGO, CA 92116
NEIL F. MICHELSEN